WORLD WAR II
& THE GREAT LAKES

SUBMARINES, BOMBERS & ORE BOATS

Wes Oleszewski

Edited by Chris Rottiers

Avery Color Studios, Inc.
Gwinn, Michigan

© 2018 Avery Color Studios, Inc.

ISBN: 978-1-892384-77-5

Library of Congress Control Number: 2018939535

First Edition 2018

10   9   8   7

Published by Avery Color Studios, Inc.
Gwinn, Michigan 49841

Cover Photos: Submarine: Author's Collection, Bomber: Library of
Congress, Ship: State Archives of Michigan, Negative No. 05708

Back Cover Illustration: Tony Strublic, Maritime Artwork
www.strublicmaritimedrawings.com

The person in this photo is my late uncle Jack McGarrity from Saginaw, Michigan. He served in World War II from the beginning to the end in the Pacific theater. A humble family man who never talked about the war, he would reach down from the great beyond and slap me behind the head if I dedicated this book to him. Thus, I will dedicate this book to all of those who served during that war, my Uncle Jack and his buddies for whom he fought so hard. Also to my Uncle Buck who served in North Africa, my Uncle Tom and Uncle Bill who were in uniform waiting to be deployed. This book is also dedicated to the neighbors that I grew up with that served and survived as well as the people who worked in the factories, patrolled the streets as air raid wardens, plowed the fields, made the bandages and did countless other jobs that saw the allied efforts to victory. This book is also dedicated to all of those who were killed in the act of liberating the planet from those who sought to rule it with unimaginable tyranny.

Acknowledgements

First off I need to acknowledge Chris Rottiers, my new editor and proof reader who turned into a major contributor. Chris' expertise in the areas of automobile manufacturing, naval operations, Great Lakes maritime history and technical writing led the way in squeezing those countless typos and inconsistencies out of the manuscript and made the end product a far better book. He also has a great knowledge of thing such as tanks… a subject of which I have only a remedial acquaintance. He pulled my fat from the fire many times in those areas. It is a great help to have a person who is a tank-buff read my chapter about World War II tanks. Chris made that chapter a lot better. Additionally, Chris and I tend to think a lot alike when it comes to research. So, when I'd be looking at some obscure detail and deciding what to do with it, he went right along with me. On occasion I'd send him a draft of a chapter and he'd proof and edit it and return it with a whole paragraph of information that I had overlooked! On one occasion I got a chapter back from Chris with a correction of some material I'd written late, late at night and the notation, "Wes, yer' killin' me here…" I've always said that good editors make authors look good - Chris is a good editor. Of course the one area that I did not let him edit was the "Acknowledgements," so any typos you may find in this section are all mine and not Chris' fault at all.

Next I have to acknowledge my wife, Teresa. Not for the usual "support and patience" and blah, blah, blah as I was writing the book, but because the entire concept of this book was her idea! That's right folks. Originally the concept that I was assigned was just not working for me as it focused on aircraft lost on the Great Lakes. While agonizing over that subject as my wife and I drove down the highway I quipped that most of those aircraft came from training aboard the two aircraft carriers on Lake Michigan during World War II. She simply said, "Why don't you write about that? The great lakes in World War II." BING! The light went on! I immediately called my

1

WWII

publisher and rattled off the some of the things produced on the lakes during the war... steel, tanks, jeeps, weapons, bombers, subs... When I said "subs" he lit up! "I served on one of those subs!" He exclaimed, "Let's do it!" Thus began more than two years of work and research and this resulting book, all thanks to my Teresa. The night that we first got together way back in college I was writing my first book and she's been with me on every one since.

Of course there is my "go-to guy" when it comes to all things concerning aviation history, especially those involving the wars - that is Brian Nicklas, AKA "The Amazing Binzo." Brian is not only one of my best friends, but he also served as the Best Man in my wedding back in 1988. We attended the Embry-Riddle Aeronautical University together and were on the student newspaper, "The Avion" staff together. Today he resides where his talents serve the aviation world the best - at the National Air and Space Museum. It is a real blessing as a writer to be able have a question, text Binzo, and get the absolute correct answer. He is also the author of the fantastic book, "American Missiles: The Complete Smithsonian Field Guide." It is a MUST for anyone in aerospace to own.

Thanks to Jim Luke and William J.Luke, for help in running down a missing keel date that no one else could find. It was carefully kept in the "Luke Collection" of Great Lakes freighter history. Thanks as well to Steve Vanden Bosch for photo research and some high resolution images. Thanks must also go to Eric Laskowski, founder of the Michigan Civil Defense Museum web site , located at www.michigancivildefense.com. His amazing web site has information and tons of amazing images that not only provided me a roadmap for the World War II era of Civil Defense, but also gave me a taste for what that era was like. I'd recommend that everyone reading this book visit his site.

Thanks also to Andrew Rottiers - who caught an error in a tank image caption and saved me from a being pecked to death by the rivet-counters out there in the world of tank history.

A tip of the hat to my long-time friend and fellow ERAU alumnus Jennings Heilig. When he heard about the subject that I was working on, he connected me with his long-time friend David Brady whose

Acknowledgements

father Cdr. Jim Brady (USN Retired) trained aboard the Great Lakes aircraft carrier *USS Sable*. He did his carrier qualifications in the Navy's SNJ aircraft. I ended up having a very long pleasant phone conversation with Cdr. Brady during which he was able to fill me in on priceless details about flying the SNJ onto and off of that carrier during World War II. Thus, a huge thanks must go out to Cdr. Brady for both his service during his long career in the Navy and for opening a page of history that a fellow career pilot such as myself can truly relish.

Appreciation must be given to my long-time fellow lakeboat chaser and outstanding photographer Dave "DJ" Story. Along with being blessed with a wonderful family, DJ is also blessed with photographic talent. He's the only boatnut I know who could shoot a full roll of film and have nearly every picture come out as a work of art. Now, in the digital age he's even better. He is also the guy I knew I could call on in the final hours of illustrating this book and say, "Hey, I need a photo for the following vessels..." and in less than a few hours they arrive at my computer. Thank you DJ, you are one of a kind indeed.

Credit must go to Walter Lewis who runs the "Maritime History of the Great Lakes" web site. He has worked long and hard to make that site easily searchable with stunning content. I often go there just for pleasure reading, yet as a research tool its value cannot be understated.

One of the most up-lifting parts of writing this book has been making contact with people and projects that seek to preserve the history of World War II for future generations. In that regard I need to acknowledge the folks of the Yankee Air Museum and www.savethebomberplant.org as they are making a monumental effort to preserve the history of the Willow Run B-24 production facility. Hats off to Dennis Norton and Elisa Guyton of that organization as well as all of the other folks there whom I have yet to meet, yet look forward to doing so.

Not enough praise can be given to Gudmundur Helgason who runs the uboat.net web site. This site is an amazing tool that allowed me to take the meager information on the Great Lakes canal-class

WWII

vessels that were lost to U-boat action during World War II and cross reference them. Much of the details that have been missing from the annals of Great Lakes maritime history concerning these war losses are now filled in my "U-boat Bait" chapter - all thanks to uboat.net.

Thanks to Mike McCollum and Dan McCollum who helped inform me concerning the POWs in Michigan's Au Train area. Also thanks to the late legend of the lakes Wally Watkins who filled my ears with neat stories of life on the lakes during his days sailing in the mid 1900s. Wally is long gone, but his stories are still in my notebook. Thanks also to the alive and well Great Lakes historian and video ace Ric Mixter who didn't do a lot to help with the writing of this book, but my putting his name in here will compel him to buy a copy… okay I'll actually send him an "author's copy." Look for Ric's "Storm" lectures as he travels around the Great Lakes.

Thanks to Andrew Dziengeleski for his service in the United States Army and his help in running down the facts of my Uncle Jack's WWII outfit.

At length there are all of the folks involved in boatnerd.com. That is a great site filled with great information and is a good place to go and relax while you're working on a 75,000 word book. Boatnerds from all over the lakes led by Roger LeLievre are on this web site… including me.

To all of these folks and anyone I may have forgotten, I thank you.

BLACK-OUT!

As a child growing up in the 1960s I resided on the east side of Saginaw, Michigan. There we were surrounded by the places of industry, some of which had been there long before many of us were born. At the end of our block on Parkwood Street was located an elongated factory known as Lufkin Rule. Opening in 1885 and having expanded over the years to encompass more than two and a half square city blocks, the factory was, at one time, America's largest manufacturer of precision measuring tools. I always noticed that although the plant had countless windows, almost all of them had been painted black!

"Why would anyone go through the trouble of putting all of those windows into such a huge building and then just paint them black?" I wondered.

It was a simple question that only a little boy like me would continually ask himself. If you did not want people to look out of, or into the building - it would be far easier to just make it all walls.

One day my five-year-old's curiosity got the better of me and I asked my Mom why all of the windows were painted black?

"That's for a black-out," she informed me, "from back during the war. They had to black out all of the lights so the enemy bombers couldn't see them at night."

She explained that all of the factories in town and every house had to comply with the black-out rules every night. My little boy's imagination ran wild as I pictured a cartoonish night's sky filled with search lights illuminating enemy bombers right over Parkwood Street

5

WWII

Aerial view of Saginaw's Lufkin Rule Plant, October 1965. Author's pre-school home at 2717 Parkwood Street is shown by the arrow. Photo - US Geological Survey

as air raid sirens went off and flack burst in the night. Of course since there was no bomb damage, I reasoned that the black-out stuff must have worked pretty darned good. When we got home I dug my plastic army helmet out of my closet and went outside to check the sky for bombers. Sure, we had won the war 17 years earlier, but ya' never know the enemy could come back. Late at night, with my army helmet on along with my plastic camouflage poncho and all of the lights out - I carefully raised the shade in my bedroom window and peeked up toward the night's sky. Outside was the glow of the surrounding factories as they, and my Dad, worked the night shift.

"Those fools! Didn't they know about the black-out? Why the enemy could come back at any time." I thought to myself.

6

Black-Out!

Other than those who went through the first years of the war, no one can actually fathom the true sense of fear that followed the attack on Pearl Harbor. For the previous two years the Germans had been bombing countries across Europe by way of aircraft. During the blitz on London, night raids by Nazi bombers had been reported widely on the radios of American households and printed as headlines in our newspapers. U-boats were torpedoing ships within sight of American beaches. In the Pacific Japanese bombers had been raiding Chinese cities for the past few years. Then came Pearl Harbor and our Naval forces in the Pacific were severely damaged by the air bombardment. Following that raid the realization set in that we really did not know the extent of the enemy's capability to drop bombs on American cities. Perhaps they indeed could mount a blitz bombing effort against Detroit, Chicago, Buffalo, Cleveland, or even Saginaw. We had plenty of factories that just could make the difference in stopping them in their effort to rule the world.

If you think there wasn't fear and near panic, take a look at this front page from December 9, 1941 and a west coast "test" of the black-out system. Author's Collection

7

WWII

Saginaw itself had three prime targets that any potential enemy would probably aim for if they had considered the production capability of each in the event of war. First there was Gray Iron Foundry which would be producing castings for aircraft engines. Next there would be the Saginaw Malleable Iron plant where a new type of steel was being produced in large quantities. Called "ArmaSteel," a moniker that stood for steel processed by arrested malleablizing the metal and giving it qualities between iron and steel. That led to the Malleable Iron plant being able to produce parts for the .50 caliber machine gun barrel support, 90mm anti-aircraft gun mounts, Hydra-Matic transmission cases and Browning Automatic Rifles. They also produced millions of cast parts for tanks. Finally, there was the Saginaw Steering Gear plant. The factory's best known product during the war was the M1 carbine rifle and the Browning 1919 .30 caliber machine gun. When asked by the government to help produce the M1 in 1943 they turned them out not by the thousands, nor by the tens of thousands, but by the hundreds of thousands! A single bombing raid on just this single, modestly sized industrial city could have set the allies back months in their efforts in advancing the war to a successful conclusion.

In fact, as early as July 8, 1938 Nazi planners were working on a project that would evolve into the Messerschmitt Me 264 - a long range four engine bomber that could reach New York City. On May 12, 1942 Reichsmarschall Hermann Goring was presented with the plans for the new bomber which had a proposed range of 3,800 miles. If launched from the Azores, which at that time were sympathetic to the Nazis, the aircraft would be able to reach any of the industrial cities in the Great Lakes region. Additionally, there was a similar four-engine long range bomber called the Junkers Ju 390 that was also intended for use against the United States mainland. Although both aircraft reached the prototype stage and actually flew, neither project could survive the lack of raw materials and the war withered industrial base of Germany by mid-war. Both projects died on the vine.

On the other side of the planet the Japanese empire was also considering a super long-range bomber that would have been capable of not only striking the American west coast, but also could hit targets

Germany's trans-Atlantic long range bomber the ME-264. Author's Collection

as far as Detroit. This proposed aircraft, the Nakajima G10N1 Fugaku, was being considered in 1943. The design resembled a B-29 with six 36 cylinder radial engines. Japan at that point in time, however, lacked the infrastructure and raw materials to fully bring the project to life. As a result, the G10N1 Fugaku never got farther than the drawing board.

No one in the United States at that time knew that these projects existed, yet the attack on Pearl Harbor by air, in itself, gave the impression that Great Lakes industrial cities could soon look like London with smoldering buildings and bomb craters. In the days following Pearl Harbor the fear that these cities may be immediately attacked caused industrial leaders to begin taking drastic action. In Detroit the Ford plants completely stopped making cars and switched to making military equipment full time the day after Pearl Harbor. Some of the plants that had already been building military equipment were put on a 24 hour a day seven day a week work schedule. That, of course meant that they would have to fully implement night shifts as well. The glow from the necessary indoor lighting would provide easy targeting for enemy bombers.

In London they found that painting the roofs, skylights, and windows black reduced the ability of German Luftwaffe bomber crews to properly sight specific targets at night. Even with these measures taken by the British, German crews were highly skilled at night time bombing and the United States Office of Civil Defense,

WWII

or "OCD" began to organize the civilian population in the art of civil defense. Since the man-power needs of front line combat units were so great, it was decided to mobilize every day citizens into a Civil Defense Corps.

OCD knew full well that black-outs could never hide an entire city. The objective of the black-out was to deny enemy aircrews, who were unfamiliar with the area, the ability to readily spot specific targets especially factories manufacturing critical war supplies. Yet, by hiding the specific targets, OCD was inviting carpet bombing - where ordinance is deployed in a wide pattern in the hope that somewhere in the drop zone the bombs will hit something critical. As often is the case during carpet bombing, large areas of civilian

Early Civil Defense recruiting poster circa 1942. Photo - Library of Congress

homes, businesses, schools and other non-war related property are also destroyed. Additionally, OCD was aware that the Nazis as well as the Imperial Japanese were indiscriminate in how they bombed populated and industrial areas. So, along with the blacking-out of large areas, the public had to be organized and prepared for the worst.

Planners realized that to fully mobilize the population would take months although some areas were designated as a priority and were mobilized right away. The formation of the Civil Air Patrol, or "CAP" was immediate. Some documentation says that the CAP was formed the day before Pearl Harbor, while other sources say it was formed the day after. Regardless of which day they were formed, the CAP was charged with patrolling the skies, conducting search and rescue operations and doing anti-submarine patrols from the onset of the war. In modern times the primary mission of the CAP includes looking for downed civilian and military aircraft and airborne security patrols post-9/11. As the author of this book, I'm proud to say that I was a CAP Cadet from 1972 to 1974.

In order to reduce casualties in an air raid it was important to limit panic and to prepare the general public literally on how to get bombed. As the war efforts began to gear up, Civil Defense volunteers became trained in areas such as first aid, fire fighting and even detection of chemical gases and how to deal with them. Guide booklets and short films were produced showing how to prepare for anticipated attacks. Every detail from having buckets of water on the stairs and along the walls ready to put out fires to how to black-out your home's windows was covered. Citizens were also formed into teams of Air Raid Wardens. These people were sub-divided into teams of "spotters" who were trained to identify assorted enemy aircraft types. Although aircraft spotters had been organized locally along the northeast coast of the United States as early as May of 1941, now the practice spread nation-wide. Located at strategic points where it was felt that formations of hostile aircraft may approach, they were instructed to dash to the nearest phone, contact the operator and say "Omni Flash!" Upon hearing "Omni Flash!", the operator was to connect the line to the nearest Army "filter center" where the spotter's information was evaluated and disbursed.

WWII

As a back-up to the telephone system, Boy Scouts and Sea Scouts were used as messengers. They would carry written information through the air raid by bicycle. That worked fine until winter set in along the Great Lakes. Once the snow was piled high, every scout just hoped the Nazis decided to pull their raid in the spring - otherwise it could take longer to move the message than it did to for the bombers to fly across the Atlantic.

Onset of an air raid would require an immediate black-out. To ensure that every home was completely blacked-out, air raid wardens walked the streets and checked that every window was covered and every light extinguished. For the factories around the lakes region this was a far bigger problem than it was for neighborhood homes. After all, it was the factories that the enemy would be targeting and those plants had hundreds of thousands of lights burning. The answer was simple; remove any non-critical outdoor lighting and paint the windows black. Thus, when one of the mandatory practice black-outs took place, plants such as Saginaw's Malleable Iron, Steering Gear, Eaton Manufacturing and Lufkin Rule, could keep running their night shift while still complying with the black-out regulations. At some factories, however, the task of blacking out windows was a real monster. The Ford Motor Company's River Rouge Complex, the largest in the world, existed on 1,096 acres of land with 7,250,000 square feet of floor space and had more than 345 acres of window glass. And that didn't include Ford's new Willow Run plant where mass production of B-24 bombers was about to begin. Mr. Ford's staff was going to need an awful lot of black paint.

Nearly two years before the United States entered the war the American Women's Voluntary Services or "AWVS" was formed as one of the earliest civilian preparations for war. January of 1940 saw the organization formed by Alice Throckmorton McLean and it went on to become the biggest women's service organization in the nation during World War II. The AWVS members provided support services like aircraft spotters, and canteen workers, message delivery, emergency kitchens, ambulance driving and the selling of war bonds among other things. Their efforts blended well into those of the Office of Civil Defense.

By 1942 the various Civil Defense organizations were expanding and becoming quite efficient. There were 15 different branches divided into corps, wardens, watchers, crews and squads as well as police, firemen and messengers - each of which had its own specific patch. All of the patches had a basic blue circle with a white triangle inside which was annotated a red symbol. Air-Raid Wardens handled threats from the sky. Their patch had a series of red stripes cutting across the white triangle. Decontamination had a red laboratory "Retort" as its symbol and had a corps of people who were trained in handling chemical weapons. Fire Watchers were trained to identify

Maureen Sullivan and Shirley Conn, posed in the uniform of American Women's Voluntary Services. Photo - Library of Congress

and combat incendiary bombs. Their patch had a red flame symbol in its white triangle. Rescue Squads had a red ladder in their patch's white triangle and were trained and equipped to find and rescue people trapped in debris. Auxiliary Firemen sported a patch with a red four leafed iron cross and were trained to, "fight blazes during air attacks." A red pick ax was the symbol for the Demolition and Clearance Crews who were set to clear the roads and sidewalks and other blocked areas after an air raid. The caduceus was silhouetted in red on the patch of the Medical Corps which included not only doctors and nurses but also volunteers who were trained in first aid. A coal shovel was the moniker for the Road-Repair Crews who would repair the bomb craters that would close many streets in areas struck by the enemy. To denote Auxiliary Police a spade-shaped red badge symbol was placed on their patch. Volunteers assigned as the "Handlers of private car transportation" were in the Driver's Corps and a three spoke steering wheel was the red symbol on their patch. Nurses Aid Corps members wore the traditional red cross on their patch. An inverted dive bomber was the image on the patch for the Bomb Squad. Their mission description, however was somewhat interesting as they were officially charged to, "Dispose of perilous time bombs." Exactly how many of those the OCD expected the enemy to drop is unrecorded, but it was enough to warrant a patch. The Messengers had what most of the scouts who were assigned that job must have thought to be the most neato of patches with a red, non-symmetrical lightning bolt as their symbol. And probably the most critical of all the corps was the Emergency Food and Housing Corps - their symbol was a simple coffee cup. Of course all of these had to be run by an over-seeing management unit called the Staff Corps. Their symbol was the standard Civil Defense logo with the blue circle, white triangle and red letters "CD" inside and a block lettering of "US" in the background. All of the volunteers were referred to as "Minute Men" or women or boy and girls depending on the task assigned.

As the war progressed, the chances of the United States mainland being attacked by enemy bombers grew exponentially remote. Yet, the blackouts continued as did brown-outs and electrical curfews which became a way of life in America. It was no longer the risk of air raids that precipitated these events, but rather of the conservation of coal. Most of the nation was powered by coal-burning power plants and in the Great Lakes region nearly all of the industrial facilities were powered by energy produced from coal. The engines that pulled the cars of iron ore from the mines to the loading docks were coal fueled. The freighters that hauled the ore down to the steel plants were fueled by coal. Those same freighters carried the coal from the lower lakes to the upper lake ports where the trains moved the ore cars. Coal was the lifeblood of Maritime transportation on the Great Lakes and with demand for wartime materials at its highest, coal was being consumed at a far greater level than ever before. Such was the working truth throughout the nation. The best way to ease the strain on the nation's coal producing capability was to simply reduce usage as much as possible on a massive scale. Thus, the power curfews, brown-outs and black-outs served to reduce the amount of coal being used.

With the war finally coming to an end and the Axis powers on the verge of defeat, the only enemy bombs to actually hit United States soil were some FO-GO, or "fire balloon" contraptions. They were designed to drift with the jet stream from Japan to North America. An estimated 9,000 were constructed and launched, but only about 300 actually made it to North America and only two were confirmed as hitting the Great Lakes area with very little damage being inflicted. In fact, the damage was so slight that the FBI and the War Department covered up the events so as to not damage war morale. Thus, the wide network of Civil Defense air raid preparedness was never needed. Likewise, neither was the blacking-out of the windows of factories and homes.

With that in mind it would be easy to look back on war-time Civil Defense efforts and scoff at them as being much ado about nothing. Such a viewpoint, however, would be highly short-sighted. One of the greatest benefits of the Civil Defense effort and the black-outs was that they served to solidify morale. They kept the public keenly aware that around most of the planet, a shooting war was taking place. It made the average citizen feel as if he or she was ready in the face of a merciless enemies.

Morale-boosting poster. Photo - Library of Congress

When Americans put on their patches and donned their white helmets and belts in the name of Civil Defense they felt connected to their sons, brothers and fathers who were serving on the front lines overseas. Each blacked-out window in each factory represented a message sent to the Axes powers. It was a message that said if they wanted to take us on - they'd have to do it house by house, door by door and window by window. Rather than feeling helpless as the war news came in, which was not particularly good in the first months of the conflict, Americans felt empowered as they were personally defending their neighborhood and their factories.

After the war, many factory managers found it just too time consuming and too expensive to remove the black-out paint from those countless windows. As a result, they just left them in place. The blacked-out windows on the Lufkin Rule plant remained that way until the company went out of business in 1967 and the property was sold. The factory was demolished in 1997. Likewise, the concept of Civil Defense also faded away with the end of the Cold War. This was largely caused by the fact that Soviet and US nuclear weapons became so powerful that in a World War III exchange there would be no shelter and no survivors. Thus, there would be no "civil" to defend.

Additionally, those major targets in the city of Saginaw also faded away. The Gray Iron Foundry is only a skeleton of what it once was. Today it's called the GM Saginaw Metal Casting Operations and has fewer employee cars parked outside than the local Wal Mart. Saginaw Steering Gear's decline started with the 1980 recession. As a part of General Motors since 1909, it was spun off from its parent company in 1999 as Delphi Automotive only to be bought back by GM after Delphi's bankruptcy in 2010. Renamed Nexteer, it was sold to Pacific Century Motors in 2013. Today Nexteer Automotive in Buena Vista Township is still producing parts for the automotive

Civil Defense volunteers looking to sign up for victory. Photo - Library of Congress

WWII

industry although Plant 2, the gun plant, on the west side of town closed in 2001 and was torn down in 2002. The Saginaw Malleable Iron plant was not as lucky. In May of 2007 the plant was shut down permanently and within the next three years the site was leveled. It remains today as nothing more than a huge cement slab. There is no need for blacked out windows anymore.

Yet the blacked out windows are symbolic of what this book is about. It is a peek back into the history of the Great Lakes region during World War II, the people who lived and died during that time, the enemy combatants who were held prisoner there, the people who guarded the area and the machines that were produced and the factories that made them. This is not a complete history of those times and events. That would take longer to write than the war itself lasted. It would also take tens of thousands of pages in hundreds, if not thousands, of books to properly tell the story. Instead this is a glimpse into some of the more interesting events that left behind those blacked out windows that inspired a five-year-old boy to ask the question while looking at the Lufkin Rule plant one day," Mom, why are all the windows painted black?"

CAUGHT OFF GUARD?

Modern documentaries and Hollywood movies like to give their audiences the impression that the attack on Pearl Harbor on December 7, 1941 and the beginning of United States involvement in World War II had caught Americans completely by surprise. In fact, nothing could be further from the truth.

During the mid-1930s, the rise of Nazi forces in Europe and the expansion of Imperial Japan in the Pacific gave leaders in the United States a whiff of the ill winds that foretold the oncoming of a second world war. Yet many still held firm to the mistaken belief that if America simply isolated itself and remained neutral, the expansion of that foreign evil would simply halt at the vast oceans that surrounded them. There was enormous political pressure on United States President Franklin Delano Roosevelt, (FDR) to keep the United States out of the conflicts abroad. Many isolationists in Congress were closely watching to ensure that the president did not make any moves that the "Axis" powers of Germany, Italy and Japan may see as hostile. But, FDR, who was a former Secretary of the Navy, knew well that war was likely on the horizon.

On December 31, 1936 the treaties of The Washington Naval Conference of 1921-1922 and The London Naval Conference of 1930, which came about as a result of World War I and were intended to somehow ensure peace through weakness, expired. Although the United States had followed the terms of the treaties, both Germany and Italy had skirted the agreements and Japan had completely ignored them all together. Thus, on the first day of 1937 FDR found

19

WWII

himself with a Navy that had been allowed to become largely obsolete. The story was far worse for the United States Army. With the U.S. Congress firmly in the isolationist camp and committed to not becoming entangled in a foreign war, less than half of the military budget that the FDR administration and War Department had asked for were approved. Some sources say that the United States military at that time ranked 14th in size in the world - behind Sweden. Other sources say that we were 19th, behind Romania. Regardless, the United States Military at the onset of World War II was in a woeful state to meet the coming crisis.

FDR also found himself with a nation ravaged from the effects of the Great Depression. Millions of able-bodied men were unemployed while countless factories sat idle. For FDR, the answer to getting those men back to work and the factories producing again was defense material production, but the Congress held the purse strings tightly.

Nowhere were the ills of the depression more apparent than in the Great Lakes region. Prior to 1937, along the harbor of Buffalo, New York the massive expanse of steel mills hardly registered a heartbeat. Port cities such as Erie, Pennsylvania and Toledo, Ohio found their waters packed with Great Lakes ships left in lay-up or simply abandoned where they had docked the day that their owner's companies had simply ceased to exist due to the depression. In Toledo, a new high-rise steel bridge had been erected to span the Maumee River as part of FDR's jobs program. As construction slowly moved along, beneath the new span lay anchored an idle fleet of modern, huge, steel ore boats with no future in sight. In the Iron Range above the twin ports of Duluth and Superior at the far end of Lake Superior, once bustling iron ore mines scraped out what little ore the management believed could be shipped. That ore would go down the lakes aboard vessels crewed by third mates who had once been captains, engineers who had once been chiefs and deck hands who were just happy to have a job. Inland, places such as Flint, Michigan saw assembly lines that, in the "Roaring Twenties," had rolled cars out like sausages - now idle. You cannot sell cars to people who are without an income. It was this massive reserve of idle facilities, materials and people that would become FDR's Arsenal of Democracy.

On September 1, 1939 Germany invaded Poland and eight months later they stormed Denmark and Norway followed by Holland a month after that. Great Brittan declared war on Germany on September 3, and Canada did so on September 9. King George the VI approved Canada's declaration the next day and with that, Canada and the Great Lakes also went to war. On May 10, 1940 the feckless Neville Chamberlain resigned as prime minister of Great Brittan. It was he who had myopically signed a treaty called the "Munich Pack" with Hitler guaranteeing "peace in our time." The date was September 30, 1938 just 11 months before the Nazi invasion of Poland. That left the prime minister's seat open to Winston Churchill. To everyone, other than a now dwindling number of hardcore isolationists, it was becoming quite evident that a second world war was in the making.

For the people of Canada, the largest contribution that they could offer in support of the war during the early days was shipping. The Island of Britain was under attack and the Nazis were determined to isolate and then conquer it. Canadian Great Lakes shipyards went into full speed production of Corvette vessels for convoy protection, U-boat killing, and mine sweeping. Additionally, large private luxury steam yachts were requisitioned and converted for military use. Canal class Canadian lake freighters were diverted to convoy duty and vessels around the Great Lakes that had been in indefinite lay-up or abandonment due to the depression were purchased by the Canadians and rapidly scrapped so that their metals could be melted down and recycled into the weapons needed to fight the war.

Next door to Canada the Americans were still clinging to neutrality but the writing was already on the wall. From the mines of the northwest iron range to the steel mills along Lake Erie, production was being increased and men who had been without work found that from mid-1938 until late 1941 there were plenty of jobs to be had. The factories that were the heart and soul of the automobile industry began to take on U.S. Government Defense contracts and the sleeping giant of United States industry began to stir.

WWII

British seamen aboard the destroyer Vanoc *"preparing the torpedo,"
before loading the tube, August 16, 1941. Library of Congress*

A flotilla of outdated World War I era destroyers that had been
mothballed on the United States east coast were rapidly repaired,
repainted, and put back into commission when on September 2, 1940
FDR signed the "Destroyers for Bases" agreement. That decree would
send 50 of these four stack flush-deck destroyers to the United
Kingdom in exchange for the U.S. taking possession of eight British
bases. Each vessel was filled with ammunition and torpedoes. This
was the predecessor to "Lend-Lease" which FDR would sign into law
on March 11, 1941. General Motors was already beginning to produce
tanks and other military vehicles prior to lend-lease and so when the
flood gates opened and the US was about to enter the war on the side
of the allies in Europe, the Great Lakes was ready to respond.

Although few were expecting the sort of total all-out production
effort that would be needed after Pearl Harbor, very few expected
the surprise attack that took place there on the morning of December
7, 1941. While true the United States Pacific fleet was caught

unprepared that day as were other U.S. military installations in the Pacific, the industrial complex of the Great Lakes was not caught completely off guard. The "sleeping giant" of American industry that Admiral Isoroku Yamamoto was said to fear the Pearl Harbor attack had awakened was indeed ready to come to life. The bulk of that monster resided in the Great Lakes with its inexhaustible supply of iron ore and its massive fleet of lakeboats to transport that resource, the region could also produce enough steel to build a fleet of warships larger than anything Japan's leaders could imagine. Likewise, a steady stream of tanks, artillery, munitions, motor vehicles, and submarines would be produced at a rate never before seen in history.

Countless products were made from the steel that had its life blood in the red iron ore that was about to be shipped in quantities greater than anyone had ever thought possible. Yet other products were also produced in record amounts. Paper, for example, was

Lend-lease tank being loaded aboard a convoy vessel circa 1941.
Library of Congress

produced in Erie, Pennsylvania in huge volumes. It turned out that by the end of the conflict, the War department had used more paper during the war than steel, and Erie's Hammermill Paper Company was a huge contributor to that. Likewise, Saginaw Steering Gear, a Division of General Motors which had previously been manufacturing steering assemblies and other components for cars, switched to making the fine parts needed for the M-1 rifle and Browning 1919 .30 caliber machine gun. Grain needed to feed the troops was harvested in the Canadian plains and loaded aboard lake freighters on the northern shore of Lake Superior to be shipped down to eastern lake ports. Meanwhile on the quiet banks of the Tittabawassee River in Midland, Michigan the folks at Dow Chemical were using their advanced know-how to create the substances that would make the "boom" of dynamite and black powder seem like a fire cracker. Products such as phenol, bromine and magnesium which were key materials used in flares, explosives, aircraft engines and even some medicines were produced in the massive quantities that only the Midland-based plant could churn out. Napalm, produced by Dow saw its first use in World War II and saved countless American lives as it was effectively used to neutralize Japanese troops who were dug in and determined to fight to the death on Pacific islands. In a more constructive, rather than destructive area, Dow developed a plastic wrap that could cling to itself yet easily be removed. This product was critical in protecting military equipment and aircraft that needed to be shipped overseas on the decks of cargo vessels. It provided much-needed protection from the ever present corrosive saltwater spray that the transporting vessels experienced. Today, we know that product as "Saran Wrap." Eventually nearly 90% of Dow's chemical production went specifically into war-time use.

The onset of war caused nearly every form of industry around the Great Lakes to operate at levels far beyond their pre-war capacity. Production in most industries exceeded levels that management would never have believed even possible just a few short years earlier.

However, there were a few exceptions to that war-time production boom. One of those exceptions involved the production of cement. Cement powder is normally used in domestic construction, but during

Caught Off Guard?

World War II the domestic construction business nearly faded away to nothing as every asset was directed toward the war effort. The Huron Cement Company, located in Alpena, Michigan normally supplied almost all of the powdered cement products to the entire Great Lakes region and much of the United States as well. By 1928 the company added additional kilns and had a production capability of 4,000,000 barrels. Like every other industry their production dropped off in the shadow of the depression. In 1936, business began to pick up and by 1942 cement production was back to the 1928 pre-depression level; then the bottom dropped out as the war began. In 1944 Huron Cement had the same basic production that they had seen in 1932! Their boats were laid up and their staff was reduced. After the end of the war, however, America started to experience a baby-boom and the economy began to steadily grow - as did domestic construction. Huron Cement saw their product demand grow nation-wide without interruption until the late 1970s. Yet, even though Huron Cement suffered a lack of business during the war, there was one war-time policy that would benefit the company during the years immediately following the war. The United States Maritime Commission had ramped up the construction of sea-going vessels of every type and size during the war years. One of those Maritime Commission built ships was the motor vessel *Coastal Delegate* that was constructed in 1945, but was launched too late to play a significant part in the war. She became part of the Mothball Fleet belonging to the Maritime Commission and Huron Cement was able to purchase her at a steeply discounted price. She was taken to the Bethlehem Steel Company in New Jersey and converted to a self-unloading cement carrier and towed to the Great Lakes by way of the Mississippi River where she entered service for Huron Cement in 1952 as the *Paul H. Townsend*. The *Townsend* sailed for the company and its subsequent owners until she was sent off for scrapping in 2017.

Although isolationists garnered a lot of press and newsreels in the late 1930s and the first years of the 1940s, there were important people in trusted positions who saw that a second world war was inevitable. Even before the first Japanese aircraft roared over Pearl

WWII

World War II era vessel Paul H. Townsend *unloading cement at 6th Street, Carrollton, Michigan, June, 1996. D.J. Story photo*

Harbor, the industrial giant of the Great Lakes was awakening and looking toward the storm clouds forming on the horizon. The Lend-Lease program had oiled the rusting wheels of industry caused by the depression and Yamamoto's legendary fear of a sleeping giant filled with a terrible resolve was soon to become a reality.

Thus, if you picked up this book thinking that the United States and the Great Lakes region were caught completely off guard by the on-set of World War II, think again.

MICHIGAN'S HEAVY BOMBER

Located 19 miles west-southwest of the Ford Motor Company's massive River Rouge plant in Detroit, Michigan is an expanse of open ground, a few huge buildings standing mostly empty and three underused runways. The place is almost as idle now as it was in 1940 when it was nothing but farm land. Then the vast stretch of land was being used as Camp Willow Run also known as the "Ford Farm for Boys," where troubled, or "disadvantaged" youth could be sent to "learn the trade of being productive and responsible Americans." There were long fields that the boys plowed and maple trees that they would tap for sap in the spring as well as apple trees whose fruit was harvested and sold. In the spring of 1941, however, bulldozers and earth movers would roll in and quickly put an end to the farm. Watching his camp for boys being cleared to make way for a new plant where the Consolidated B-24 bomber plant would soon reside, the elderly dedicated pacifist Henry Ford, then in the throes of dementia and sometimes suffering from hallucinations, quipped that it had taken 29 years to cultivate and grow the trees but it took just 29 minutes for the bulldozers to take it all down; it was April 18, 1941.

In the first week of January 1941, Edsel Ford, the son of Henry Ford, boarded a plane headed for San Diego, California and the Consolidated aircraft factory where the B-24 heavy bomber was initially being produced. Also aboard the plane was Edsel's sons, Benson and Henry II along with the most brilliant man in the manufacturing industry Charles Sorensen - the man who had

27

WWII

Ambassador Joseph Grew (left) and Edsel Ford (right) on the ramp at Willow Run in early 1943 near a B-24 bomber. Grew was the Ambassador to Japan and was in Tokyo on the day of the Pearl Harbor attack. (Sorry about the propeller blade in Grew's head. That's just the way that the photo is presented). Library of Congress

perfected Ford's assembly line production methods of car building. They were on their way to see what the B-24 looked like and how Consolidated built the aircraft.

This had been a long rough road for Edsel who had to convince his father that the Ford Motor Company absolutely must get onto the defense industry bandwagon. The senior Henry Ford was dead set against his company building any sort of weapon. He hated the concept of war and reportedly referred to soldiers as "murderers in uniforms." Yet with the threat of World War II looming the powers that be in Washington D.C. had their eyes on the massive Ford plant in River Rouge, Michigan. They knew the senior Ford had his heels dug in against manufacturing any type of military equipment. On July 30, 1938 on his 75th birthday Henry Ford had publically accepted the "Grand Cross of the German Eagle" from representatives of the Nazi government. The award was in thanks for Ford opening a truck plant in Germany. That plant, which was supposed to build only non-military truck components was actually secretly building engines for the Junkers Airplane Works. Hitler personally directed that Ford should be presented with the medal which was garnished with four swastikas. As war approached, the U.S. and Canadian media put out a rumor that Ford was a Nazi sympathizer. Later it was said that the United States government would take over Ford facilities in the event of war. First Lady Eleanor Roosevelt publically stated that the president could take over Mr. Ford tomorrow if an emergency existed. With all of that hanging over their heads it took both Edsel and Sorensen to convince Henry Ford to allow his company to make B-24s. Yet he agreed to do so only if the aircraft were to be used for the defense of the United States. That was good enough for Edsel even though he knew all too well that the bombers would be used to fight in the upcoming conflict.

Consolidated Aircraft Company was founded in the Great Lakes community of Buffalo, New York by aviation pioneer Ruben Fleet. He flew the inaugural air mail run carrying a letter posted by President Woodrow Wilson himself. In 1936 Fleet moved the company to San Diego, California where it specialized in building huge sea planes, or "Flying Boats." In 1939 Consolidated was able to obtain the rights to a new and highly efficient wing design; the "Davis airfoil." This was the brain child of aeronautical engineer David R. Davis. It was initially adapted to serve on the Consolidated twin-engine flying boats, the PB2-Y and PB4-Y, but would later become a key element in the design of the B-24 four-engine heavy bomber.

In January of 1939, assured that war was on the horizon, the United States Army approached Consolidated with a proposal to have them produce the Boeing B-17. Consolidated declined and instead offered to build their own "better" version of a heavy bomber equipped with their new Davis airfoil wing design. So intrigued was the Army at the thought of this new technology that they offered

WWII

The Consolidated PBM-3 "Mariner" flying boat sports the elongated oval fuselage that would be adapted into the B-24 giving the heavy bomber its unique rectangular appearance with its set-back cockpit.
Library of Congress

Consolidated a contract to design a "3,3,3, bomber." The aircraft was to have a range of at least 3,000 miles, fly at a speed greater than 300 miles per hour and carry a bomb load of at least 3,000 pounds. Once the army saw Consolidated's basic bomber design in March of 1939, they offered the company the opportunity to build a prototype. Fleet's factory was given nine months to build the new aircraft. The prototype design was very forward thinking with a high wing stature, roll-away bomb bay doors and crew sleeping quarters for long distance missions.

Monikered the "Model 32" the prototype was ready for its first flight on December 29, 1939 just one day prior to the contracted delivery date and just over three months after Hitler invaded Poland starting World War II. The aircraft, soon dubbed the XB-24, bettered only one of the "3s" which was the bomb load where it was able to carry a maximum load of 4 tons instead of the 1-1/2 tons specified in the contract. It, however, fell short on speed as it topped out at 275 miles per hour. It also had a range of just 2,400 miles. Of course this model "A" of the bomber was equipped with R-1830-33 Wasp engines that did not have turbo superchargers which resulted in short-falls in performance. The turbo superchargers, mounted on each engine, essentially take the thin air of the upper atmosphere and compress it before feeding it to the engine. This fools the engine into performing as if it were at a lower altitude therefore allowing an increase in range and speed in piston engines.

Initial flight testing of the Model 32, now designated the XB-24, went very well. Consolidated's Chief Test Pilot William B. "Bill" Wheatley along with a crew made up of George Newman, Jack Kline and Bob Keith made the first flight from Lindbergh Field in San Diego.

With the threat of war on the horizon the number of employees at the Consolidated Aircraft Company jumped from 3,000 to 16,000 in about a year. When the new parts factory, then under construction in San Diego, was opened Consolidated added approximately an additional 15,000 employees. Image is from June 1941. Library of Congress

WWII

In spite of positive test results the Army initially only ordered seven of the big bombers. The French government, however, ordered 175 (although some sources say it was 120) and the British ordered 160. When the Nazis captured France, the 120 aircraft ordered by the French were transferred to the United Kingdom and eventually the very first B-24s to see action would be British. It was the British who monikered the big bomber "The Liberator." Ironically, test pilot Bill Wheatley was killed on June 26, 1941 while doing the delivery checkout of B-24 AL503, the first Liberator II, scheduled for delivery to the British. A loose bolt fouled the aircraft's elevator control just after takeoff and the B-24 crashed into San Diego bay killing all aboard.

It was the outstanding long range of the B-24 that the British were really interested in as German U-boats were ravaging the convoys that kept Britain supplied with everything from arms, food, and fuel. Now, with the B-24, the British would have the long range bomber capable of seeking out and destroying the German U-boats that were close to bringing Britain to its knees. The only problem was that production of the B-24s was painfully slow. At best Consolidated could turn out about one B-24 per day and the crash of AL503 delayed production of the Liberator II by two months. A world war would demand a far greater production rate; enter the Ford way of assembly.

When Edsel Ford and Charles Sorensen first saw the B-24 at San Diego what they were looking at was the largest and most complex flying machine that either of them had ever seen. Edsel was an aviation buff who, at the age of 14, had constructed a single engine airplane out of wood and fabric powered by a Model-T engine. He had the help of a friend, Charles Van Auken, who volunteered to fly the aircraft. Of course there was little choice since Edsel was forbidden to fly it under orders from his father. The aircraft hardly broke ground before a gust of wind sent it crashing into a nearby tree. Van Auken escaped with just a bump on the head, but Edsel always carried a love of aviation. Gazing at the B-24 it was clear to him that this was no wood and canvas airplane and it sure wasn't powered by a Model-T engine.

Michigan's Heavy Bomber

Standing one-inch shy of 18 feet tall the B-24 was 66 feet long and had a wing span of 110 feet. The aircraft had four huge radial engines each of which provided more power than all three of the Ford tri-motor's aircraft engines combined. It was a monster - much to Edsel's delight. Inside was a maze of wires, tubes, cables, ribs and stringers that made the beast come to life and fly. More than 1,700 different rigid aluminum tubes had to be hand-fitted. There were more than 400,000 rivets in the airframe each of which had to be set by hand. The wing area alone took up 1,048 square feet of sheet aluminum. It looked like a large puzzle that would take an enormous amount of man-hours to produce.

As Sorensen walked around the plant at San Diego his keen eye saw countless problems in the way that Consolidated was producing the aircraft. First off, each piece was manufactured and then carried to the spot where the aircraft was being built. This was the same mistake that early car manufacturers had made. Ford's assembly line was the other way around; you bring the machine you are constructing to the parts rather than the parts to the machine. Another problem was that the largest parts were being assembled outdoors. That meant that when the hot California sun was shining, the huge metal structures would heat up and expand. But when you were working in the cool of the night they would contract and the dimensions would change as dictated by the temperature. The problem there was that none of the construction was truly uniform. Building each aircraft was like making a custom tailored suit. So, the parts from one B-24 would not be interchangeable with another. If battle damage caused a tail to need replacing in the field, the tail taken from another aircraft, along with all of its plumbing, would not fit. There was a serious lack of standardization. During the visit Sorensen had confided to Edsel that those Consolidated people know nothing about mass-production.

When Sorensen brought this point up to Mr. Fleet, who ran Consolidated, a loud argument took place. Finally, Fleet challenged, "Well how would you do it?!" Sorensen simply replied, "I'll tell you tomorrow."

That night Sorensen sat in his hotel room and sketched out the floor plan for what would later become the Willow Run B-24 plant.

WWII

Founder of the Consolidated Aircraft Company Ruben Fleet (left), Charles Sorensen (center) and Edsel Ford (right) tour the Consolidated facility in California on January 8, 1941. It was on this tour that Sorensen said to Ford, "These people know nothing about mass production."

Considering the size of each aircraft the plant would require an 80-acre footprint. The aircraft would move along an assembly line just like cars. The airframes would be broken up into six manageable sub-sections consisting of the nose, aft fuselage, tail, center wing, engines and outer wings. All of the piping and electrical wiring, cables and other vital internal fixtures for each sub-section would be constructed in modules in another part of the plant and sent to the moving line to be installed. Each module would be identical to every other one of its breed, so they would all be interchangeable in the field. Once the center wing was installed and the landing gear was attached and completed, the aircraft would roll the rest of the way along the line on its own wheels. The best part was that all of the work would be done indoors under climate controlled conditions so that every fitting and every rivet hole matched perfectly on every aircraft. Sorensen's calculations showed that using this method, Willow Run could turn out one B-24 every hour, 24 hours a day, seven days a week. When Sorensen presented his plan to Mr. Fleet he was told to "Get serious."

Consolidated wanted Ford to simply build parts for planes and ship those to California for final assembly. Sorensen replied that Ford would build the whole aircraft, or nothing.

Upon returning to Detroit Edsel put out a press release on January 8, 1941 stating that Ford was immediately beginning the construction of a new plant to build the largest, most expensive and most destructive bomber in military history and would do so in numbers never before seen; 400 per month. Even more astounding, Edsel also

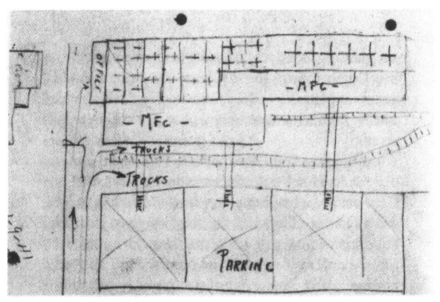

This image is of one of the actual hotel room sketches that Charles Sorensen made of what would become the Willow Run B-24 bomber plant. Sitting up until four o'clock in the morning at the Coronado Hotel and using a pencil and hotel note paper Sorensen made a stack of drawings showing how to mass-produce the bomber. It is also a drawing that aviation legend Ruben Fleet of Consolidated Aircraft looked at and scoffed, "Get real." Image courtesy of the Yankee Air Museum

stated that they hope to have the plant in production before the end of 1941! The plant would cost the government $200 million. The press went wild. There was just one problem; Ford did not yet have any official approval from Washington, or Consolidated!

Almost immediately Roosevelt's Office of Production Management balked at the idea and insisted on just parts. The other auto-makers in Detroit called it impossible and scoffed. Yet the people at Ford kept sending in more and more detailed drawings and up-dated figures. Finally, on March 3, 1941 Ford received their official contract from the government to build 1,200 B-24s. Oddly, the contract was not for the proposed $200 million, but was for $480 million. Apparently the shadow of war had gotten so dark that in less than two months even the most audacious of plans were now worth the risk.

Willow Run's creek waters had only been free of ice for a few weeks when a legion of construction and earth moving equipment came thundering across the ground. Soon the first of 100,000 yards of concrete was being poured. It took 38,000 tons of structural steel to build the aircraft plant. Additionally, some 10 million bricks were laid by hand. Thereafter 11 acres of warehouses sprung up where the apple trees had once been. An airfield measuring 1,434 acres was cleared in the center of the property. Henry Ford, however, had insisted that the creek of Willow Run itself should not have the flow of its waters interrupted by the construction of the new plant. Thus, workers laid down steel pipe where the original creek had been that allowed Willow Run creek to flow underneath the new bomber plant.

Railroad tracks and a new modern highway led from urban Detroit to the new Willow Run plant. The stage was set for a facility that would eventually employ more than 42,000 workers. The plant was dedicated on June 16, 1941 and all appeared in readiness for Ford Motor Company to apply its assembly-line technique to the building of the huge B-24 aircraft.

When it came to the actual production of the B-24s far more than just a factory building and the grounds upon which it sat were challenging the Ford Motor Company. If they were to apply assembly-line technology to the production of this aircraft new tooling and jigs would be required to produce the assorted components. Of course Ford and Mr. Sorensen were able to apply the use of "mass production fixtures" in order to make the assorted sub assembly modules for the aircraft. The mass production fixtures were simply large steel holding frames customized for each individual module. Each of these fixtures had four or more wheels on the bottom so that they could be easily moved about by workers on the production floor. For example, a subsection of the aft fuselage portion of the aircraft that contained a series of hydraulic tubes, air tubes, wiring harnesses and hull ribs would begin by having a prefabricated and pre-formed piece of the aircraft's outer skin locked in place. Whatever hull ribbing was needed would be installed and riveted to the outer skin as well. It would then be moved to a designated place on the assembly floor where workers would install the proper pieces of aluminum tubing. At the same time other workers would install a bundle of electrical wiring with a cannon plug on each end. Then the entire assembly would be moved to the next designated place along the assembly-line where it would meet the aft fuselage section of the aircraft. The assembly would then be installed in place like a giant piece of a giant puzzle. Since the ends of the tubing in the cannon plugs on the wiring were all common to the other modules that were to be connected on each end it was a simple matter for the technicians on the assembly-line to add the piece into the final aircraft and roll it on to the point where the next pieces would be added. Thus, rather than having assembly workers crawling around inside the partially constructed fuselage of the bomber and attempting to work around and over one another to install their specific pieces as Consolidated had been doing, Ford could now cut the assembly man-hours required to the absolute minimum.

One item in the construction of the B-24 that gave Mr. Sorensen the greatest degree of concern was the production of the center wing. Acting as the backbone of the entire aircraft the center wing consisted of the main wing spar and all four engine mounts for the aircraft engines. It was the most complex portion of the aircraft and required the most labor to construct. Thousands of rivet holes had to be drilled in precise locations and scores of access panels had to be cut into the aluminum skin that covered the center wing unit. At Consolidated that process could take days and as many as 550 man-hours to complete. In Mr. Sorensen's eyes it was a showstopper. The solution to this problem was proposed by William Pioch who was the chief tool design engineer at Ford. He dreamed up the idea of something he called the "final machining unit."

Utilizing overhead cranes attached to rails in the ceiling of the plant each 30-ton center wing unit would be picked up, inverted and transported, nose-down, to the location of the final machining unit. The center wing would then be lowered into the unit and locked in place. A series of drill presses and machine cutters would then close in on the center wing unit and simultaneously machine every single hole needed. The same crane would then remove the center wing from the final machining unit and move it down the assembly-line to be joined with the rest of the aircraft.

The entire process would require six men and one hour of time. In other words, the process was reduced from 550 man-hours to just six man-hours, a man hour reduction of 99%. The cost of the machine was $250,000. There was another benefit other than the savings in man-hours, each and every center wing unit would be identical and interchangeable with every other center wing unit made by Ford.

There were also to be plenty of other new

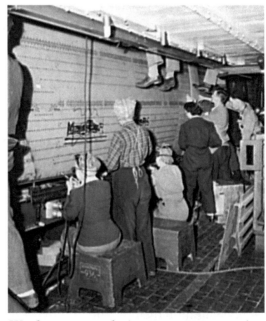

Workers completing a center wing section for a B-24 in the vertical position. Note the feet of the person on the upper portion of the work stand. This is classic Sorenson where the part is brought to the workers rather than the workers going to the part. Library of Congress

equipment never before used in the manufacturing of Ford automobiles that would have to be applied at Willow Run. X-ray machines were needed to examine critical metal parts, provisions for handling toxic chemicals used in the production of aviation components, molds and hot baths for the shaping of Plexiglas window components ñ all of these and countless others would be installed at the new plant. Plus, there was one entirely new building that had never before been needed at a Ford Assembly plant; a huge school for training aircraft workers. The cost was just over $500,000 and Ford now had the capacity to train 8,000 students in the fine art of handling and understanding the smallest components that made the huge four engine bombers come to life.

By the first week of December, 1941 the Willow Run aircraft plant, at that time the largest factory under one roof in the world was nearing completion and slightly ahead of schedule. Then, the bombs and torpedoes began to fall on Pearl Harbor. In a heartbeat "slightly ahead of schedule" was far from being good enough so far as the B-24 was concerned. On December 8th, the day after Pearl Harbor Edsel Ford received a telegram from General George C. Kenney that stated that the Undersecretary of War was directing industry leaders to take all necessary steps to immediately increase the manufacture of munitions to the highest possible level and ordered that all production must at once be placed on a 24-hour per day seven day per week schedule. Almost immediately he received a second telegram from the Assistant Secretary of War for Air Robert Lovett. That message said the government was raising its expectations for production and stated flatly, "the vital part which we are counting on for the Ford Motor Company to play" at Willow Run would be that of the "Keystone in the arch of the big government plants" And it was for that reason that Lovett's department was most anxious to get the Willow Run plant into operation at the earliest possible date. Edsel replied that the board fully realized the, "gravity of the situation and importance of the earliest completion and operation" of Ford's aircraft engine and bomber plants.

Unlike his pacifist and diehard antiwar father, Edsel Ford knew full well that the world was now at war and it was something that he had expected. Henry Ford simply ordered that, "We might as well stop making cars now." One step that the elder Ford did take was to send a telegram to his nemesis in the White House, FDR. Henry Ford simply wished the president, "The strength and wisdom necessary for the task you have received."

Edsel now turned to the most hated man in the Ford Motor Company for help with the manpower situation that now loomed over the company; that man was Harry Bennett. It was said that Bennett was feared by every employee in the Ford Motor Company. A two-fisted tough thug, he had become Henry Ford's personal muscle and ran what was described by "American Mercury Magazine" as the "most powerful private police force in the world" After years of having Bennett around, Edsel new that there was nothing that Bennett knew better than how to fight and there was also nothing that the man liked to do more. Now the entire nation was in its greatest fight for survival since the Civil War and within the Ford Motor Company Bennett would play a key role in that fight. Edsel directed him to begin safeguarding the company's plants and personnel from air raids. As far as anyone knew at that point in time enemy planes could come roaring overhead at any moment just as they had in London and at Pearl Harbor but the axis powers had one problem, they'd have to go through Harry Bennett in order to get to the Ford plants! Pity be upon them indeed.

Considering the near panicked tone of the messages that Edsel Ford had received from the very top of the United States war machine his first instinct was to drive out and check on the progress of the Willow Run plant. Although the school and office facilities were far from complete the production plant was fully enclosed and ready to start building. In fact, the first components for the first B-24s would actually be produced on December 9th. Yet, as Edsel walked into his brand-new production plant and the fact that B-24 mass production required an enormous amount of space, it suddenly washed over him that, the building was starkly empty. Every footstep that Edsel took across the brand-new concrete floor, which was as smooth as glass and the wooden floors of the assembly bays, seem to echo in the distance. He had boasted that the first bombers would be rolling off

Michigan's Heavy Bomber

Perhaps the most feared and loathed man in the automobile industry Harry Bennett ran a private security force for Henry Ford. When it came time to secure the Ford facilities at the outbreak of war, Edsel Ford called on Bennett's talents. Image, Wayne State University

the line in May of 1942. Now, as he gazed across the cavernous empty plant, we can only imagine what sorts of doubt may have gnawed at him.

Yamamoto's sneak attack on Pearl Harbor had galvanized the resolve of the American people like tempered steel. Many people in the Great Lakes region knew that Ford had opened a new bomber plant at Willow Run and the instant the word went out that they needed manpower for around-the-clock production people flocked to Willow Run. Yet, men were also being drafted into the Armed Forces, the result being a shortage of "manpower" which was soon to be replaced by "woman power."

WWII

Legions of women flocked to the Ford plants. With each B-24 requiring 400,000 rivets, each of which had to be set individually by hand, the term "Rosie the Riveter" would soon be applied en masse not only at Ford, but later in defense plants across the nation. Many accounts state that the actual "Rosie the Riveter" was Rose Munro, a Kentucky expatriate who came to Willow Run shortly after Pearl Harbor and was seen working by a government publicist seeking a symbol to recruit women and build morale. Unexpectedly, Willow Run suddenly became a news media star. Popular magazines

Rosie the Riveter became a World War II icon symbolizing the need for women to get to work in American industry and to help win the war. The original Rosie was discovered at Ford's Willow Run B-24 bomber plant and is often celebrated today by the Yankee Air Museum at Willow Run. Library of Congress

such as "Look" and "Life," ran glowing stories about the world's largest bomber plant. Newspaper such as the "Washington Post," the "Christian Science Monitor" and the "New York Times" trumpeted the facility as being a linchpin in FDR's "arsenal of democracy." They told of the plant's huge dimensions comparing its length to the height of the Empire State building and talking of how many baseball diamonds could fit inside. They talked of so many bombers coming out of this plant that they would blot out the sun over Germany and Japan. They told the free world that the fight was not only taking place on the battlefield, but right in the heart of Detroit while ignoring the fact that Willow Run was actually in Ypsilanti.

In the first weeks of 1942 the Willow Run plant begin to feel growing pains. In his original concept for the plant Edsel Ford had envisioned that workers would drive into the plant by the thousands along a brand-new roadway that he had constructed linking Willow Run to workers based in Detroit. Yet with the onset of the war the Office of Price Administration had set up mandatory rationing of food products and gasoline as well as items such as rubber tires. Suddenly the workers who would be manning the huge bomber plant could not afford to drive their cars the distance between Detroit and Willow Run. The result was a shantytown of government supplied trailers housing new workers. The conditions there led to a decrease in worker morale and increase in absenteeism. Additionally, nearly as fast as Ford could educate new workers in their bomber plant training school many of those same men were being called up by

Trailers, tents and almost no sanitation made living in "Bomber City" very harsh. This led to high absentee rates and hurt production.
Library of Congress

their draft boards. Most hurtful, however, was a rash of wildcat strikes that plagued the plant.

Most of the leaders in the aviation industry were highly critical of allowing a car company, such as Ford, to get into the business of building a complete aircraft. Considering that Edsel Ford had flatly stated that the very first bombers would begin rolling out of the Willow Run plant in May of 1942 the critics of the Ford production effort were quick to highlight the growing pains of the plant. Ford executives argued that changing over from building cars to building aircraft was not an effort that could take place overnight. The effort cost millions of dollars and tens of thousands of man-hours. Some machines that were used to mass-produce automobiles could, in some cases, be readily changed over to making aircraft parts. But many mass production devices simply could not be so easily modified or didn't exist and had to be designed and built. Still the critics were not easily silenced and there was only one thing that would quiet them and that was the actual production of a B-24 bomber from the heart of Michigan's automobile country.

On May 15, 1942 the very first B-24 Liberator was rolled out of the Willow Run plant. Although it had been assembled largely with parts shipped in from Consolidated in California that fact was easily painted over by the morale building value of the huge bomber being rolled out of the plant that was intended to produce one exactly like it every single hour. Harold Henning, Ford's chief test pilot, would be at the controls of this first Michigan assembled B-24.

Following the approved checklist for the B-24, Henning perform the standard walk around and preflight - first checking the landing gear and inspecting the horizontal stabilizer and tail assembly as well as checking all four engines to ensure there was no oil leaking. Crouching down as low as he could get without folding himself in half, Henning ducked into the open Bombay doors and climbed up toward the cockpit. Taking his seat, he first checked all four fuel shutoff valves to verify that each was in the "on" position and also checked to make sure that the cross feeds were properly set and confirm that each engine was receiving fuel from its main cell. All four fuel gauges indicated the proper amount of fuel required for this test flight. He adjusted his seat, however, it was pretty much where it had been countless times as he had adjusted it prior to today's test flight. By now Henning's flight engineer had taken his seat and both men confirmed that they had crossed checked the fuel valves and gauges. Henning called "generators" and his engineer replied "off." The way that the B-24 was wired required that the generators be kept off at this phase in order to prevent draining the batteries should there be a faulty reverse current relay and also because the generators could not charge unless engine RPM was above 1,400. The pilot next called for "carburetor air filters" and his engineer replied, "as required." Continuing down the checklist Henning called for "mainline battery selectors" and his copilot turned that switch to the "on" position and checked the level of each battery and then turned the selector to the "off" position as today's start would be done from an auxiliary power cart located outside of the aircraft. The B-24 was a monster of an aircraft and the crew could not simply jump in and start her up. The pre-start checklist took a good deal of time as the crowd of assembly-line workers and Edsel Ford himself stood outside watching and waiting.

A fire guard armed with a huge fire extinguisher stood near engine number three as the crew began the process of starting the B-24's four engines. Upon Henning's call his copilot snapped all four ignition switches to the "on" position. Henning "cracked" all four throttles by moving them slightly forward. Next the pilot called for the boost pumps and his copilot threw all four switches energizing the pumps. As the fuel pressure rose above 4 pounds each engine was primed by depressing that switch for one second and then releasing it.

While many in the crowd held their breath Henning called for "start engines." Cranking around for several turns the propeller on engine number three seem to agonize as it spun. It is quite likely that many in the crowd wondered if it would actually ever start. Of course this crew had started and ran all four engines a number of times very early that morning before the crowd and the press arrived. Henning, his crew, and Ford management wanted to make darn sure that this aircraft would both start and run flawlessly as a part of the roll-out

45

show. After the private run-up, the B-24 was quietly wheeled back into the factory to await the public roll-out. With a slight billow of white oily smoke engine number three came to life and soon thereafter engine number four, number two, and number one would all roar to life. With a sound that only a B-24 can make the first Willow Run-built monster taxied out onto the new concrete runway. Henning and his crew did a run-up on each engine starting with engine number four, then three, then two, and finally number one. Advancing the throttles on each engine Henning throttled them up to 2,000 RPM individually to check the magnetos. At completion of the pre-takeoff checklist Henning positioned the olive drab painted B-24 along the runway centerline and upon clearance from the control tower advance the throttles to full power. Like a thumb in the eye to the Willow Run critics the giant bomber clawed its way into the air. She could have been mistaken of a homesick angel.

Although the delivery of the first B-24 was essentially on-time, mass production of the bombers was still a faraway goal. Aside from the issues of manpower, the production of B-24's was suffering from a new issue; quality control. Although the entire plant had been designed to produce identical parts interchangeable with each and every aircraft, it required properly trained people completing each task exactly to specification. Through what remained of 1942 on into most of 1943 Ford was training large groups of line technicians. Yet after months of technical training on very specific areas in the assembly process, no sooner would many of the men get acclimated to the production process they would be spirited away by the military. By mid-February 1943 the B-24 training program had taken in 20,177 workers yet before their training was completed more than 11,000 had quit. In a single month more than 1,700 had been drafted by the military and nearly 1,500 had gone to enlist. This constant turnover resulted in low quality aircraft coming off the assembly line. In October of 1942 Charles Lindbergh, who had been hired by Ford as an aviation expert to consult in their B-24 program, flew one of the aircraft that was fresh off the assembly line. His report back to Edsel Ford was not a good one. Lindbergh described the B-24 as being essentially one of the unruliest aircraft he had ever attempted to fly. The aircraft was extremely heavy on the controls and poorly rigged, he found an abundance of defective riveting and faulty workmanship. In short, the Ford-built Liberator was a lemon.

Another serious headache for Willow Run management was the never ending series of changes in the aircraft's design dumped upon them by the United States Army Air Corps. When you're building an aircraft one at a time by hand, as Consolidated was doing, it's relatively easy to implement changes - both minor and major. However, Ford's 1940s assembly-line technology did not lend itself at all well to any sort of changes in design. Stamping machines, for example, use dies in order to rapidly produce exactly identical parts. Those dies also must be designed and constructed. A single small change, such as a bulge or an indentation that may be required to accommodate some other change in the aircraft causes a domino effect in blueprints, milling, machining, testing, and expanded man-hours. Although military leaders were begged by Ford to freeze the design of the B-24 - the changes kept coming.

Ford workers operating drill presses. Note the time-keeper at the lower right. Library of Congress

WWII

Ford found a solution to this complex mountain of problems, not by throwing money at it or reverting back to the traditional form of constructing aircraft, but by way of micromanagement of the assembly-line process and the innovative recruitment of manpower. Edsel Ford ordered Harry Bennett to send his recruiters into the deep south of the United States to recruit anyone and everyone who wanted to work. The company bought thousands of bus tickets and soon scores of people who had never before even seen a factory were being trained to build the B-24. Black, white, educated, illiterate, it didn't matter. If you wanted a job, there was one waiting for you at Willow Run. Many arrived carrying only a gunnysack containing their worldly possessions, yet still they came to build the bombers and do their part for the war effort. Southern blacks who were eager to escape the Jim Crow laws arrived in droves. Ford also found places for the handicapped. Persons missing limbs or who were deaf or even blind found a useful job somewhere in the bomber plant.

One specific group of individuals who are normally considered to be out of the mainstream found a very useful place at Willow Run. Dwarfs, or as they prefer to be called "little people" were critical in the construction of the B-24. These individuals were not hired in spite of their size, but rather they were hired because of their size. The enormous middle wing section of the B-24 required some critical riveting that had to be done after that section had been affixed to the fuselage. If this critical riveting was not done properly the aircraft would not hold together during flight. The problem was that people of "normal" size could not fit inside the center wing assembly. For that reason, the little people were tasked with crawling into the center wing section and doing that very important riveting. There were also other areas of the aircraft that benefited from their size and skill. When FDR toured the Willow Run plant, he was astonished to see the little people at work. So much so in fact that he had the open top limousine that he was riding in stopped and he opened the door to shake their hands. Frankly, they were just as critical to the B-24 as the center wing itself - their contribution helped win the war.

As a part of the stabilization of the labor force at the bomber plant Edsel Ford personally pleaded with FDR to do something about that critical housing shortage in the area around the factory. From that conversation the president directed that immediate federal housing should be constructed adjacent to the factory. In spite of Henry Ford's objection, "bomber city" was constructed at a pace that only a war emergency could create. Soon other housing very near the plant sprang up. Additionally, a continuous bus service shuttled workers to and from the factory. The buses were normally filled to capacity and arrived and departed about every 8 minutes around-the-clock.

May 26, 1943 dawned to find the Ford company absent one of its leaders. Edsel Ford had died during the night from stomach cancer at the age of 49. The company would eventually be taken over by Henry Ford II, Edsel Ford's son. Yet not even the loss of the man who conceived the huge bomber plant could stop the flow of Michigan's heavy bomber production. With the labor force stabilized the B-24 lemon very quickly evolved into the B-24 Liberator. Greater attention to detail and quality lead to a better flying aircraft.

Charles Sorensen and Edsel Ford's B-24 bomber assembly line on the roll in 1944. Photo from the Yankee Air Museum Collection

WWII

B-24 on its test flight over Lake St. Clair (Note the Great Lakes freighter in the background). The B-24 test pilots and crews slept on cots in the assembly plant waiting for their next shift of flight tests aboard the huge bombers. Photo from the Yankee Air Museum Collection

Additionally, an in-house army of quality control officers kept stopwatches running at each and every station along the assembly-line. They did time studies, plotted every move that every worker made and then micromanaged that to make better use of time.

July of 1944 saw a total of 400 B-24's rolled out of Willow Run. Thus as Allied forces were fighting their way across France, in Detroit that July an average of 13 new Liberators per day were rolling onto the field at Willow Run. This meant that every single new aircraft had to be test flown and ferried off to a dispatch airfield. During test flights a load of steel dummy bombs were taken aloft and dropped into Lake St. Clair. The tiny Lake between Detroit and Lake Huron became one of the most heavily bombed sites in North America. To this day thousands of dummy bombs lay on its bottom.

50

Michigan's Heavy Bomber

Along with the shortage of men to work in the plant there came a shortage of male pilots needed to ferry the B-24s to their dispatch fields. That gap was sometimes filled by bold young ladies in over-sized men's flight suits. With pant legs rolled up and a devil-may-care swagger that most men could only wish to match, these WASPs, or Women Airforce Service Pilots, flew nearly every type of aircraft in the United States World War II military inventory - including the B-24. In their day, however, they never got the credit that they deserved and earned. Not until my generation of professional aviators were women pilots truly accepted as the equal to their male counterparts. As a professional pilot I can state without doubt that the WASPs were damn good pilots, equal to the female pilots of today, because I have trained and flown with many a female pilot and frankly a lot of them fly better than some of the men.

New B-24s parked on the ramp at Willow Run awaiting flight test and ferry service. This photo contains 23 of the big bombers- that is one short of a single day's production at the plant during its peak.
Photo from the Yankee Air Museum Collection

51

WWII

B-24s, however, were not the only product that Ford turned out for the war effort. 4,291 invasion gliders were constructed using lumber milled at Ford's Kingsford lumber. 12,314 armored cars were constructed at Ford plants. 277,896 Jeeps, 93,217 trucks, 26,954 tank engines and 2,718 tanks were also constructed by Ford. In addition to that the most complex machine that Ford built, the B-24 Liberator, saw 8,685 come off the assembly line at Willow Run. At its peak the plant employed more than 42,300 workers. Overall more than 80,700 individuals had participated in the construction of B-24's in Michigan. On June 28, 1945 the last B-24 was rolled out of the hangar at Willow Run.

Although the B-24 always remained heavy on the controls and unable to take as much damage as its cousin the B-17, the Liberator was produced in greater numbers than any other United States aircraft during World War II. The objective had been to produce so many bombers that when flown together they would blackout the sky

June 28, 1945 - the final B-24 rolls out of the hangar at the Willow Run plant.

A fly-over of Willow Run. In the background is the enormous assembly plant for the bombers. The two white arrows indicate the tiny portion of the plant that remains today as the Yankee Air Museum. Photo from the Yankee Air Museum Collection

over enemy territory. Although that was a good motto for morale building purposes, the simple fact that the Willow Run factory was producing one bomber every hour seven days a week went a long way toward making that threat look achievable.

Production of the B-24 ended just before VJ day. Over the next two years the aircraft were flown back to the United States and some were scrapped at Willow Run. Most, however, were flown to the desert in the western United States and parked as nothing more than war surplus. In the end the B-24 was a machine created to help win the war and it served its purpose fully, yet in peacetime it would serve no one except the scrap dealers. By the time the war ended aviation technology, both civilian and military, had advanced beyond the design capabilities of the B-24 thus making the B-24 itself outdated. Although not all of the Liberators were constructed in Michigan many of the forward fuselages were and other components that went into B-24s constructed in other plants around the country were prefabricated in Michigan. In spite of getting off to a stumbling start, the assembly-line method of building wartime bombers proved itself and helped bring victory to the Allied forces in World War II.

After the war the plant that made the B-24 remained active in the automobile industry. But as the plant went from Ford's ownership into the hands of Kaiser-Frazer and at length to General Motors the production of American made automobiles declined. In the end GM built transmissions in the facility until 2010 when the Willow Run plant ceased operation. Soon the bull dozers and wrecking crews came calling looking to turn the vacant plant into another of lower Michigan's empty cement slabs.

Enter the Yankee Air Museum.

In 2004 the Yankee Air Museum's facility near Willow Run had burned to the ground. Fortunately, many of the museum's historic aircraft survived and after raising $5.5 million the museum acquired part of the plant before it could be demolished. The area is under 4% of the original plant yet measures 144,000 square feet of hangar space. This section of the plant is the final inspection area - the end of the line were the completed B-24 bombers were rolled out for their test flights. The organization intends to turn this site into one of the best aviation museums in the nation, but it will take additional funding and a lot of volunteer work. Their efforts can be found on the Internet at: www.savethebomberplant.org.

A PROUD CANADIAN VETERAN

No sooner had war been declared by the nation of Canada than one of her most experienced and well-worn veterans of the lakes joined the fight for liberty against Nazi aggression. She was the *Maplecourt*, a 46-year-old lady of the lakes who had been requisitioned by the government during the previous world war.

Maplecourt had a long and storied history on the Great Lakes. Having gone from the upper crust of elegance to the lowly state of an abandon wreck, twice, she endured the toil of the salvage business, nonetheless, the boat was a veteran. She held the rare distinction of having been cut in half three times to allow her to pass through the tiny locks of the Canadian canals along the St. Lawrence River. Additionally, she had left her original bow on the bottom of Lake Erie. Now she was being called up in the opening days of Canada's entrance into World War II. She would venture out into the salt water of the North Atlantic and face the teeth of the Nazi U-Boat wolf packs in order to do her part to help win the war.

Long before anyone imagined anything as horrific as a world war the vessel that would one day be called upon to serve in two of them came to life. At exactly 2:30 on a bitter cold Saturday afternoon a brand new steamship slid down the launching ways at Cleveland's Globe Iron Works. The year was 1894 during the thick of the Victorian era as well as the industrial revolution. Ladies and Gentlemen of the upper class had come from all over the region to witness this event as the sleek steel hull met fresh water for the first time. Tugs had worked for hours in order to free the launching slip

WWII

In an era when steamship cruising was a way of life, the proud vessel
North West *was a true lady of the lakes. Library of Congress photo courtesy of Steve Vanden Bosch*

of ice and when the 383-foot-long hull splashed into the water its wake threw huge cakes of ice onto the opposite shore as fine ladies bundled in their winter's best wraps squealed with delight. Christened the *North West* the steamer that would one day become the *Maplecourt* was one of the new class of "Palace Steamers."

This type of vessel had first sailed the lakes from the mid 1840s until the early 1850s and were designed to be as extravagant as the finest hotels of the day. They also had below deck spaces for large numbers of immigrants who were packed in like sardines. The boats moved people west where new opportunities waited for both rich and poor alike. By the late 1850s, however, dismal economic times and competition from the newly expanding railroads sent most of the big palace boats to the lay-up wall where they rotted away. The 1890's saw the return of the palace steamers as the way west was still the choice of many, but the destinations were now pursued for pleasure and sight-seeing.

Although her steel hull was a generation more modern than the wooden hulls of her Palace Class predecessors, the new *North West* easily matched their accommodations. On her upper deck she had 140 first class staterooms and another 18 huge Palace Class staterooms. Below decks and forward there were sardine accommodations for 350 "emigrants." In order to keep the non-emigrant passengers happy a crew of 150 were employed to make every aspect of the boat function to perfection. She also had "an electric lighting plant" powerful enough to energize all 1,300 electric lights onboard. Many of those were located in her fine dining salon that measured 38 by 52 feet and was adorned in white, gold and carved cherry wainscoting. She also had a lady's deck salon finished in fine Mahogany which sported a grand piano. For the palace class ladies there was also a "lady's reading room" located on the far aft deckhouse which had an open fireplace in its center.

Twin quadruple expansion steam engines working twin propellers provided the *North West* with a total of 7,000 horsepower. That was enough to propel her sleek white hull across the lakes at a top speed

Passengers loved the elegant North West, *but she never sailed at a profit to her owners. Instead she was simply a promotional device for the western railroads of tycoon James J. Hill. Library of Congress photo courtesy of Steve Vanden Bosch*

of 20 miles per hour. Her owners, the Northern Steamship Company placed her into service on the Buffalo to Duluth route. Oddly, the *North West* and her sister the *North Land* always sailed with a full load of passengers, yet financially always ran at a loss! Their owner, railroad tycoon James J. Hill, felt that the boats and their routes were good advertising for his western railroads and so he kept them sailing. That worked fine for the *North West* - until 1911.

Preparing for the 1911 summer cruise season both the *North West* and her sister ship *North Land* were rafted together in the slips of the Lehigh Valley coal dock complex just north of Tifft Street in Buffalo, New York. Today the remnants of the extended south slip where she was tied up is still somewhat visible as part of the Tifft Nature Preserve just north of Tifft Road and Highway 5. At four o'clock on the morning on June 3, 1911 fire broke out in the paint locker aboard the *North West* and quickly turned her upper wooden structure into a flaming mass. Her sister ship the *North Land* was towed clear by a Buffalo fire department fire boat and only suffered some scorching. Yet, the *North West* was gutted and soon sank from the weight of the water that the fire companies had poured upon her to extinguish the blaze. It took until noon before the last of the flames were smothered.

In the days following the blaze newspaper stories stated that the *North West* was raised and would be quickly towed to Cleveland and repaired. Local managers of the boat stated unequivocally that she would be fully repaired and returned to service in time to catch the end of the 1911 cruise season. But the owners of the Northern Steamship Company had a different perspective. What they saw was the burned out hulk of a vessel that financially had always lost money. Her palace accommodations were completely in ashes. It would take more than $250,000 in 1911 dollars (which is just over $6,250,000 in 2015 dollars) to get her back into a suitable condition. It was far better business to simply abandon her to the insurance company. She was reportedly "well insured."

Thus, the hulk of the once proud *North West* was left in the backwaters of the Lehigh Valley Coal slips near where she had burned. For six long winters and summers she sat, her white hull paint chipping away and rust finding its way into every area of opportunity.

A Proud Canadian Veteran

The 1911 fire that gutted the North West *could have spelled her demise. Instead it led her into new adventures. Author's Collection*

He upper hull was scorched and stained with black soot and her two remaining smoke stacks showed the scars of the fire and the fading of abandonment - only their white stars gave any indication of her former glory. Then there came the drums of a distant war.

Canada's Governor General declared war on Germany on August 5, 1914. This was just one day after Great Britain had declared war on Germany. With that the nation entered into a protracted and bloody struggle that would kill on a scale that gave new meaning to the phrase "Led like sheep to the slaughter." By 1917 the allied forces were short of men and material as the development of new weapons killed men at levels never before seen in human history. As the war meat grinder went on, the losses of men and material only got worse. One of the greatest needs was for ships. There was a new German war machine known as the "U-boat" or as they called it the "Unterseeboot" and it was decimating allied shipping and their crews in alarming numbers. In 1916 alone the allies lost 415 ships to U-boats - that was half of

59

WWII

their fleet at the time. Anything that could float was needed to aid in the war against the Germans and so in August of 1915 Charles Finnegan purchased the hulk of the old *North West*.

Finnegan's problem was that in order to get the hulk to the Atlantic and into the war, she would first have to be towed through the locks of the canals system that led to the sea. The smallest of those locks was able to accommodate a vessel no longer than 261 feet and the hull of the *North West* was 383 feet long. The solution was one that was being used frequently during the war. They would place her in drydock, cut her in half and float the two halves through the canals and then re-drydock them in Montreal and rivet them back together. The vessel would then be rebuilt as a cargo carrier to support the war effort.

On the overcast and rainy late autumn day of October 27, 1917, Mr. Finnegan's charred boat was towed into a drydock at Buffalo and the task of removing hundreds of rivets and winching the boat in half took place. She was broken apart just in front of her boilers and aft of where her pilothouse had once been. Then her open hull was rigged with a temporary water tight bulkhead covering her bottom, holds and ballast tanks so she could float as two separate sections. The job was done at a brisk pace because the United States was now in the war and had been so since the sixth day of April. Thus, every hull that could float was being requisitioned on an emergency basis. Huge steamers were even being constructed of wood in the effort to beat the Kaiser, but then something odd took place.

As of this writing I've not uncovered the exact reasoning, but the two halves of the *North West* changed ownership five times between the day that she was halved and the day that the war ended on November 11, 1918. First she was sold to Theodore Hofeller, then to Samuel J. Feldman, all in the remaining two months of 1917. Then she was sold to the Susquehanna Finance Corporation in 1918. At length the boat was sold to Canadian J.F. Darcy of Montreal. Mr. Darcy had the same plan as everyone else and that was to float the two sections down the canals and onto salt water to profit from the war effort. Oddly, that process began some two weeks after the war ended!

A Proud Canadian Veteran

Both sections of the *North West* started out for the Canadian canals November 17th - which is a bad time to begin any trip across the Great Lakes. With the stern in the lead and the bow section tied to it with a thick towing hawser they safely made it through the Welland Canal and then sat at Port Dalhousie, Ontario waiting for better weather before trying to sail the length of Lake Ontario. At Buffalo on the morning of November 28, the wind was blowing a steady 12 miles per hour and the lake was fairly pleasant. But, just a bit to the west in Erie, Pennsylvania, the winds increased to 42 miles per hour and the barometer was rapidly falling as a massive late autumn low pressure system was sweeping in. At Oswego, New York on the far eastern end of the lake the winds were also 12 miles per hour, but had made a rapid shift from due north to due south during the previous 24 hours. In the hours ahead the winds there would increase to 46 miles per hour with driving snow and sleet. It caught the two halves of the *North West* and their tugs out in the open lake just a few hours west of the mouth of the St. Lawrence River.

To most vessels, riding out the choppy seas brought up by a simple 12 miles per hour wind was no problem. At worst you would simply take on ballast and get a lower profile to the waves and winds. Yet, for two halves of a powerless vessel with no ballast and no pumping capability, any amount of water shipped aboard could be fatal. Worse yet, the tugs that were towing the vessel halves were able to make less than six miles per hour headway in calm seas while pulling the deadweight of the high-riding vessel halves. In the confused beam sea, they were almost standing still.

Only the stern section of the *North West* made it into the safety of the St. Lawrence River. That was after the stern and its crew had managed to limp out of the storm and into Rochester, New York on the lake's southern shore. During the storm the bow section had been smashing into the stern where it became necessary to cut loose the bow in order to try and save both sections. The bow later capsized and sank near Scotch Bonnet Island on the northeastern end of Lake Ontario. Only 11 crewmen on the bow escaped in the boat's life raft, however, two of them died from hypothermia before the raft drifted into Wellers' Bay, Ontario where the survivors sought shelter in a fishing hut. The 9 survivors were soon returned to the United States.

It was estimated that the cost of building a new bow section for the half vessel that Mr. Darcy now owned would be about $500,000, (approximately $6,944,000 in 2015 dollars). But, considering Atlantic merchant fleet losses during the war - he thought it was worth the investment and the vessel got a completely new bow section and, on January 22, 1920 it also got a new name; *Maplecourt*.

By 1921 the Canada Steamship Lines purchased the *Maplecourt* from Mr. Darcy and after briefly running her in the salt water trade it was decided to bring her back to the Great Lakes in 1922. This time the process was reversed and she was placed in the care of the Montreal Drydock Company and again her rivets were removed and she was sent back up to the lakes by way of the Canadian canal system. Once on Lake Erie the Buffalo Drydock Company was given the task of putting her back together. She reentered lakes service at the beginning of the 1923 season. *Maplecourt* sailed without incident until October 30, 1929 when she ran onto the Magnetic Reefs on Lake Huron. For the second time in her career she was declared a total loss and turned over to the insurance underwriters. Famed Great Lakes salvage expert Thomas Reid refloated her in 1930 and she was purchased from him by John E. Russell of Sin-Mac Lines, a Canadian salvage outfit. Later, in 1936, she was purchased by another salvage company, United Towing and Salvage. Then came the onset of another world war.

As Canada entered the war, even heavily-worn vessels such as the *Maplecourt* were needed. Once again the U-boats threatened, but this time they had far greater range and could come right up to the Canadian Maritimes and hunt. Thus from the salvage yard the Canadian government requisitioned the old steamer. While younger passenger liners were ripped apart and melted down for wartime re-use, the older *Maplecourt* had one advantage over them. Since she had been working fairly steadily through the depression years and, unlike many younger vessels her engine equipment was in good running order, she could go straight to work once she was again on salt water. For the third time she was taken apart to allow her to transit through the St. Lawrence River canal system. This time her bow section was separated forward of the pilot house. In Montreal she was again put back together, but this time she would not miss out on the war. Defensive armaments, such as deck guns, were installed on her bow and stern and she was ready to fight.

In charge of the old World War I veteran *Maplecourt* was Captain Emrys Herbert Humphries of Vancouver. His Chief Officer was William Robertson of Montreal and the third officer serving on the old lady's bridge was Andrew Dube of Hamilton, Ontario who was a native of fresh water sailing. Down in her engine room Chief Engineer Frank James Esson looked after her triple expansion engine which had been installed in 1919 to replace her original quadruple expansion engine. Second Engineer William Small, Third Engineer Charles Cornelius Hendrik Luyten and Fourth Engineer George Young were also in charge of the engines. The remaining crew consisted of Radio Operator Arvo Aho, Able Seaman Dedier Aucoin,

As the Maplecourt, *the old vessel went to war in order to do her part to preserve freedom. Although she looked good she was truly unfit for ocean service. She would never return to the Great Lakes. Author's Collection*

WWII

Ordinary Seaman James Bennett, Fireman and Trimmer Raymond Berry, Able Seaman Edison Bowes, Steward Claude Brent, British Army Private (DEMS gunner) George Frederick Brimicombe, Fireman and Trimmer Garfield Campbell, Fireman and Trimmer Roy Davis, Able Seaman Edward Dewhurst, Fireman Joseph E. Doucette, Mess Room Boy Clarence Gallant (age 19), Chief Cook J.B. Kelly, Second Cook Harold Langille, Ordinary Seaman (DEMS gunner RCNVR) John Alden Lockhart (age 19), Ship's Carpenter Ray MacGougan, Able Seaman Elmer C. MacLeod, Fireman and Trimmer James Malloy, Fireman William Matheson, Fireman and Trimmer Michael Morrissey, Fireman James Mount, Fireman and Trimmer Albert O'Hanley, Fireman and Trimmer Earl O'Hanley (both of St. Peters Bay, Prince Edward Island, but of different parents.), Boatswain (Bosun) Adrien Poitras (an Army veteran from World War I), Steward Roland Potvin, Able Seaman Clarence Richards, British Army Private(DEMS gunner) Wilfred Harold Riddle, Ordinary Seaman Joseph Shaw, Oiler Albert Shea, and Ordinary Seaman Earnest F. Trefry who together took the *Maplecourt* to war in the first weeks of January, 1941.

During *Maplecourt's* first crossing of the Atlantic she endured a wicked gale that forced her to limp back to Boston Harbor in a leaking condition. She was placed into drydock, repaired and again put back out to sea.

On February 6, 1941 Captain Günther Hessler raised the periscope of the U-107 and in its sights was a Canadian freighter. Captain Hessler had been stalking the vessel for nearly eight hours and had already shot one torpedo at her four hours earlier and missed. The steamer was a straggler from her convoy and presented a ripe target for the U-boat. The U-107 had been on patrol since January 24, and had already sunk two British vessels, the *Empire Citizen* on February 3, and the *HMS Crispin* that same day, all off the coast of Ireland. Now he had a Canadian vessel in U-107's sights - the *Maplecourt*.

Just 120 miles off of Rockall, Ireland Captain Hesslerhad maneuvered U-107 so that he could shoot with his stern tubes. He fired a single torpedo and watched as it impacted the *Maplecourt* just aft of her engine room. The steamer sank rapidly. He was sure that he saw crewmen abandon the vessel in two lifeboats. He lowered his periscope and noted the position as 57°33'N, 17°24'W. It was the last vessel that U-107 would sink on this 37-day patrol. Captain Hesslerhad, however, would sink another 18 ships on his next two patrols, although none were Canadian flagged. He survived the war and after a brief allied imprisonment the British Royal Navy would commission him plus another U-boat commander, Alfred Hoschatt, to write a six volume book series titled "The U-boat War in the Atlantic" documenting in detail that part of the war. U-107 was not as lucky as Captain Hesslerhad when on August 18, 1944, off the western coast of France, south-west of St. Nazaire, she was spotted by a British Sunderland flying boat. The Sunderland, a repurposed airliner, used depth charges to sink the U-107 taking her entire crew of 58 down with her.

No survivors of the *Maplecourt* were ever found and she was listed officially as "lost with all hands." Her position, however, was initially mistakenly given as 55°39N/15°56W and her date of sinking has been incorrectly reported as February 7th, 8th, and even the 10th. *Maplecourt's* career on the lakes had been long, but her service in World War II and that of her crew came to a swift and sudden end. "Lost with all hands."

FORTRESS SOO

Rather than expanding their empire south through the Pacific and making a star-crossed attack on the island of Midway, or continuing to exercise the battle of the Atlantic with wolf packs of U-boats, the Japanese or the Germans could actually have won the war by bombing one single target on the Great Lakes; the Soo Locks.

United States manufacturing was the heart of the Arsenal of Democracy and the blood was iron ore. As the prospect of world war began to grow and the gears of Lend-Lease began to turn, there were plenty of ore boats available. Nearly the entire Great Lakes fleet had been idled during the Great Depression as had their crews. Old lakeboats that should have been sold for scrap in the decade of the 1930s remained intact and simply laid up in out of the way slips because the price of scrap was so depressed that it was simply not worth it to tow them to the scrap yard. With war on the horizon these obsolete vessels were dusted off, repainted and made ready to be pressed into service one last time. They would haul ore from upper lakes ports such as Marquette, Ashland, Superior, Duluth, Two Rivers and Escanaba. There was, however, one strategic problem that the war planners quickly realized. Of those half dozen iron ore ports only one, Escanaba, did not require that vessels transit through the locks at Sault Saint Marie, "the Soo" as it is affectionately known. There is a 22-foot difference between the average level of Lake Superior and Lake Huron. These two fresh water seas are connected by the Saint Marys River which had been blocked by a series of rocky rapids until 1855. In that year the first series of locks, a tandem pair,

WWII

Sault Saint Marie and the famous Soo locks that allow vessels to transit between Lake Superior and the lower lakes. Had the Axis powers bombed this site they could have crippled the American steel industry. Library of Congress

were opened and for the first time large vessels could transit the river without being portaged. As the needs of the industrial revolution grew, so did the locks and the flow of iron ore.

Transferring raw iron ore from the mines in the north western Great Lakes region to the blast furnaces on the lower lakes required an efficient form of transportation, the "oreboat." As World War II loomed in the future the process of moving iron ore down the lakes was the same as it had been for nearly a century. The ore was dug from the ground, transported a short distance by rail car to gigantic loading "pocket ore docks." There the rail cars, atop the massive piers, had their hopper doors opened and the ore fell into bins. The bins were rigged with shoots that were lowered toward the open hatches of an oreboat and gravity fed into the vessel's hold.

A standard iron ore dock operates by gravity. Railroad cars loaded with ore are positioned on top of the dock and open their hopper doors to allow the ore to fall into storage bins. The chutes to those bins are then lowered down into the open hatches of a Great Lakes ore boat and the bin doors are opened allowing the ore to slide down into the vessel's cargo holds. Library of Congress

The fly in the red ore ointment was that Lake Superior had a total of 15 individual ore docks, many of which could handle the loading of four vessels at once, while below the Soo locks there was only Escanaba and its five docks. The storage capacity of the Lake

WWII

In 1940 a total of 77% of America's iron ore was shipped from Lake Superior ports to the nation's steel mills. All of that had to go through the locks at the Soo. Library of Congress

Superior pocket ore docks was 1,139,000 tons while the Escanaba docks had a capacity of just 262,000 tons.

For the Axis powers the easiest way to anesthetize the monster of the arsenal of democracy would have been to clog up its coronary artery - the locks at Sault Saint Marie. With the locks out of commission, for even as little as a year, the flow of iron ore would have dwindled as would the production of tanks, jeeps, ships, submarines, guns, artillery of every sort and aircraft engines would all have ground to a near halt as the production of steel slumped. It would have been an event nearly as devastating as Pearl Harbor.

In mid 1939 Canada entered the war and began stationing guns and soldiers around their nation's lock at the Soo. Likewise, the American Army used troops stationed at Fort Brady near the locks to stand guard. All of 20 soldiers were assigned for this duty. There was no real military concern about the Japanese at that time. They were thousands of miles away from the Soo and mainly flexing their muscles in Asia. The Germans, however, were waging an active war in the Atlantic and it was Hitler's machines that many in the lakes shipping community felt may pose a threat to the locks. Soon the idea began to sink in to the military leaders in the United States that remote possibilities were still possibilities. Although the U.S. was supposedly neutral, the Nazis may get the idea that no steel meant no Lend-Lease of military hardware from America to Britain. That may just make the Soo a tasty target for German saboteurs or worse.

On August 4, 1940 an article appeared in the "Detroit Free Press" that speculated on how the locks may be attacked by air. Although the locks were 720 flying miles from the waters of the Gulf of St. Lawrence and just 670 miles from the New Jersey coast, those waters were highly patrolled and any bomb-laden hostile aircraft departing from there would have to fly over Canadian or US territory for several hours in order to hit the Soo. There was, however, one other, more practical spot from which to launch an attack. James Bay, at the southern end of Hudson Bay, was just 402 miles away from the Soo locks. Flying a strike from there would allow the hostile aircraft to cruise over a nearly unpopulated stretch of Ontario and perhaps remain completely undetected. It was envisioned that some sort of aircraft could be smuggled into the sparsely-guarded northern mouth of Hudson Bay, in pieces, by U-boat. Then the enemy could go ashore on one of the remote islands in James Bay, assemble the aircraft and fly off to bomb the Soo.

Of course military leaders in both the U.S. and Canada worried little about such a raid. The current U-boats were far too small to carry any sort of aircraft below decks and if carried on the deck while running on the surface (which was where most U-boats spent the majority of their time) the odds of the rough north Atlantic waters simply sweeping it into the sea were good. Additionally, once in James Bay the parts of the aircraft would have to be ferried ashore without getting wet. Imagine trying to move the engine of a military bomber from the submarine to the beach in the U-boat's tiny dingy. Even if they did get the parts ashore, assembled, fueled and armed,

WWII

they would then need some sort of a runway from which to take off. This was a threat that only non-aviators could dream up. Yet, the U-boat and airplane speculation helped to highlight the vulnerability of the Soo locks - especially to sabotage.

It was also speculated that the real threat may come from someone sneaking aboard an oreboat and stowing away. Then, under arms, the saboteur would commandeer the vessel and ram it into the lock gates or, worse yet, use an explosive to sink the boat in one of the narrow channels below the locks.

On February 15, 1941 the United States Department of the Interior assigned the 702nd Military Police Battalion to the task of securing the American canal at Sault Saint Marie. A unit consisting of 545 MPs made their way to the great white north and quickly found that the Great Lakes winter had done exactly what they had been deployed to prevent - the locks and the canal were both closed - locked tightly in the grip of ice. Their job involved ground security operations and keeping a sharp lookout for saboteurs. Since the US

Being a true choke-point in the flow of iron ore, protecting the locks at the Soo became an immediate concern to the War Department. The locks were a crowded place and had been so since the early part of the century when this photo was taken. One aircraft with a few bombs could effectively put the locks system completely out of operation. Library of Congress

was not currently at war with Germany, Italy, or Japan, sympathizers for those nations were allowed to freely walk the American streets. The dreaded "fifth column," a group that seeks to topple a social order from within - or what today we would call a "sleeper cell" was thought to be able to suddenly rise up and create havoc at the Soo locks. So, ice or not, the MPs went immediately into action guarding the frozen canal in a town where everyone knew everyone else. The real policing would have to wait for the 1941 tourist season.

Of course once winter released its grip on the Soo the MPs of the 702nd found very little to do other than check passes and paperwork. No spies ever did any evil deeds or sabotage at the Soo during the 702nd's tour. There was, however, one story that circulated around the Sault area in the later years of the war. The tale involves a Japanese spy who took up residence in the historic Ojibway Hotel posing as a Chinese citizen. According to the story, the spy simply sat in his hotel room recording all of the vessel passages as well as the placement of defenses around the locks. Someone reported his presence to the FBI and he was subsequently taken into custody just weeks prior to the end of the war. True, or not - it is a fun story to tell.

Once the United States was actually involved in the shooting war, the powers that be in the War Department began to take the possibility of threats to the Soo under more intense consideration. Although the submarine assembled aircraft theory was nonsense, the War Department considered that a squad of German paratroopers could do a great deal of damage. They could easily overwhelm the MPs as well as Fort Brady's troops and set to work vandalizing the locks. In reality it would take more than a 100 paratroopers and nearly four tons of explosives set by demolition experts to put all of the locks out of commission. Yet there was the chance that some sort of air assault could be done. In fact, the German HE-139 seaplane could be catapult launched from a small ship in Hudson Bay. Able to fly 2,858 miles, the four engine float plane easily had the range to make the round trip to the Soo. If three or four of these aircraft were carried on-deck, similar to the Doolittle raid, they could carry a sizeable number of paratroopers and their equipment to the target. Granted the Nazi troops could never hold their position very long, they could still do some real damage. The greatest damage, however, would likely be to U.S. national morale.

On March 28, 1942 the Army deployed the 131st Infantry Regiment to the Soo to replace the MPs that had been guarding the locks for the past year. Earlier that month the 100th Coastal Artillery Unit had been deployed along with their anti-aircraft weapons. Interestingly, the 100th consisted of all African-American soldiers transported up north from Camp Davis, North Carolina. Although there was a degree of shock displayed by the locals due to the fact that the population was now suddenly integrated, the men of the 100th were soon widely accepted as true protectors of the city and the locks. Additionally, the soldiers found that although the weather was bitter cold, there were no Jim Crow laws. Thus they were welcome to go where ever they wished in spite of their color. It was a far cry from the deep south, where many of the men were from.

Soon the park adjacent to the locks and the locks themselves,

Guard towers and chain-link fences were used to help secure the locks from marauding enemy saboteurs who never existed at the Soo. Army Corps of Engineers photo

which had always been wide open to the public, was now cut off from the tourists. A chain-link fence was erected and extra lighting was in place. A series of guard towers were erected and a close watch was being kept on anything or anyone that moved around the locks.

April of 1942 saw the protective strength of the locks being increased as members of the Army's 399th Barrage Balloon Battalion arrived at the Soo. The barrage balloon is a simple, passive, anti-aircraft device. A steel cable is hoisted aloft by a large blimp-like balloon. The most difficult thing for a pilot to see from the cockpit is an elevated cable or wire, so if a large number of barrage balloons are sent aloft their wires would form an invisible and deadly thicket for low flying aircraft - especially dive bombers. Just one of these cables can rip off a wing and send the aircraft and its crew to their doom without expending any ammunition and without being manned.

Barrage balloons, however, do have some draw-backs that would

Barrage balloons were a simple, passive, anti-aircraft device. But when one got loose in a storm and its steel cable crossed some power lines it did more damage than an enemy bomber. Author's Collection

manifest themselves in upper lakes climate. Storms in August and October of 1942 caused some of the balloons to snap their cables and fly away. In the October adventure the balloon drifted away dragging its long steel cable across the ground. That cable came in contact with power lines and knocked out power to wide areas including some war production plants. Thereafter the balloons were reeled in and stored when nasty weather threatened and during the winter months when poor weather and high winds are normal at Sault Saint Marie.

Soon the number of troops stationed at fortress Soo would add up to between 7,000 and 12,000 soldiers - depending on which source you read today. Bristling with anti-aircraft guns, search lights, machinegun nests, barrage balloons and guards with rifles at the ready, the Soo was likely the most heavily defended location in the 48 United States and was certainly the most heavily protected in the Great Lakes region. In its August 17, 1945 edition, the *Chicago Tribune* reported that the Soo was protected by 51 barrage balloons, 48 anti-aircraft guns, (located everywhere from back yards and parks to local tennis courts) and stated flatly that fortress Soo was, "the most heavily guarded inland city in the United States."

Each vessel that wanted to pass through fortress Soo needed to comply with a special set of Lake Carriers Association security procedures involving a search of the boat and its cargo to ensure that no stow-away saboteurs were aboard. Of course there was far too much traffic and far too few Coast Guard officers to do such searching and not interrupt the flow of cargo. Thus, the vessels were required to police themselves. One of the boat's officers was required, before entering the canal, to check every inch of the vessel. When that "inspection" was complete the vessel needed to raise a yellow flag with a black ball in the center. That was the international signal flag for the letter "I" which was short for "Inspected." In his book, "Iron Fleet" author George Joachim tells of researching the log books from several vessels which indicate that the inspections by the officers on these lakeboats were quite superficial as some took as little as 15 minutes. Likewise, the "I" flags became a real pain. They tended to shred in the wind and were simply a bother to go out and raise. At least one oreboat went as far as to take a sheet of metal

Through the war years armed sentries became a common sight as the oreboats passed the Soo. Michigan Historical Archives

and paint it yellow with a black ball and weld it to the forward spar as a fixed "I." In the end it was the word of the oreboat crews themselves that provided the best onboard security - just about everyone knew everyone else. Any suspicious saboteur would probably stick out like a sore thumb. Yet there could always be that one exception.

On May 8, 1941, the *Industry*, a coal boat working the Indiana Harbor Canal apparently had a saboteur aboard posing as a watchman. Working with her sister ship the *Commerce* the two service boats were busy delivering coal to fuel the big lakers and were employed by the Hopkins Coal and Dock Company. The canal itself was just 260 feet wide in 1941, but with the use of a good tug boat the big ore carriers could easily slip in and out while delivering ore to the Inland Steel plant. U.S. Gypsum also had a facility on the canal as did Youngstown Sheet and Tube. It was first thing in the morning and as the *Industry* went about her work, suddenly in mid channel the boat took on a list and began to sink. Her fleet mate was nearby and came to her aid, tied up alongside and passed hoses over to start pumping her out. When her captain and a crewman went below they found that during the night someone had opened the boat's sea cocks. They also found that one of the boat's watchman, who was supposed to be aboard that night, was mysteriously missing. At the time it was thought that it had been an attempt to sink the little coal boat in the channel and block the canal. The event, no doubt raised eyebrows in the pre-war environment, but may have been as little as a pay dispute or disagreement with the captain.

Over all it is very hard to find any real sabotage or enemy agent activity that took place on the waters of the Great Lakes during the World War II era. The enemy completely ignored the flow of iron ore and other bulk materials along the inland seas that turned out to be the life blood of the war effort. This was due in large part to the fact that in the first years of the war, from late 1939 to late 1942, the Germans and Japanese were making huge gains in their conquests. But, by the autumn of 1943 the Germans and Japanese were both beginning to lose ground as the allied forces grew in strength and capability. By then it was too late to think about placing any sort of strangle hold on the growing Arsenal of Democracy. The Axis powers were too busy defending what they had taken. For Germans, even though Hitler refused to believe that any sort of defeat was taking place - their close companion Italy had already fallen and taken up arms against them. Meanwhile the Japanese were watching as the ships that kept their soldiers fed and armed were being devastated by the U.S. Navy. In such chaos the locks at the Soo were effectively safe from the enemy, even though at the time no one in the War Department realized it.

One hard fact that the War Department swiftly addressed in the beginning involved the locks themselves. When war broke out there were four locks on the American side and one on the Canadian side. The Canadian lock itself measured just 898 feet in length and could be used by any vessel of the ore fleet depending on their load. On the American side, the northern most lock, the Sabin, had been opened in 1919 and measured 1,350 feet long and 80 feet wide. It could thus accommodate any of the 1940s ore fleet, some of which could lock through two boats at the same time. Likewise, the Davis lock, which opened in 1914. It was a twin to the Sabin and was located just to the south of its sister lock. It could also handle any oreboat on the lakes at that time. The problem came with the two most southern locks - the Poe and the Weitzel locks. The Poe was opened in 1896 and had taken 15 years to build. It measured 800 feet in length and 100 feet in width and in its hay day could lock as many as six ore boats through, three abreast. By the time of World War II, however, the Poe's 16-foot depth restricted it from passing most of the ore fleet when carrying a load. So, for war-time iron ore transportation purposes it was pretty much useless. The southern-most lock, the Weitzel, was also useless so far as the ore boats were concerned. Opened in 1881 the Weitzel was 515 feet long, 80 feet wide, narrowing to 60 feet at the gates and it was just 11 feet deep. The restrictions in depth meant that just three locks at the entire Soo could be used for war time

With the onset of World War II and the demand of iron ore spiking, the Weitzel Lock (left in the image) with its narrowed entrance and shallow depth was seen as expendable. It was dug up and reconstructed as a new wider and deeper lock to support the greater volume of war-time traffic. Library of Congress

WWII

St. Marys Falls Canal, Sault Ste. Marie, Michigan. Detroit District view looking upstream from control tower showing construction of concrete wall sections for Macarthur Lock, May 1, 1943. Photo Thomas Manse Collection

movement of iron ore - and that was not enough.

Another problem for the War Department was that in the history of lock building at the Soo it had taken 11 years to build the old Weitzel lock, 15 years to construct the Poe, and a decade each to build the Davis and Sabin. The War Department quickly decided that there was need for a new, modern lock at the American Soo - but they didn't have a decade in which to do the job. The solution was the same as it had been for every other war time problem; manpower and the sleeping giant of American industry.

August of 1942 found the residents of the Soo shaken by huge explosions as one of the locks was systematically destroyed by dynamite. Of course it was not saboteurs that had set the charges. Instead it was construction workers who were demolishing the antiquated Weitzel lock. March of 1942 had seen the beginning of a population boom in Sault Saint Marie as a flood of construction workers and equipment began to arrive. Their mission was to build a new lock and to do so in world record time. Soon more than 9,000 construction workers were busy around the clock ripping out the old Weitzel lock, deepening the channel and constructing a new lock measuring 859 feet long, 80 feet wide and 32 feet deep.

Most of the digging and work requiring floating equipment was done in the months when the ground was not frozen and the water was free of ice. In the winter months a huge temporary wooden shelter was constructed over the work space and heaters equipped with fans were used to allow the crews to continue to do important tasks such as pouring cement. On July 11, 1943, just a little over 15 months after construction had started and seven months ahead of schedule the McArthur lock was activated. The self-unloader *Carl D. Bradley* was the first vessel to pass through the brand new McArthur lock. Locking

Completed in record time the new McArthur *lock was opened in just over 15 months of construction. The first lakeboat through the new lock was the self-unloader* Carl D. Bradley. *Author's Collection*

WWII

upbound she was 638 feet long and was the largest vessel on the Great Lakes at that time. Oddly, she was not an ore carrier, but rather a career stone carrier. It was a reminder that all of the bulk cargoes carried through the Soo were critical to the war effort.

What also may seem a bit odd is that the lock itself was named for an active duty General. At the time of the lock's construction, General Douglas McArthur, the lock's namesake, had been kicked out of the Philippines by the Japanese and with a legion of United States army soldiers, including my uncle PFC Jack McGarrity, was in an island-hopping campaign trying to fight his way back. Of course the Davis and Sabin locks had been named after Colonel L.E. Davis and Mr. L.C. Sabin both of whom were engineers. The Poe had been named for General Orlando M. Poe who was responsible for the design and placement of many of the lighthouses on the lakes and was also in charge of the Soo canal for a time. The lock, however, had been given his name a year after his death. The Weitzel lock had been dedicated to General Godfrey Weitzel. He was active in the Army Corps of Engineers and supervised the building of his namesake lock and, like McArthur was still on active duty at the time of its opening. So, naming the lock after an active duty general was not totally un-heard of and was likely a great morale booster for the American public.

As the war went on, both the Pacific and European fonts began to push back and box the enemy in and by 1944 the manpower being used to guard fortress Soo was systematically reduced. The threat of Nazi paratroopers striking within the United States was effectively gone. Hitler's paratroopers had been massacred in the Soviet Union and the insanity within the Nazi high command had plenty to focus on other than the Soo locks. Likewise, the Japanese were being strangled in the Pacific as the United States Navy had grown into a force beyond anyone's imagination. The Japanese were of little threat to the Soo locks.

Of course it is worth noting that feeble attempts were being made to fly bomb laden balloons from Japan to North America riding on the jet stream. Although the locks at the Soo were not a direct target, the Japanese actually came fairly close. One of their balloon FO-GO,

or "fire balloon" weapons was reportedly sighted in the vicinity of Sault Saint Marie and fighters were scrambled to the area. The balloon vanished into clouds before it could be engaged. Two others were confirmed as hitting lower Michigan. One landed in an open field near the town of Dorr after having dropped its incendiary somewhere totally unnoticed and the other bombed a farmer's field in Farmington Hills. Both locations were about 270 miles out of the range of fortress Soo's anti-aircraft batteries.

In fact, the only Axis bombs to drop anywhere near the Soo locks were the Japanese "Fo-Go" or "fire balloon." Those landed hundreds of miles south of the locks and were more a result of happenstance than of targeting. Army Air Corps photo

By the end of the war all of the troops had been removed from fortress Soo and it reverted back just being a passageway to the lower lakes and a tourist attraction. Oddly, neither the Nazis or the Imperial Japanese ever considered attacking the locks. Many traces of the fortifications, however, remained well after the war. In fact, as late as the 1980s local folks talked about some war time structures that remained in the area. Today, one very noticeable fortress Soo structure remains and is still serving the same purpose it did during the war. The McArthur lock still raises and lowers hundreds of vessels upbound and downbound every season.

Today the McArthur Lock continues to raise and lower lakeboats. Seen here are the World War II vintage lakeboats Alpena *(foreground leaving the McArthur Lock) and the* Middletown *entering the Poe Lock circa 2005. D.J. Story photo*

FLAT TOPS ON FRESH WATER

With the devastation of Pearl Harbor still smoldering it suddenly became clear to most of the United States Navy's brass that the days of the huge battleship's domination of war at sea were at an end. From that point on the once admonished aircraft carrier would rule the waves when it came to Naval conflicts. There was just one problem - the United States had just three carriers on duty in the Pacific Ocean while the Japanese had nine. To make matters worse the Imperial Navy was about to commission an additional five carriers in 1942. The U.S. also had five carriers whose construction had just been started in 1941, but even if they were to be launched in 1942 the Japanese would still have nearly a two to one advantage in the Pacific. With the devastation of the US Navy's battleship fleet on December 7, the nation was in a terrible position. If the Japanese decided to attack the U.S. mainland, they could easily do so.

Of course the US Navy had no choice other than to rush assets from service in the Atlantic Ocean through the Panama Canal into the Pacific. The carriers *Hornet* and *Yorktown* were immediately transferred to duty in the Pacific joining the *Lexington*, *Saratoga* and *Enterprise* while *Wasp* and *Ranger* remained in the Atlantic. The message that Pearl Harbor had sent was very clear; the key to waging the war in the Pacific would be aircraft carriers.

Aircraft carriers, however, are useless without aircraft and the pilots trained to fly them. Basic military pilot training began taking place in mass across the United States more than a year before Pearl

WWII

Harbor. At make-shift fields across the country, both the Army and Navy geared up to meet their needs as the foreshadowing of war grew. Although the basics of takeoff and landing as well as airborne maneuvering could be taught at these simple airfields, landing on the pitching and rolling deck of an aircraft carrier at sea was unique and required an actual aircraft carrier in order to properly qualify not only pilots, but Landing Signal Officers (LSO) as well. Following Pearl Harbor every carrier in the US fleet became a highly critical asset and none could be spared for any training of pilots and LSOs. Fortunately, this gap in United States preparedness was quickly solved on the Great Lakes.

Months before Pearl Harbor the Navy's valuable escort vessels were being heavily utilized in the North Atlantic for U-boat detection. This duty kept them away from being used for the protection of the high value aircraft carriers that otherwise could have been used to do training on the open sea. Seeing this and knowing that war with Germany, Japan, or both was inevitable Captain John J. Manley dreamed up the concept of converting Great Lakes sidewheel passenger liners for carrier training duty. He thought that their conversion could be most economically done on the lakes as could the training. There, on the inland seas and land-locked away from enemy submarines, training carriers would not require any sort of escort protection. He took the concept to Captain William Amsden who in turn passed it along to Commander Richard F. Whitehead, aid to the head of the Navy's Great Lakes Training Station. The proposal fell upon deaf ears at the highest levels of the Navy brass - until after Pearl Harbor. Chief of Naval Operations, Admiral Ernest J. King was presented with the idea and he immediately placed it into action.

Logical choices for the vessels to be converted to carriers were the huge Great Lakes sidewheel passenger steamers. The reasoning for this was in large part due to their width, or "beam" as it is called in maritime-speak. The largest of these sidewheelers, the *Greater Buffalo*, was 536 feet long and had a 96-foot beam including her wheel buckets. Her predecessor, the *Seeandbee*, although only 519 feet in length, had a 98-foot beam over her buckets. That length and

86

Flat Tops On Fresh Water

Having been in almost constant use through the depression, the passenger liner Seeandbee's *engine workings were in great condition as she was being considered for wartime use. Thus, she was the first vessel selected to be converted into an aircraft carrier to train Naval aviators on the Great lakes. Author's Collection*

beam allowed for both boats (on the Great Lakes a civilian "ship" is properly called a "boat") to support a satisfactory sized flight deck. Additionally, both boats were in active service when the war broke out and thus their engines and propulsive equipment was in excellent working condition.

"Requisitioned" from the Cleveland and Buffalo Transit Company in March of 1942, the *Seeandbee* (which stood for C & B - or Cleveland and Buffalo) was the first to be converted. Assigned a remarkably high 14A priority by the Navy Department, the contract to the American Shipbuilding Company called for the conversion to be completed by the first day of September of 1942. The Navy Department, however, made it quite clear that they expected the job to be done by the first day of August. America was at war and

WWII

shipbuilding was now a top priority as was the training of naval aviators. The new training carrier was needed without delay.

At Cleveland's Ninth Street Pier the initial stripping of the boat's upper works was started. Yet, before the *Seeandbee* could be towed to Buffalo there was one safety feature that the shipyard management insisted on putting aboard. Carefully, a dockside crane hoisted aboard a Cleveland city fire engine. The previous February a fire aboard the ocean liner *Normandie* in New York Harbor had wrecked the vessel and raised suspicions about sabotage. This incident was fresh in management's mind and they were going to take no chances with this 14A project. So the stripped hull of the *Seeandbee* was initially moved and eased into a slip at Michigan Avenue and the fire department pumper was placed onto her deck for the trip to Buffalo. Oddly, when the boat reached her destination and the fire engine pumper was placed ashore it was found that the pumper didn't pump! The vehicle was totally inoperable and the whole effort had been completely pointless other than making some city managers feel a bit more at ease.

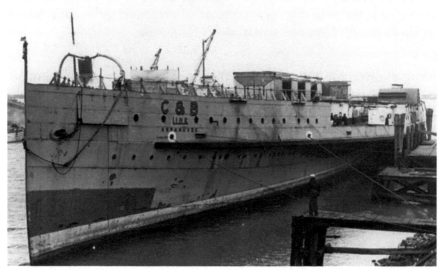

Stripped of her upper cabins and smoke stacks the Seeandbee *was ready to be towed from Cleveland to Buffalo for the rest of her conversion. US Navy photo*

Flat Tops On Fresh Water

Once at Buffalo the framing for the flight deck was constructed atop the *Seeandbee* and a carpet of three-inch-thick teakwood was applied as the landing surface. This was similar to the landing surface then on the active carriers in the Pacific as well as some that were then under construction. *Seeandbee* was the only vessel on the lakes ever to sport four smokestacks, now her four midships funnels were redirected to her starboard side and just ahead of them was constructed a no-frills pilothouse and flight operations observation deck. The vessel had no hangar deck and thus no elevators for handling aircraft. Any aircraft that remained on her deck at the end of the day had to be lifted off with a shore side crane. She also had no facility for fueling aircraft or servicing them. In order to stop aircraft at touchdown, a single trap wire was strung across her aft deck to catch the plane's tail hook. In addition to the single trap wire, a set of arresting cables were also rigged forward to aid in catching aircraft that botched their landing. The new carrier was designated auxiliary vessel IX-64 and renamed *USS Wolverine*.

Here we see the support structure needed to give the sleek hull of the Seeandbee *her new, longer, wider flight deck that would allow aircraft to land and take off. US Navy photo*

WWII

Although the Navy Department had wanted the *USS Wolverine* ready by August first in spite of her being contracted for September first, the American Shipbuilding Company split the difference and had her out on August 12, 1942. Most of the delay was caused by shortages of materials or common bureaucratic red tape. The man who solved the problems and kept things moving was Lt. Commander E. A. Eisele. He made the miracles happen by getting to know bridge tenders, railroad engineers, shipyard workers, tug captains and truck drivers. He knew how to light the fire inside them as to how important this single project was to the war effort so when he needed something such as rail cars filled with steel moved he could call the railroad engineer at home on a Sunday and get him to come down and fire up his locomotive and shove the cars. When an inbound freighter was due that would cause a bridge opening and delay his crew from getting to the job site on time, he got the bridge tender to hold the bridge. He then went to the city council and had bridge hours set up for that span. If steel was slow coming from the mill he found local sources and got what was needed. Frankly, the new carrier should have been christened the "Eisele."

During the conversion one technical issue came up that was solved through sound engineering and improvisation. No one really knew for sure just how much force a landing aircraft would apply to the arresting wire when the plane's tailhook captures it. If the wire's breaking mechanism that was to be installed on the *USS Wolverine* was not strong enough to handle the load, the first Naval aviator to attempt to land could easily find himself swimming in Lake Michigan. Some quick calculations found that the force was equivalent to about one and one half tons moving at about 35 miles per hour. On shore an area was cleared and a pickup truck was loaded with scrap steel slugs until it weighed about a ton and a half was positioned so that it could reach a speed of 35 miles per hour. A volunteer was selected to drive the rig with a trap cable attached to the rear of the vehicle. With the driver wearing football pads and catcher's pads, the truck sped down the kludged test track. As he hit 35 mph, the engineer hit the breaking mechanism. They forgot Isaac Newton's first law of motion; "An object in motion will tend to

Flat Tops On Fresh Water

Her conversion completed the former Seeandbee *has now become the US Navy auxiliary vessel* IX-64 USS Wolverine. *She is the first sidewheel aircraft carrier in the Navy. US Navy photo*

remain in motion with the same speed, in the same direction unless acted upon by an outside unbalanced force" The truck stopped suddenly, but all of that scrap steel used to increase its weight by more than a ton kept going! Fortunately, none of it penetrated the cab and no one was hurt. Yet after the experiment the guys who were doing the test had a lot of scrap steel to pick up.

No sooner had the *USS Wolverine* cleared Buffalo upbound for Chicago than the second passenger liner was requisitioned - this vessel was the *Greater Buffalo*. Although the *Seeandbee* had been launched in 1913, the *Greater Buffalo* was 11 years younger. Her conversion was nearly identical to that of the *Seeandbee* with the exception of her flight deck. Rather than teakwood, the *Greater Buffalo* was given a steel deck similar to those on the new Midway class of carriers that were being constructed in 1943. Two different

WWII

Immediately after the USS Wolverine *was put into service, work was going forward on converting her former fleet mate the* Greater Buffalo. *Author's Collection*

types of steel decking were placed on her deck in a checkerboard pattern to test them for operational use. Additionally, eight different types of non-skid coatings were then applied to the deck in order to test them out. This second vessel would not be ready until March of 1943 and would be designated as auxiliary vessel IX-81 *USS Sable*.

USS Wolverine qualified her first Naval aviator on September 12, 1942. In October she gained a distinction that no other Great Lakes vessel is ever likely to achieve. That happened when Admiral Ernest J. King boarded the freshwater flat top and went out to observe her in action. Of course with the admiral aboard his command flag was flown from the *USS Wolverine's* mast, and for a day she became, not only the first carrier on the lakes, but the first vessel on the freshwater seas, in modern times, to be a United States Navy flagship.

Although stripped of her plush upper deck passenger accommodations in favor of a flight deck the *USS Wolverine* retained plenty of space below decks to support naval crewmen. Located amidships and one deck down from her main deck she retained a spacious yet spartan galley. Originally meant to feed more than 500 people, both passengers and crew, the galley now easily functioned to feed her sailors. One deck up from the galley was a spacious crew mess. Moving forward along that same deck would be found the crew's showers and the head followed by the berthing area. The bunks were the standard Navy issue of that era and folded down from the bulkheads. One deck below was the officer's quarters. All the way aft on the first enclosed deck was located the sick bay, dispensary, "water closet," and ward room "Officer's country." One deck below and fully aft a lecture hall was established and with it an adjacent yeoman's office. Forward of that area was located a C.P.O.'s (Chief Petty Officer or Chief's) area and then a flight of steps leading to the next deck topside. In all, the *USS Wolverine* was a fairly nice place to serve during war time as each night she put in to the great city of Chicago.

One of the lesser places to serve aboard the *USS Wolverine* was in her fire hold. That was the place where her boilers were stoked with coal. Although nearly all of the U.S. Navy's fleet had been converted to oil fuel by the late 1930s, the task of shoveling coal would live on with the Great Lakes aircraft carriers. Both the *USS Wolverine* and the *USS Sable* were coal burners and both were hand-stoked which meant that Navy blue-shirts had to be in the firehold shoveling the coal. Of course on the lakes many of the steamers were still hand-stoked and their black gang crewmen got a real snicker when newspapers reported that the Navy men were complaining about the hard work. In fact, the work was a bit too hard as the fire troughs in the boilers of both vessels were longer than the men were able to shovel and this resulted in coal landing too close to the firebox doors. As a result, the gate bars in the bottom of the troughs were only partially covered and that resulted in an uneven heating and thus a lack in boiler efficiency. It took a while before the Navy men learned the fine art of pitching the coal the full length of the boiler. Additionally, each steamer had nine boilers with a total of two dozen doors that had to be fed and the Navy could only assign one stoker at a time to the fire hold. Although the learning curve was steep and the work was back breaking the crews did not have to worry about enemy torpedoes or dive bombers.

WWII

For pilots the act of flying on and off of one of these Great Lakes carriers pose a number of differences from doing so on the ocean. Training operations were conducted nearly year-round which meant that the pilots sometimes found themselves flying over huge fields of ice and through snow in order to get to their carrier. Additionally, both of the sidewheel carriers squatted much lower in the water than their saltwater counterparts. Although this gave the illusion that the operational carriers were farther away and the pilots were higher on their initial approaches, the aviators quickly overcame that sensation.

Also, the weather on the Great Lakes tended to be much worse than the weather found in the South Pacific. Autumn brought gales

In March of 1943 the former Greater Buffalo *was ready to enter the war as the auxiliary vessel IX-81,* USS Sable, *seen here. Note the "S" on her stern for "Sable." That letter was there to clearly identify her as the* USS Sable *and not her sister carrier the* USS Wolverine. *Pilots who landed on the wrong ship when both were doing carrier landing qualifications had no excuse. US Navy photo*

of wind and ice cold rain while spring and summer often brought thick areas of fog. In the winter of 1942 ñ 43, the weather on Lake Michigan almost completely shut down carrier operations. During that period of time, the escort carriers *USS Core* and *USS Long Island*, both based in San Diego, California, temporarily took over the training duties of the Great Lakes flattops.

Aircraft used in the training operations were based on land at Naval Air Station Glenview. As operations ramped up, however, the space at Glenview became too crowded and nearby Douglas field was utilized. Douglas, which had other military operations, was soon declared unsuitable and Allendale field was pressed into operation. Flights of aircraft would depart the inland fields and in formation, guided in part by radio commands, would fly out over the lake and

A US Navy SNJ aircraft taking off from the deck of the USS Sable. *It is well worth mentioning that Cdr. Jim Brady, USN Retired, who did his initial carrier qualifications aboard the* USS Sable *during World War II was kind enough to give this author a phone interview and fill me in on details for flying the SNJ aboard the fresh water flattops. US Navy photo*

WWII

meet the carriers. They would make their landings and takeoffs aboard the carriers and then return to Glenview or Douglas.

Each pilot had to make eight landings on the paddle wheel carrier's deck in order to be "carrier qualified." These landings were accomplished either in the type of aircraft that the pilot would be assigned in combat, or, if there were none of those available for the qualification, they would be accomplished in the Navy's SNJ training aircraft.

The SNJ itself was a handy training aircraft in its day serving as an advanced trainer. Basic flight students learned in the Navy's Stearman aircraft and then transitioned to the more complex SNJ. When it came to landing on a carrier, the SNJ lacked one feature; a tail hook. This device was standard on all active duty carrier aircraft and was a simple hook attached to a metal bar. During takeoff and normal flight, the tail hook was stowed in a retracted position. As the aircraft made its approach to the carrier the pilot would drop the tail hook in order to trap the arresting cable on the carrier's deck. Since the SNJ had no tail hook, ground mechanics rigged up a simple solution. They cobbled a tail hook out of metal and attached one end to the lower aircraft fuselage near the tail. On the hook end they simply tied a rope and passed it through the fuselage, up into the cockpit and tied the free end to the armrest of the pilot's seat. As the pilot set up his landing approach, all he had to do

One pilot who did his carrier qualifications aboard the USS Sable *went on to become the 41st President of the United States - President George H.W. Bush.* National Archives Image

96

Flat Tops On Fresh Water

Carrier qualification is, and always will be, one of the most dangerous skills to be learned by a Naval Aviator. Here a pilot stands a perfectly good F6F Hellcat on its nose after missing the arresting wire on the USS Sable. *That was not a good day for him. US Navy Image*

in order to drop his tail hook was un-tie the rope and let it go. It was crude, yet it was inexpensive and it worked.

For the remainder of the war the *Wolverine* and *Sable* stayed in constant operation qualifying new carrier pilots. In total 17,820 naval aviators were carrier qualified by way of these two vessels. One pilot in that crowd who completed his carrier qualification on August 24, 1943 aboard the *USS Sable* would go on to become the 41st president of the United States - his name is George Herbert Walker Bush.

When the concept of training pilots on Great Lakes carriers had first been proposed, the objective had been to train 30 pilots per day. By the height of the war in 1944 that rate had risen to 60 pilots per day. Additionally, the original qualification requirement of eight carrier landings per pilot had been increased to 14 carrier landings

97

per pilot. Those statistics, however, did not come without a price. With a total of 136,429 carrier landings that had taken place, more than 110 aircraft had been lost in Lake Michigan - some sources say that the number is three times greater than that. Overall, 21 pilots had been killed during training. Remarkably, none of those fatalities were attributed to shipboard operations.

On November 7, 1945, a little under two months after the Japanese surrender and the end of World War II, the *Wolverine* and the *Sable* were officially decommissioned. Both were left at their pier at the foot of Grant Avenue in Chicago. The purpose for which they had been converted had been fully served and there was no longer a need for the two vessels, either military or civilian. They would simply go to scrap along with millions of tons of other war

Together the USS Wolverine *and the* USS Sable *were the only two sidewheel aircraft carriers in the world During their duty on Lake Michigan the ships were based at what became "Navy Pier" in Chicago - seen here. US Navy Image*

surplus; the *Wolverine* was the first to go. It was sold for scrap and towed to Jones Island, Milwaukee, Wisconsin on November 28, 1947. Just over seven months later on July 7, 1948 the *Sable* was sold to Canadian scrappers. The problem, however, was that the vessel was too wide to fit through the Welland Canal. This was solved by cutting away the vessel's two paddlewheels and placing them on her deck. She was then towed through the canal and scrapped at Hamilton, Ontario. Although there were many ideas for preserving one of these vessels which included everything from a floating dance hall to a specialized carrier of gigantic pieces of equipment, there were no funds available for such conversions. Thus, the *Wolverine* and *Sable* became the first and the only paddlewheel aircraft carriers in the United States Navy and the only aircraft carriers to ever operate on the Great Lakes. Their contribution to the effort to win absolute and complete victory in World War II can never be understated.

To this day Great Lakes scuba divers are locating and recovering aircraft that were lost in training on the two Great Lakes flat tops. Although the fresh water has done much to preserve those aircraft, zebra mussels have done much to damage them. Yet World War II aviation historians and preservationists manage to work miracles finding and bringing the once abandon aircraft back from the depths of Lake Michigan. As you read this, somewhere in a hangar there are aircraft preservation teams doing the meticulous chore of preserving an aircraft that once sought to qualify a pilot aboard the *USS Wolverine* or the *USS Sable*. May their efforts always succeed.

MYTHS AND
HAIR-BRAINED IDEAS

Whether concocted in the news media or carefully plotted in the War Department or somewhere in between, war-time hatches some pretty hair-brained ideas. Shortages, threats, paranoia and the simple human need to try and help the war effort spawned some concepts and actions that, from a historical perspective, just make you shake your head. Alongside that there are some persistent myths that seem to emerge out of the war that linger on to this day.

One of the craziest hair-brained ideas came about as the result of the need for Great Lakes vessels to carry iron ore, coal, and other bulk materials. It was early May of 1942 and most of the U.S. Navy's heavy battle ships that had been stationed in the Pacific were still on the bottom of Pearl Harbor while German U-boats were knocking off allied merchant ships in the Atlantic so close to the United States shoreline that residents of coastal cities could stand on the beaches and see them burning. Meanwhile American and Canadian shipyards were just beginning to come up to speed in order to replace the lost tonnage.

On the Great Lakes every vessel that was not critical to the manufacturing industry, such as the Canadian canallers, were requisitioned to salt water service. Older ore boats that in the 1930s were considered uneconomical and too small to compete against the 550 and 600 footers were taken out of lay-up and placed back in service. Yet it still was not enough to satisfy the needs of the arsenal of democracy. More lakeboats were needed. At that moment in history someone came up with the absolute most hair-brained idea to add to the fleet; resurrect the ghost fleet from "The Great Storm of 1913!"

In early November of 1913 one of the most horrific and deadly storms in maritime history hit the lakes. Lasting just over three days, the storm was a white hurricane that took advantage of the hubris of many lake captains and shattered the illusion that, "no wind can blow that can take down one of these boats." All together a dozen lakeboats were lost with all hands. Of those, eight were sunk on Lake Huron; the 550 footer *James Carruthers*, the 524 footers *Issac M. Scott* and *Charles S. Price*, the 450 footer *John A. McGean*, the 436 footers *Argus* and *Hydrus*, the 256 footers *Wexford* and the *Regina*. As World War II began, those big laker's all rested on the bottom of Lake Huron and someone decided that they could be raised, refurbished, and added to the inventory of the Great Lakes maritime fleet.

It was reasoned that the fresh water would not have caused the steel hulls of these eight giant lakeboats to deteriorate and if they could be raised not only would their hulls have been of use in the war effort, but also their cargoes could be salvaged and used. The *Price*, for example, had onboard an estimated 7,000 tons of coal that was thought to be salvageable. Additionally, her hull was worth an estimated $300,000. When the values of all eight of the 1913 storm's Lake Huron victims were added up, it seemed reasonable to raise them all. The news papers of the days stated flatly that "salvage men" said the task could be done.

Yet, there was just one little problem with this hair-brained scheme; no one knew where seven of the eight wrecks were located. In fact, as of this writing in 2017, one of the eight, the *James Carruthers*, is still missing. The most recent wreck found was that of the *Hydrus* discovered by famed wreck searcher David Trotter and his team in 2015. Yet in 1942, there was this idea that finding those wrecks would be so simple that all they had to do was just "drag the lake." Of course they said that the whole process would take time and cost a great deal of money, but it could be done. The news papers showed a map of Lake Huron and the places where the wrecks were thought to be located.

Myths And Hair-Brained Ideas

Of course at that time the only known location of any of the November 1913 storm wrecks was that of the *Price*. She had been found floating upside down about a dozen miles southeast of Lexington, Michigan. Only a small portion of her bow remained above the surface. Three days after the storm a tug took a hard-hat diver, William H. Baker, out to the wreck and lowered him down until he could read the boat's name on her bow. Two days later she slowly sank to the bottom in 64 feet of water where she came to rest upside down. Other than the *Price* no one knew where any of the others rested in the vastness of the fresh water sea called Huron.

On May 8, 1942 famed wrecking captain Thomas Reid reported that he had ventured out to again find the *Price*. His crew eventually did re-locate the wreck and gave the press a juicy story about how her $80,000 cargo of coal must still be aboard and the hope that she could be raised. The *Price*, however, remains on the bottom of Lake Huron to this day as she will forever more. In fact, had the wreckers actually managed to raise the wreck they would have been in for an $80,000 disappointment. You see, most of her coal cargo is no longer aboard. When the *Price* capsized the weight of her cargo blew out her hatches and dumped most of it on the lake bottom. Modern scuba divers have discovered huge coal piles laying on the lake bottom several miles from where the *Price* rests today.

As for the other vessels that went down in the 1913 storm, they have been found one by one in recent years - and almost none of them are where the 1942 newspaper map said the salvagers thought they may be. Some, such as the *Regina*, are so close to land you feel as if you could swim ashore from the wreck site. Discovered on July 1, 1986 by research divers Garry Biniecki, John Severance and Wayne Brusate, the wreck is just six miles east of Lexington harbor. She rests at anchor and upside down. In the summer of 1988 the *McGean* was discovered by David Trotter who would also later find the *Argus* and *Hydrus*. The *Scott* was also discovered by divers in the modern era. All of these discoveries involved the use of modern electronics none of which, in 1942, had been developed to the point of being used in this manner.

WWII

No attempt was ever seriously made to raise or salvage any of the 1913 storm victims on Lake Huron. To this day they remain where the sank and are protected by the Great Lakes states and Canada in whose waters they were lost.

Another hair-brained idea sprouted from the supposed threat of saboteurs sneaking aboard a Great Lakes vessel, hijacking it in a critical waterway and then using it to somehow block vessel traffic. The War Department's answer to this was to place two to four armed Coast Guardsmen aboard each vessel that needed to transit the locks at Sault Saint Marie.

This solution, however, created problems of its own. In a time when manpower was extremely limited, the Coast Guard could not afford to put two or more experienced guardsmen on every vessel that passed through the Soo. The answer was to assign young, newly-trained recruits to that task. Picture if you will a seasoned Great Lakes vessel captain, first mate, second mate, third mate, chief engineer, second engineer, and crew squaring off with a green, recently graduated from boot camp, teenage Coast guardsmen sporting a side arm; the formula is unpleasant. One vessel man remarked that once on board all these guards did was eat - because they were only needed while the vessel was loading, unloading, or passing through the Soo. The rest of the seven or eight days that made up the trip involved nothing for them to do other than watch the water go by. Yet, instances occurred where there were confrontations between ships officers and these Coast guardsmen. Finally, after vehement protests by the Lake Carriers Association, the War Department came up with an even better solution. They inducted all of the United States Great Lakes ships officers as auxiliary Coast Guard officers and removed the armed guards from the vessels.

When it comes to myths, one of the most pronounced and persistent from World War II and the Great Lakes involves Nazi U-boats. The myth goes like this:

A U-boat on a one-way mission to interrupt shipping on the Great Lakes sneaks into Lake Ontario by way of the St. Lawrence River. Before the submarine can do any damage it is detected by either the United States Coast Guard or the Canadian Coast Guard and under

Myths And Hair-Brained Ideas

This infamous photo of a junked cold war era Soviet submarine being towed away to the scrap yard annoyingly pops up on social media every now and then claiming that it is a Nazi U-boat discovered on Lake Ontario. Please do not believe for a heartbeat that there is any truth in this myth. Author's Collection

their gunfire it sinks. Of course neither the Canadian, nor the United States governments want to upset war morale by releasing the information that a German submarine has invaded the inland seas, so the whole incident remains classified forever.

This myth gained new life with the advent of the Internet and social media. Conspiracy sites and good old-fashioned hoaxers seem to perpetually give this nonsense a rebirth every so often. Let's look at the facts and allow this author to help put this insanity to rest once and for all.

WWII

First off, the only way for an oceangoing vessel to reach the landlocked Great Lakes was by way of the St. Lawrence River which in spots is strewn with rapids and boulders. Prior to the construction of the modern day Seaway in the late 1950s, which allowed deep draft vessels to navigate around the rapids, a series of five narrow canals and two dozen small locks existed at the onset of World War II. Any enemy vessel seeking to enter the Great Lakes would have to either transit those locks and canals, or shoot the rapids.

The majority of the locks along the St. Lawrence River were so small that only vessels of 261 feet or smaller and drawing less than 14 feet of water were able to pass. The most commonly used type of U-boat in World War II was the type VII. Of those only the type VIIA would've been short enough to fit the locks. Unfortunately, all of the type VIIA U-boats drew 14 feet 4 inches of water when they were without crew, provisions, torpedoes, or mines. So, if any such vessel did manage to somehow get through those two dozen heavily guarded locks, they would have to re-arm and refuel somewhere on the lakes. Picture if you will a group of German sailors slogging ashore at Oswego, New York seeking to purchase provisions, German torpedoes and TMA mines plus a tanker full of diesel fuel.

Of course, the other alternative would be to shoot the rapids up stream. For anyone not familiar with the movement of floating vessels, navigating one in the rapids going up stream is absolutely impossible. Additionally, the U-boat's depth of just over 14 feet would have found every single boulder along the rapids punching holes through her bottom. They'd be better off trying to get through the heavily guarded locks.

Thus, in spite of Internet hoax sites that display photos of rusting Soviet submarines residing in a boneyard and claim that this is a German U-boat discovered on the Great Lakes, this author can state without doubt that no U-boat *Ever* entered the Great Lakes during World War II; it is a complete impossibility.

SILENT KILLERS

When the Japanese were attacking Pearl Harbor they focused primarily on the big battle ships of the US Navy. Other than some targets of opportunity, smaller vessels were largely ignored. In fact, some of the sailors who were manning the four US Submarines *Norwhal*, *Dolphin*, *Cachalot* and *Tautog* that were moored in the harbor during the attack saw, as the Japanese planes flew past, the pilots of the rising sun smile and wave at the US submariners! Apparently those pilots had no idea that submarines would soon become one of the critical tools that would cut off and starve the forces of their empire. Many of those American subs would be constructed on the Great Lakes.

Immediately after the Pearl Harbor bombing, Admiral Harold Stark, Chief of Naval Operations ordered all 22 submarines stationed in the Pacific to commence unrestricted submarine warfare against anything flying the flag of the Empire of Japan. Of course he knew full well that this tiny fleet could do little damage to the Japanese. The forces of the emperor were rapidly storming across the southern Pacific and Indian Oceans and seemed nearly unstoppable. In rapid succession the Japanese attacked Wake Island, Guam, and landings by invasion troops were made in the Philippine Islands and later Borneo. Within weeks of Pearl Harbor, the Japanese conquered Java. Yet the submarine was the only weapon that the United States could use in those first months of the war to hit back at the Japanese. Soon the Empire of Japan had overtaken nearly one quarter of the Pacific Ocean, the outlook was grim.

WWII

A view of the Manitowoc Shipbuilding Company, circa 1941. Library of Congress

A year and a half before the raid on Pearl Harbor Charles C. West, the head of the Manitowoc Shipbuilding Company met with his most valued and trusted staff at New London, Connecticut. They had been summoned by Mr. West to immediately come by train in order to meet with him and visit the Electric Boat Company. Their purpose was to learn all of the ins and outs of building submarines. His employees must have been a bit puzzled because the Manitowoc Shipbuilding Company had never built anything like a submarine. In fact, all of the submarines that they had ever heard of were over 300 feet long and drew 17 feet of water - there was no way to get them out of the Great Lakes. The Canadian locks along the St. Lawrence River that allowed access to the ocean were not designed to accommodate vessels longer than 260 feet. The only other passage to the sea was by way of the Chicago Sanitary Canal and the Mississippi River. Although the canal was long enough for a sub to

Silent Killers

pass, the Mississippi route had a choke point at the Chain Rocks Channel between St. Louis and Grafton were nothing drawing more than nine feet of water could pass. Still, the loyal members of Mr. West's company headed east and made the trip to New London anyway. Without doubt a lot of discussion and speculation went on during that train ride.

Throughout the winter of 1939-1940 many people clearly saw war brewing as the Nazis swept across Europe and the Japanese across China. Canada soon joined the conflict and the only question was when the United States would be drawn into the war. As a part of the military build-up, smart business men such as Mr. West stepped forward to lend whatever support their companies may be able to give. Manitowoc Shipbuilding Company's best bet was in building small vessels that could fit through the St. Lawrence canals. Yet, vessel-man West was always an innovator and he had created a concept that could possibly send vessels larger than 260 feet and drew more than nine feet of water out of the Great Lakes by way of the Sanitary Canal and the Mississippi.

Manitowoc Shipbuilding already used "floating dry-docks" for much of the repair work that they were often contracted to perform. A floating drydock was essentially a flat-bottom barge with high sides that were actually ballast tanks that could be flooded allowing it to sink. Once the vessel that needed repair was secured within the floating drydock the water was pumped out and the vessel would be lifted completely out of the water. The drydock itself, even with the vessel aboard, drew only a few feet of water. Mr. West reasoned that his shipyard could build something such as a destroyer, place it into the floating drydock and lift it up until it could be carried right over Chain Rocks Channel.

Mr. West submitted the floating dry-dock concept to the United States Navy, but found them uninterested. Leaving the drawings behind with Rear Admiral Claude Jones, he dejectedly returned to Manitowoc. It appeared as if his unique idea as well as the opportunity for his little company to support the war effort had fallen on deaf ears.

In the summer of 1940 Mr. West was summoned back to the admiral's office. This time he found a very receptive United States

109

Navy. But, instead of a destroyer's bow-on image, his concept drawing now had a simple circle drawn upon it. This time Admiral Jones was much more than interested in Mr. West's scheme of drydock floating a vessel down the Mississippi from the Great Lakes. In fact, he very bluntly told Mr. West that the Navy wanted his shipyard to build submarines! While Mr. West was contemplating this sudden proposal the admiral asked if the change over from destroyers to submarines would be a hindrance to the concept of drydock barging? Mr. West quickly and cautiously informed Admiral Jones that no one at the Manitowoc Shipbuilding Company, including himself, had ever seen a submarine let alone built one. He asked for a few days to study the problem with the top people from his shipyard. The admiral agreed to West's request, but added a note of urgency. He also stated the people from the Electric Boat Company would give the Manitowoc Shipbuilding Company's staff all of the help and training needed to make the project happen.

A single day after his meeting with Admiral Jones, ship builder West met with Commander Armand Morgan who was in charge of the Submarine Desk at the Navy's Bureau of Construction and Repair. This meeting had been arranged by the husband of Mr. West's niece, Lieutenant John Prescott. At dinner the previous evening Lt. Prescott was struck by the amount of doubt and trepidation that Mr. West had over the thought of having to serve his country by building submarines. During their meeting Commander Morgan was impressed by the thoughtful degree of questions that the Great Lakes shipbuilder asked about subs and their construction. The naval officer sent for some submarine blueprints for Mr. West to examine. Over the course of the meeting Morgan was so impressed by this novice in the world of submarines that he enthusiastically encouraged the vessel-man from Manitowoc to take the contract by all means. He also ensured Mr. West that he would see to it that they Navy provided the best people they had to support the Manitowoc Shipbuilding Company in their effort to build subs.

Mr. West caught the next train to New London.

Over a two-day period, the members of the Manitowoc Shipbuilding Company team gathered at the Electric Boat Company

110

in New London to tour that facility and study submarines under construction at assorted points in their building process. On the third day Mr. West accompanied by his son John and Manitowoc Shipbuilding Company employee Armin Pitz took a car ride up to Portsmouth, New Hampshire. There they visited the navy yard where finished submarines were docked. Since there were no completed subs at New London at that time, this was their chance to study the finished version.

Sailfish was the moniker of the submarine that the Manitowoc Shipbuilding Company team had been invited to tour. Along the way their guide informed them that this sub had just been completely rebuilt, and renamed as she had originally been christened the *Squalus*. The name sounded familiar, and soon their guide went on to say that the boat had sunk just over a year earlier taking the lives of 26 of her 59-man crew.

On May 23, 1939, while performing a series of dives during sea trials, after a recent overhaul, *Squalus'* aft torpedo room suddenly flooded followed by her crew quarters and both engine rooms. Her crew were able to shut water-tight doors and stop the flooding, but in the initial onrush of water 26 of her crew were drowned. The boat then settled to the bottom in 240 feet of water. By luck her sister ship, the *Sculpin*, discovered *Squalus* and called for help. In a daring feat of submarine rescue and using a newly developed sort of diving bell called the McCann Rescue Chamber and with the aid of four hard helmet divers, 33 crewmen were rescued from the stranded sub. The four divers, Chief Boatswain's Mate Orson L. Crandall, Chief Machinist's Mate William Badders, Chief Torpedoman John Mihalowski and Chief Metalsmith James H. McDonald were all awarded the Congressional Medal of Honor for their work during the rescue and salvage of the *Squalus*.

That part of the Manitowoc Shipbuilding Company staff's tour sent a very clear message to them all; duty on a submarine was extremely dangerous and the slightest defect in any part of the boat's construction could cost the lives of a brave crew. The work at the Manitowoc Shipbuilding Company must be done with nothing less than perfection - every time.

WWII

One of the advantages that the Manitowoc Shipbuilding Company had as it entered into the submarine building business was their ability to improvise and think "outside the box." In the case of submarine construction, they decided to divide each boat into 16 sections. Each of these sections would be fabricated indoors so the Wisconsin autumn and winter weather would not slow the work. The individual sections would then be moved by way of a 60-ton transporter to the construction ways where the final assembly would take place. The boats would then be side-launched, Great Lakes style. Thus, whenever you see video clips of World War II submarines being side-launched, the boat in that image is one of the Manitowoc subs.

Building submarines in modular units indoors and then transporting those modules to the launching ways for final assembly gave the Manitowoc Shipbuilding Company the advantage of speed in building. Seen here is one of the modules, circa 1942. Note the markings of "FRONT END BOTT" and "AFT END BOTT" on the jigs. This module is standing on end. Library of Congress

Silent Killers

Although the sectional method of building subs was being employed at the Plymouth navy yard, their sections were essentially shells of hulls. This was due to the fact that the Plymouth yard lacked cranes with enough strength to lift a fully equipped hull unit. The Manitowoc units were planned to be fully equipped units that would require little more than welding in place and attaching their internal workings to the previous unit. So, when the final section was welded in place the vessel would be nearly complete. Of course, Mr. West's yard also lacked cranes with that capacity - so, he simply had his engineers design and build cranes strong enough to do the job. Designed and built several months before Pearl Harbor, those cranes turned out to be the famous Manitowoc 3900, which lived on for many decades as one of the most useful cranes in the world. In fact, just eight days after the attack on Pearl Harbor the Navy ordered the Manitowoc Shipbuilding Company to immediately build and ship their largest cranes to that location. Their job was the salvage of useful equipment and the clearing away of wreckage caused by the Japanese attack. The Manitowoc Shipbuilding Company had not launched a single sub, yet their skills were already aiding the war effort.

Construction of the first submarine at Manitowoc took place on February 12, 1941 when the steel for the *Peto* arrived at the shipyard. Four months and six days later the first section of her hull was rolled out of the assembly building and hoisted onto the construction ways. Finally, at 11:15 in the morning on April 30, 1942 the *Peto* was launched sliding sideways into the water. Over the course of the war the *Peto* would sink the Japanese vessels *Tonei Maru*, *Kinkasan Maru*, *Konei Maru*, *Kayo Maru*, *Tatsuaki Maru*, *Aisakasan Maru* and *Chinkai Maru*. Her victories deprived the Japanese a total of 29,139 tons of shipping capacity.

With the bombs and torpedoes dropped by the Japanese at Pearl Harbor, a flaw in the Manitowoc Shipbuilding Company's submarine contract with Navy emerged. As the United States Congress declared war on the Empire of Japan and the Nazis declared war on the United States the ocean waters that surrounded America suddenly became official war zones. The problem was that under the contract to build the subs the Manitowoc Shipbuilding Company was supposed to deliver each boat to New London for the Navy to test and accept. That meant that a civilian crew would have to man each boat from New Orleans to New London. However, maritime law forbade civilians from manning a war ship in a war zone and no insurance company would cover such activity under any circumstances. The Navy, however, could not accept and crew a boat until its sea trials were completed and that had to be done by a civilian crew. Until the Navy officially accepted the boat it belonged to the builder and had to be insured. It was sort of a catch 22 and the solution was one that was, at first, unpalatable to some in the Navy. The subs would all have to do their sea trials on Lake Michigan.

The Manitowoc Shipbuilding Company had gone to great lengths to retain the core of highly skilled staff through the years of the Great Depression. That effort paid off as World War II began and those skills could be adapted to building submarines. Here a crew is seen installing equipment for a boat's diving plane in August, 1942. Library of Congress

Some of the Navy brass felt that the weather on Lake Michigan could cause delays in delivery as there were normally four months each year when the lake was locked with ice which would prevent sea trials from taking place. Yet, the Manitowoc shipyard officials pointed out that the same ice that restricted sea trials would also block the boats from sailing to Chicago to be shipped down the Mississippi River, so what was the difference? Additionally, there was no real alternative to conducting the training and sea trials on the lake, no matter how much the brass objected. So, with that, the Manitowoc boats would all do their trials on fresh water.

For the Manitowoc Shipbuilding Company, the problem now was turning the precision building of one submarine into mass production. Through savvy management, Mr. West had been able to retain a large core of his highly experienced workforce through the thin days of the Great Depression. Now, when he needed their skills the most, they were available to go to work. Not only would that core group of about 500 skilled craftsmen build the subs, but they would also pass on their skill to more than 8,000 new shipyard workers who would soon come flooding into the company. Together their efforts would go far toward winning the war.

After launching of the *Peto* no other subs came off the builder's ways at Manitowoc Shipbuilding Company in 1942. The *Peto*, however, was ahead of her contract date. The government had contracted for only one submarine in 1943. But Mr. West demonstrated that he could do a lot better than that and delivered a total of nine boats that year. Remarkably, that production rate covered the Manitowoc Shipbuilding Company's contract all the way through September of 1945. In 1944 the company delivered a Baker's dozen subs plus another five the following year. The submarines were sliding down the launch ways nearly as fast as they could be given sea trials and towed to the Gulf of Mexico. Each and every one was delivered to the Navy with quality assured by the Manitowoc craftsmen.

Jumping straight into the fight the Manitowoc submarines immediately went to work sinking enemy vessels in the Pacific. In 1943 Manitowoc Shipbuilding Company boats sank 21 Japanese ships. The following year, they scored victories over 80 Japanese vessels. By 1945, however, the pickings were getting a bit scarce and only 31 Japanese vessels were sent to the bottom by Great Lakes built submarines. Yet the sinking of Japanese vessels was not the only, nor even the primary mission of the submarines. Other missions such as reconnaissance, special operations, cutting enemy communications and supply lines, weather reporting (which was far more important than most folks would realize), mine laying and the rescuing of downed pilots played a huge part in every patrol. The most noticeable part of the submarine's activities, however, will always be the sinking of ships.

Overall during the war, the submarine as a weapon consisted of just over 1% of the United States Navy's arsenal, yet they managed

The concept of transporting subs down the Mississippi River by way of floating dry-docks worked. Soon Manitowoc subs were making the 12-day trip to the Gulf of Mexico as fast as they could be constructed. National Archives

to sink more than 30% of Japanese war vessels and more than 60% of Japanese merchant vessels. Although the vast majority of the Navy's submarine fleet did not come from the Great Lakes, the Manitowoc Shipbuilding Company contributed its share. From the shores of Lake Michigan 28 World War II submarines entered the fight.

Interestingly, two of the subs constructed at Manitowoc torpedoed and sank two ships that had also been constructed on the Great Lakes. On February 5, 1944 the *USS Pogy*, which had been constructed by the Manitowoc Shipbuilding Company, was under the command of Lieutenant Commander R. M. Metcalf. Named for a Lake Tahoe trout, the *USS Pogy* was launched June 23, 1942. She began her 12-day trip down the Mississippi River on the first day of February 1943, under a civilian crew and was re-commissioned to the Navy upon reaching the Gulf of Mexico waters. Following the standard Navy fit-out and crew training she set sail for Pearl Harbor by way of the Panama Canal. This meant that she first had to navigate the U-boat infested Caribbean Sea. After transiting the canal, she headed for Pearl Harbor arriving there on April 5, 1943. Just 10 days later the *USS Pogy* set out on her first war patrol.

By February of 1944 the *Pogy* had racked up a respectable kill list of eight enemy vessels including one Japanese destroyer, the *Minekaze*. The Great Lakes built sub departed Midway Island on her fifth war patrol on January 15 in the company of the *USS Skipjack*. The *Pogy* was supposed to have departed the previous day but remained at the dock for an additional 24 hours to allow her number 1 periscope to be removed so that a gritty bearing could be replaced. Now both subs headed off to their assigned patrol areas. Shortly after midnight on February 20 she was patrolling 27 miles west, southwest of Iriomote-Jima Island, east of Taiwan. Her radar showed a series of targets at 20,000 yards bearing 005 degrees at a speed of just seven knots, or a smidge over eight miles per hour. After about 40 minutes, *Pogy's* radar showed two of the targets falling further behind the rest of the convoy; stragglers! It was the sort of targets that the crew of the *Pogy* referred to as "Pogy bait."

WWII

What Commander Metcalf couldn't possibly know was that one of those targets was the *Taijin Maru*. She had been constructed for World War I service at the American Shipbuilding Company in Cleveland, Ohio. Launched in 1917 as the *Gijones* she was sent to the high seas by way of the St. Lawrence River and turned over to the Mathiesen interests of Oslo, Norway. Surviving the war, she was eventually sold to the ravenous Japanese who needed every freighter they could get in order to expand their Pacific empire. Renamed *Taijin Maru*, this product of the Great Lakes was now flying the flag of the rising sun and was stocked with rice and other supplies for Japanese troops.

Before Lieutenant Commander Metcalf attacked the *Taijin Maru* he first torpedoed her running mate in the convoy, the *Nanyo Maru*. Clearing the area where the attack had taken place, the crew of the *Pogy* heard a total of 47 depth charges being dropped where the Japanese thought the sub would likely be located - the enemy's guess was way off. In his log Lieutenant Commander Metcalf later wrote of the encounter with the *Taijin Maru*,

"04:46; with a range about 8000 yards, the *Pogy* slightly forward of the target's port beam, he changed his base course 180°. Cursing the day he was born, we reversed course, too, and commenced trying to gain bearing again. By this time, it was beginning to get light (sunrise 06:18). 05:08; fired tubes 3,4, and 5, 110° starboard track, torpedo run 2,600 yards, divergent spread, target zigzagged toward as we fired and the leading torpedo of the spread hit him..."

Taking into consideration how many enemy airbases were nearby, Lieutenant Commander Metcalf decided it was best to dive his boat and depart the area submerged and did not resurface until 6:30 that evening.

After its fifth war patrol was over the *Pogy* received a letter of commendation from the office of the commander of Submarine Squadron Four it read in part: "The *Pogy* has completed five successful patrols since reporting to the fleet in April 1943. The first "freshwater" submarine has sunk 13 ships for 73,000 tons and damaged 4 ships for 14,313 tons in just 11 months she has cruised over 50,000 miles on war patrol and returned from the fifth needing very little overhaul. The performance of the ship reflects great credit on the builders, the officers and crew and primarily on Lieutenant Commander Metcalf. The present commanding officer put the ship in commission as executive officer, organized the crew and fire control party, and has maintained the *Pogy's* high-efficiency for its invaluable war service. The excellence of the fire control party in obtaining 50% hits at an average range of over 2000 yards is deserving of special mention."

Setting a record in World War I, the construction of the second Great Lakes vessel to be sunk by a Great Lakes born sub had taken just 29 days in 1918. She started out as hull number 201 at the Great Lakes Engineering Works in Ecorse, Michigan and was named *Crawl Keys* upon her launch. She too was sold to Japan and renamed *Keizan Maru*. As war broke out in the Pacific the vessel went to work for Japan in the coastal and island supply trades.

Launched at Manitowoc on April 9, 1944 the *USS Kete* arrived in New Orleans reporting to U.S. Naval Station Algiers on August 28. Reaching the Panama Canal on September 9 she was assigned to Submarine Squadron Three. On October 15 she reached Pearl Harbor and was subsequently deployed to the island of Midway on October 31. Suffering some mechanical issues with her engine and her bow planes she remained at Midway until Christmas Eve when she was ordered to the island of Saipan. Once on station, she was to conduct lifeguard duty approximately 60 miles southeast of Okinawa. For the better part of a month she remained on station watching for downed U.S. Navy pilots. At the end of January, she was ordered to Guam. During the entire patrol, no enemy vessels or other targets were spotted by the crew of the *Kete*. On the last day of January, 1945 the *Kete* departed Guam under the command of Lieutenant Commander Edward Ackerman. She was assigned to patrol in the vicinity of the Nansei-Shoto Island chain.

With her crew likely itching for a fight with the Japanese, their wish came true on March 10, 1945. The *Kete* detected three slow-moving medium-size freighters which would be easy prey. Steaming as a part of the Kagoshima-to-Naha convoy the three Japanese vessels were north of Okinawa. The *Dokan Maru* and the *Keizan Maru* were all carrying desperately needed supplies and reinforcements for the Imperial soldiers who were being starved out of existence on what remained of the Japanese held Pacific islands. The three vessel convoy was escorted by several Japanese coastal defense vessels.

Leading the convoy was the *Sanka Maru* which was carrying 590 replacement troops plus an additional 13 gunners of her own along with 51 crewmen. When the *Kete's* torpedo hit her, the vessel exploded and sank almost immediately, there were no survivors.

Dokan Maru was loaded with barrels of fuel, a large amount of assorted ammunition, 20 cars as well as other war supplies consigned to her. She also carried 29 passengers along with 23 gunners for protection. Only 24 of those aboard her survived after the *Kete's* torpedoes hit.

Keizan Maru was carrying perhaps the most lethal cargo. In her hold were a dozen aerial torpedoes, 500 barrels of gasoline and 30 Shinyo explosive suicide motor boats! She also had aboard 1000-tons of general equipment, 54 soldiers, 10 Escort troops and 43 crewmen. When the Great Lakes built submarine *Kete* torpedoed the Great Lakes built *Keizan Maru* all of her deadly cargo went to the bottom with her.

Seeing the freighters that they were escorting exploding and going to the bottom of the Pacific in front of them, in the space of just a few minutes, the escort vessels for that doomed convoy simply turned around and returned to Kagoshima. There was nothing left for them to escort.

Unfortunately, those three victories would be all that the *Kete* and her crew would ever see. The vessel radioed a message to fleet headquarters stating that she had only three torpedoes left after trying to sink a small enemy cable laying vessel. She was returning to Pearl Harbor by way of Midway Island on March 20. On that same day she sent out a radio report stating her position with a longitude and latitude location putting her just 18 miles due east of Suwanose-Shima Island which is 211 miles north, northeast of Okinawa. That was the last that was ever heard of the *Kete*. United States Navy officials surmised that she was probably attacked and sunk by a

Silent Killers

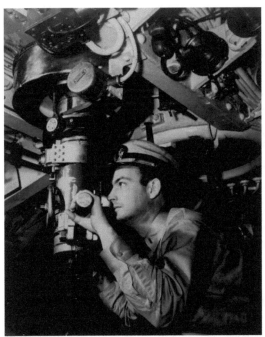

Aggressive commanders and crews who functioned as a highly skilled team used the submarines to choke the Japanese supply lines, rescue downed air crews and provide highly valued reconnaissance and countless other key tasks that helped win the war. The tiny town of Manitowoc, Wisconsin played a key role in that effort. National Archives

Japanese submarine which itself was sunk by the United States Navy shortly thereafter.

Of the 25 Manitowoc Great Lakes subs that fought in the Pacific, only four were lost. Combined the entire freshwater sub fleet sank approximately one half million tons of Japanese shipping. They sent to the bottom of the Pacific a total of 132 Japanese vessels.

Many of the Manitowoc boats continued to serve in the Navy long after World War II had concluded. One in particular that I feel compelled to mention here is the *USS Jallao*. She was launched on March 12, 1944 - just a few days short of one month before the *Kete*. Transiting the Panama Canal on August 12, *Jallao* arrived at Pearl Harbor on September 22 and departed on her first war patrol on October 9 under the command of Lieutenant Commander Joseph Icenhower. Once out of Pearl she was instructed to join the wolfpack of Commander B.A. Clarey and his submarine *USS Pintado*.

By the way, the term "wolfpack" is often associated with German U-boats, but the actual name is American. Although the Germans used a group tactic similar to the U.S. wolfpack they actually did not

121

WWII

call it that during the war. Admiral Karl Dönitz, the famed U-boat service commander, described their tactic with the term "Rudeltaktik" which translated means "tactics of an animal pack." It is likely that after the war documentary producers and authors took this translation and applied the name that was actually used by U.S. Navy submarine commanders during the war. Since the U-boats got so much glamour post-war, the term became common to describe the "tactics of an animal pack" and was easier to pronounce than rudeltaktik by most Americans. If you read the logs of the U.S. Navy's submarine captains from the autumn of 1943 on, they openly use the term wolfpack repeatedly, but the Germans do not.

Some modern sources state that *Jallao* only sank one enemy vessel in her career. Those texts are exactly 50% wrong - she actually got two. A careful reading of her Navy records shows that on her very first patrol, where most submarines traditionally refrain from torpedo actions, especially in wolfpacks, Commander Clarey's wolfpack had gotten wind of an elusive target. On the moon-lit night of October 25, the Japanese light cruiser *Tama* was speeding through their patrol area and, perhaps wanting to give Lieutenant Commander Icenhower a bit of a test, the wolfpack's commander gave the shot to the *Jallao*. Torpedoing a naval war ship was a good deal trickier than hitting a slow moving merchant ship. Cruisers and destroyers had more speed than the subs and drew less water than a freighter. Taking up the challenge the *Jallao's* crew set to the task of calculating the range, speed, and course of the *Tama* and fired three torpedoes. Commander Icenhower would have preferred to fire five fish, but he had trouble with two of his outer doors. The torpedoes were set for 15 feet of depth, but went right under the *Tama* and could be heard exploding in the distance more than three minutes after they were fired. The crew of the *Tama* must have seen the tell-tale traces of the torpedoes as the cruiser immediately turned to hunt the sub that had fired them.

Commander Icenhower saw this coming and had turned his boat perpendicular to the *Tama* and was rapidly moving away. Now he set his fish to a depth of just 10 feet and waited for the *Tama* to cross his stern. She did exactly that and when she was 700 yards off,

Commander Icenhower fired his stern tubes. All three fish hit the *Tama* and she exploded, broke in half and sank rapidly. Onboard the *Pintado* Commander Clarey watched the entire show and as the *Jallao* surfaced a message of congratulations was sent to her.

For *Jallao*, however, this would not be the start of a long string of victories. She would spend most of the rest of the war doing lifeguard duty and reconnaissance. On one occasion she did have the chance at a really big prize as one of the imperial navy's few remaining aircraft carriers passed so close to her (about 200 yards) that Commander Icenhower noted in his log that all he could see in his periscope was "paint."

Icenhower described the carrier as being of the *"Hayayaka* class," which is a passenger liner converted to a carrier. That term in itself has a bit of odd World War II history to it. The *"Hayayaka* class," category name often seen in U.S. Navy reports of that era, is completely fictional because there was never a Japanese carrier by that name! It all began with the rescue of two Japanese sailors who were among the crew of the cruiser *Mikuma*, which had been sunk during the Battle of Midway. After three nights on a raft Chief Radioman Katsuichi Yoshida and fireman third class Kenichi Ishikawa were picked up by the submarine *USS Trout*. Upon delivery to Pearl Harbor, Yoshida was taken directly to a hospital suffering from crushed ribs, but Ishikawa was in good shape and freely talked to Naval Intelligence. During his interview he gave a lot of information about the Imperial fleet that was taken quite seriously including the fact that Japan now had two new aircraft carriers that the U.S. Navy had never before heard of; they were the *Chokai* and the *Hayayaka* - both of which were supposedly former passenger liners that had been converted into aircraft carriers. This was shocking news in that the U.S. knew at that time that Japan had 11 active carriers and one training vessel prior to the battles of Coral Sea and Midway. In those two battles the U.S. Navy had cut that number down with five sunk and one badly damaged. Intelligence suggested that there were three more being readied for service in 1942, but now it appeared as if there were actually five more ready to come out! Fortunately, the castaway Japanese sailor was making it all up. Yet, the name *"Hayayaka"* remained attached to that class of carrier through the rest of the war.

On that same morning, November 13, 1944 at 06:40, *Jallao* fired all six forward tubes at the departing *"Hayayaka* class," flattop. Their target was 1,200 yards away at the time of the firing. Minutes later aboard the sub they heard nothing other than a couple of end-of-run detonations of the fish. Of course that brought the carrier's three destroyer escorts back upon the sub. They only dropped five depth charges and none of them were even close to *Jallao*. Commander Icenhower noted that there was no way he could have missed such a large target at such close range. Officially there was no explanation other than bad luck ever given for this miss. In fact, the issues with the Mark XIV torpedoes had been largely fixed many months before, so as of this writing - it was just bad luck.

On her final patrol of the war *Jallao* spent most of her time performing lifeguard duty and dodging occasional enemy aircraft. While patrolling 94 miles north, northeast of Ullung-do Island off the coast of modern day South Korea, *Jallao* got a radar fix on a vessel 17,000 yards due east. It was 20 minutes before 10 o'clock on the evening of August 10, 1945, the day after the United States had dropped the second atomic bomb on Japan obliterating the city of Nagasaki, as the sub closed on its target vessel. After he maneuvered into a position ahead of the steamer, Commander Icenhower allowed the Japanese vessel to sail right into his firing position - it was 01:45 on August 11. Spaced 1/4 ahead, 1/4 inside the bow, 1/4 inside the stern and 1/4 length astern four torpedoes were fired. Two direct hits were heard to hit the ship and Commander Icenhower saw both explosions. He then turned to fire the stern tubes. Now his target, the steamer *Teihoku Maru*, began to circle in hopes of evading more hits. It was pointless. Commander Icenhower turned his bow back and fired his remaining two torpedoes from there. One hit exactly midships - there was a huge explosion and the *Teihoku Maru* sank. Four days later Emperor Hirohito recorded a radio address that would be heard across the Empire; the war was over.

Jallao was ordered to continue to patrol in the Tungeru Strait until September first and then her war patrol was over. From there it was on to Guam and finally San Francisco on September 28, 1945. Of course she went on to serve in the cold war and remarkably saw modernization and service in the U.S. Navy until June 26, 1974 when she was turned over to the Spanish Navy to serve them until New Year's Eve 1984 when she was decommissioned and scuttled.

So, why highlight the career of this single Manitowoc-made submarine, the *Jallao*? Simple! The publisher of this book, Mr. Wells Chapin of Avery Color Studios served aboard the *Jallao* in the mid 1960s as the lead radioman and crypto officer. When I mentioned that my wife had the idea for this book and it would include Manitowoc submarines, he nearly jumped through my phone saying "I served on one of those boats! Let's do it!" Thus, because of the *Jallao*, you have this book.

TANKS ALOT

Immediately after the Japanese raid on Pearl Harbor the big automobile manufacturers in the Great Lakes region went all out ramping up war production. One of the greatest needs would be for tanks and other assorted armored vehicles. Ford, Studebaker, Plymouth and Pontiac all ceased producing cars for the civilian market and changed over to making fighting machines. The changes required by the auto industry to shift production from peacetime to wartime had a nearly instantaneous negative economic impact on the workforce - they had to lay off nearly all of their workers.

On February 2, 1942 the very last family car rolled off of the assembly line at Pontiac Plant A in the city that to this day still carries that company's name. The time was 1:31 in the afternoon and it was at that moment that the last of the production crew were given their pink slips. In order to completely change plants from car production to tanks, torpedoes, diesel engines, and other assorted military vehicles, machinery had to be changed, new assembly lines built, and the new tooling designed and built to create the implements of war. All of this took time, but there was a war going on and time was a scarce commodity.

Tank production in the United States during the two-year period from 1938 to 1940 totaled only 331 units. That total consisted of 325 light tanks and six medium tanks. One year later that total would grow to 4,052 which included 2,591 light tanks and 1,461 medium tanks. Yet, the Arsenal of Democracy was only warming up in 1941 as the following year totals for Tank production would balloon to

WWII

24,997. That inventory was divided up into 10,947 light tanks, 14,049 medium tanks and a single heavy tank. Production numbers for the year 1943 would reach an all-time record for the United States. A total of 29,497 tanks would roll off the assembly lines which included 8,212 light tanks 21,250 medium tanks and 35 heavy tanks. 1944 would see the first reduction in tank deliveries as a total of 17,565 tanks rolled out of the production facilities. That year saw 4,043 light tanks, 13,468 medium tanks and 54 heavy tanks. In the final year of the war a total of 11,968 American tanks were produced. That total included 2,801 light tanks, 6,793 medium tanks and 2,374 heavy tanks. Overall World War II production of tanks totaled 88,410 of which 30,996 of those were built in the Great Lakes region.

During the post-World War I era, the people of the United States basked in the false comfort of isolationism. Politicians bought into

In 1941 the Arsenal of Democracy was only warming up when it came to tank production. The following year totals for tank production would soon balloon to 24,997. Library of Congress

and promoted this mindset, gained votes, were elected to office and proceeded to pander to the isolationist ideal. As a result, all of the states military and National Guard units were allowed to wither and decay due to the isolationist mentality and a lack of funds because of the depression. Within the military itself tank warfare, or "mechanized warfare," was seen as little more than an interesting experiment as late as 1928. The War Department considered tanks as being nothing more than a tool to, "facilitate the uninterrupted advance of the infantryman in an attack." Much in the same way that aircraft carriers were myopically relegated to a support role for the battleships, tanks were thought to be simply a support tool for the infantry rather than the spearhead of the attack. It would take a distant enemy's actions to forever alter that perception. As early as 1930 Brigadier General Adna R. Chaffee Jr. had organized a unit of light tanks acting as an individual armored force. Still there were critics and nay-sayers. Then, in 1939 the Germans introduced the world to Blitzkrieg in Poland and later in France and the critics of tank warfare were silenced.

It was clear that war was on the doorstep of the United States and there was the real fear that Americans may soon have to face the Blitzkrieg not only "over there," but perhaps right here as well. The War Department decided that it needed a tank construction plant and they needed it where the materials and manpower for building such a machine were close at hand. That location was farmland just outside of Warren, Michigan north of Detroit and it would become the home of the Detroit Arsenal Tank Plant. Constructed by Chrysler over the winter of 1940-1941 the plant was not a former automobile plant, but a facility built from the ground up to mass produce tanks. Some 25% of all U.S. built tanks would come out of Chrysler's Detroit Arsenal Tank Plant. Delivery of the first tank produced, an M3 "Lee," named after the famous civil war general, took place on April 24, 1941. With a total output of 17,947 units the Detroit Arsenal was the leading producer of tanks in the Great Lakes region. If one looks at the records, the number of tanks produced up to December 25, 1945 was an astounding 22,234. It was also the only plant to build the M4A4 "Sherman" tank and most of these were shipped overseas to the British through lend-lease. Many Great Lakes built tanks were used to replace the light tanks lost by the British trying to stem the German advance prior to their evacuation at Dunkirk, France. In turn, Detroit Arsenal Tanks saw their first action in North Africa where they were used to eventually hand the Germans a defeat of their own.

The Arsenal Tank Plant's starting point was a railroad siding that ran through the plant on one side. Two large roll-up doors, one on each end of the railroad loading dock allowed box cars filled with parts and materials to be rolled in and unloaded regardless of weather. A loading dock that was constructed at the same level as the box car's floor allowed efficient access to the contents of the cars. Those contents were then stacked in a specific order in an indoor material storage area. That area was one of four primary work areas inside the plant. The second area was a walled-off section of the plant that contained a tool supply area as well as a heat treat department, a tooling and machine shop, and a paint shop.

Most of the floor space in the plant was taken up by the sub-assembly area. That area consisted of 10 assembly lines that manufactured the major components that would be placed into each tank. The first line was used to manufacture the main turrets of the tank. Bearing rings on which each of the turrets would swivel were constructed in the second line as was the .75mm gun rotor. The third line was where the track bogie mounts were assembled. Fourth in the line was the area where the sponsons, or the sides of the tank hull, were manufactured. Normally much of the tanks ammunition was stowed in the sponsons. Along the fifth line the rubber tires for the track bogies were assembled along with the bogies themselves. On the sixth line the top deck of the tank was assembled and prepared for mounting. Guns and their mounts were assembled on the seventh line. Transmissions for the tank were assembled along the eighth line. Tracks for each tank were assembled on the ninth line, laid in place and the tank was then simply rolled onto its track. The tenth line in the sub assembly area contained the pantograph acetylene cutting tables and finishing equipment for the tank sprockets that would drive the tracks.

All of these sub assembly lines used overhead cranes to move the parts along the line to the fourth section of the plant which was a moving final assembly line. That line began with the installation of the tank engines, turret assemblies and then the build-up of the tank hulls. Once the top deck and bogies of each tank had been installed it was cabled to the tank ahead of it on the line. That way each tank pulled the next along the line in a continuous flow of armored vehicles.

Directly outside the plant was a test track where every tank was test-driven. The finished tanks were then loaded onto railroad cars outside of the plant and taken away on the same railroad tracks that had brought in the parts needed to build them.

Fisher Body in Grand Blanc, Michigan was the first converted automobile plant to enter into tank production for the war effort. April of 1942 saw the plant turning out M4 Sherman tanks. These tanks were powered with two 6046 six cylinder engines from Detroit Diesel. Over all the Grand Blanc plant turned out 7,608 of the M4A2 Sherman's. The tanks were used by the United States Marines in the Pacific for as long as they were being produced. Production stopped in May of 1945. By then the M4A2s had also been sent by way of Lend-Lease to the Russians and had become a staple of the Canadian Army in Europe.

Two months after the Fisher Body plant began tank production and at about the same time as the Imperial Japanese Navy was still stinging from their devastating defeat at the battle of Midway, the Ford Motor Company also began to produce tanks. Ford's Highland Park plant, just north of the city of Detroit, produced the M4A3 Sherman beginning in June of 1942. This tank was powered by the Ford GAA-V8 engine. The real downside of the tank and why it was produced in the smallest number of any Sherman type was that the army had already standardized its M4's and M4A1's in Europe with the Continental aircraft radial engines while the M4A3 used a V-8 500 hp engine. After the Battle of the Bulge, December 16, 1944 to January 25, 1944, which was Germany's last major offensive in Europe, American forces suffered heavy Sherman tank losses forcing the remanufacturing of M4A3's which were then sent to Europe in

Ford V-8 assembly line for the M4A3 tanks, circa 1943. Automotive War Council

1945 as replacements for the tanks that were destroyed. Late in the war with two different types of engines and the supply chain already set in favor of the Continental radial engine built M4 and M4A1, the Ford built M4A3 tanks had been regulated to training units in the United States until modified to replace the Sherman losses in December of 1944 and January of 1945. Ford only produced the tanks for 15 months and stopped production in September of 1943.

At the outbreak of war there was a real problem with obtaining engines for the tanks. Originally the Ordnance tank designers had to decide between using a diesel engine produced by the Guiberson Company of Dallas, Texas or use a gasoline powered aircraft engine from the Wright Aeronautics Company in New Jersey. But neither manufacturer had the capability to produce the massive amount of tank engines needed while also meeting the needs of aircraft and watercraft production. In late 1940 it was decided that the

Continental Motors Company would have to be contracted to "rehabilitate" its old plant in Detroit and build the Wright engine there specifically for tanks. The expected rate of production was contracted at 20 engines per day. At that rate they figured there would be no problem in filling the needs of at least lend-lease and probably even the needs of the United States Military if we entered the war. The engine would be the Wright Whirlwind R-975 and soon the demand for it would increase beyond anything that the people in the Ordnance Department had ever imagined.

Formerly used in aircraft, the Wright Whirlwind R-975 was a radial engine. This engine had become popular in aircraft such as the Beechcraft Stagger Wing, but faded in popularity in the late 1930s as other, more powerful, radial engines were developed. The United States Army, however, found it to be well suited for use in powering light tanks. As the war erupted and production demand for the R-975

Although mass production was under way for the Detroit diesel tank engine, the air-cooled Wright Whirlwind R-975 tank engine soon became the standard. Automotive War Council

greatly increased, auto companies involved in tank production believed that in-line power plants would work better in the field, be easier to maintain, and produce - so they began pressing their case with the Army brass and the Ordinance Department to approve the change to inline engines. At first the Ordnance tank designers were reluctant to change the engines being installed in the tanks from air-cooled aircraft to engines normally used in land vehicles. The need for tank engines, however, had become critical by 1941 and the folks at General Motors Cadillac Division insisted that their engines and transmissions would be fine in tank operations. They convinced the War Department of that in October 1941 when an M3 tank powered by a Cadillac engine ran from Detroit to the Aberdeen Proving Grounds in Maryland - a distance of more than 500 miles. After that, the tank manufacturers had a choice of engines.

Sherman M4 tank in France shortly after D-Day. Note the added armor and the hedge row cutter on the front of the vehicle. Library of Congress

New tanks from the Detroit Arsenal Tank Plant were soon sent to coastal ports on the Atlantic and Pacific seaboards. They were loaded aboard cargo ships by crane. It is worth noting that most tanks constructed for World War II had a weight restriction. The upper limit was to be under 40 tons and that was not because of materials shortages, railroad restrictions, or even the capacity of cargo ships. The restriction was due to the fact that all of the tanks had to be loaded aboard the cargo ships by way of shore-side cranes. Those cranes normally had a lifting weight limit of about 40 tons. So to insure that the tanks could be loaded at nearly every dock where cargo ships were moored, the individual tank had to be under the 40-ton weight restriction of the loading cranes. This was the case until the "heavy" M26 Pershing tanks were introduced in late 1944. Built in relatively small numbers, 2,464 total, these were shipped from ports that could handle their 41.23-ton weight. The first M26 tanks arrived in Europe in early 1945 and headed toward the battle zones. Earlier the introduction in battle of the first Great Lakes built tanks occurred during the North Africa campaign. There the M4A1 Sherman tanks saw their first action of World War II. At the other extreme, the M26 tanks saw only limited service in Europe having arrived in significant numbers in the first months of 1945. Later, when they were shipped to the Pacific to fight on Okinawa, they arrived after the island was in American hands.

Although the tanks that were built in the Detroit area plants used local labor to man the factories, the component parts needed to build the tanks came from all around the Great Lakes region as well as from distant locations in the United States. For example, Timken-Detroit Axle Company supplied tank transmissions for some of the assembly plants, but the Detroit Arsenal made its own transmissions on site. General Motors Buick Division, Reed Roller Bit Company, Caterpillar Tractor, and Ford Motor Company all eventually had to get into the transmission production business by the end of 1942 in order to keep up with the demand for tanks. The Gary Armor Plant in Gary, Indiana was constructed during the war specifically for supplying armor for tanks and was the largest of its kind in the world. Detroit's Standard Steel Spring Company was dedicated to making

WWII

Detroit's automobile plants successfully switched from making peace-time cars to war-time tanks at a combined rate that no nation on Earth could match. It was another element that led to victory.
Library of Congress

the springs that went into the bogies upon which the tank's treads rode. Malleable Iron Foundry in Saginaw, Michigan cast track blocks, track frames, and covers as well as grouser bodies and ends. By the end of 1943 that company had cast 1,700,000 tank blocks.

Of course this is just a thumbnail view of the mountainous volume of war materials that we call "tanks." Around the country other tank plants turned out armored vehicles of every sort. Additionally, incredible amounts of spare parts were produced and shipped overseas. Although the facilities of the Great Lakes region served the war effort well, it was not alone in the fight. Today there are museums that proudly display tanks made near the lakes, yet many of the factories that produced those machines are now gone. Grand Blanc's Fisher Body plant today is nothing more than a vast vacant slab of concrete. We should never forget the monumental effort put forth by this country, its industries, and its people at a time when evil tried to rule the world and was stopped by steel made in America. We can all look back and say, "Tanks a lot."

U-BOAT BAIT

At the onset of World War II the Canadians were the first from the Great Lakes to get into the fight and support the British by way of ships. Part of that support came in the form of Canadian vessels sent from the lakes to the Atlantic to aid the British in their struggle with the Axis Powers. Later, as the United States entered the war, US flagged canal sized vessels also joined the fight. Although the earliest of the canal sized vessel losses to U-boats were

The continuous convoys kept Great Brittan alive in effect providing a forward base from which the Allied Forces could liberate Europe from Nazi occupation. Library of Congress

in the north Atlantic, the real carnage to those vessels took place in the Caribbean Sea, Gulf of Mexico, and central Atlantic. Known affectionately as, "canallers" these small steamships were originally constructed to fit through the small locks along the St. Lawrence River. Vessels no longer than 261 feet were able to fit through the smallest of those locks and make the passage from the Great Lakes to the Atlantic Ocean. Thus, a small maneuverable propeller driven vessel evolved that could efficiently make its way through the winding river and its tiny locks. Considering that most of the traffic in these locks service ports in Canada, that nation had the largest fleet of canallers. By Great Lakes standards these boats were short and shallow with the ability to carry a very modest load. Additionally, they were slow and somewhat cramped for their crews. They were not designed for long-distance high seas sailing. Most of the canallers were designed exclusively to move assorted cargoes up and down the St. Lawrence River and occasionally, when needed, across the Great Lakes. For many years they served Canada quite well, but when World War II broke out they would extend their service for King and country.

In the United States a number of canal sized vessels were produced to meet the urgent needs of the first World War. Yet the late entrance of the US into the conflict left many of those vessels still on the builder's ways and nearing completion when the war came to a sudden halt. Some of those vessels eventually did what they were intended to do - they went through the locks on the St. Lawrence river and out to find work making short hops along the coasts of the great oceans. When the next world war broke out they found themselves in the fight - on both sides.

Great Britain was rapidly becoming the last bastion of freedom in Europe and the nation's need for every sort of product became an issue of life and death. Canada responded and quickly prepared their fleet of canallers to join convoys headed for Britain. Largely crewed by Canadians, the tiny boats set out onto the saltwater seas and directly into the teeth of the German U-boat menace. Countermeasures needed to protect the convoys from the U-boats were nearly nonexistent in the early months of the war and the men

The canaller Donald Stewart *is a typical example of her class of vessel. They were designed to fit through the short, shallow locks of the St. Lawrence canal system. Speed was never a consideration. When removed from the Great Lakes and placed onto the high seas they simply became U-boat bait. Author's Collection*

who sailed in the convoys were fully aware of the hazards, yet they went anyway. Proud Canadians, some who had never sailed on saltwater and had spent their careers on the Great Lakes eagerly signed up to join the convoys.

Their slow speed was what made the canallers vulnerable to the torpedoes and deck guns of the U-boats. All too often the tiny vessels found themselves as "stragglers" falling behind the main body of the convoy. It was there that many would come into view of the U-boat captain's periscope only to be later entered in the log book as a kill with the notation: "straggler." In this chapter we will take the records left to us by the U-boat captains and use them as well as Allied records, Great Lakes maritime records and news media to document and remember the crews of those brave little canallers.

WWII

It is important to keep in mind that the captains and crews of the U-boats were, for the most part, simply sailors fighting for their country. Although there were some Nazi extremists among them, the rules of the German Navy forbade sailors and officers from joining any political party, and "Nazi" was indeed a political party. Thus, most U-boat crews saw themselves as military men duty-bound to follow the orders of their commanders. To us on the Allied side they were the enemy, they were the villains, they were the dirty filthy dogs lurking in the ocean to kill our boys. That is the way of war, it is an ugly and horrible business. Thus, it is not the objective of this chapter to glorify the actions of the U-boats. Rather, it is the objective of this text to present to you a record of the actions. It is also important to keep in perspective the fact that although the German U-boats conducted unrestricted submarine warfare in the Atlantic Ocean, our own United States Navy submarines also conducted unrestricted submarine warfare against the Japanese in the Pacific. It was a time when the entire planet was involved in the horror of war.

For the Great Lakes canallers the carnage began on July 5, 1940. It was then that the canaller *Magog* was sighted by Captain Otto Kretschmer of the U-99 at 12:51 local time at a position 58 miles west, southwest of the Fastnet Rock lighthouse off the southern tip of Ireland. She had originally been with convoy HX-52 bound from Philadelphia and later Halifax, Novi Scotia to Liverpool but she had fallen behind and strayed into the U-99's crosshairs. The canaller was hauling lumber but that made no difference to Captain Kretschmer. She was British raw tonnage and as soon as U-99 was ready the U-boats Commander fired its first torpedo. That torpedo exploded prematurely but still damaged the canallers rudder. Seeking to conserve his torpedoes for juicier targets Captain Kretschmer surfaced the U-99 and ordered his crew to sink the *Magog* using the deck gun. After some concentrated firing Captain T. Swales Doughty ordered the canallers crew to abandon ship by way of the lifeboats. Once the crew were safely away from their vessel Captain Kretschmer decided that a second torpedo would be needed to sink the canaller. That one struck the *Magog* at midship and the vessel broke in two. The Germans maneuvered alongside the lifeboats and

Kenordoc *seen here in happier days when she went about carrying her cargos on the Great Lakes. Author's Collection*

questioned the crew. Captain Kretschmer then returned to his patrol leaving the survivors and their lifeboats on the open sea. They were later picked up by the Swedish merchant vessel *Fidra* and safely landed at Queenstown, Cork, Ireland.

Captain Kretschmer and the U-99 struck again on September 15, 1940. Just after noon Captain Charles Ernest Brown was guiding the Great Lakes canaller *Kenordoc* toward England. The little boat was carrying a full load of lumber as a part of convoy SC-3 en route from Halifax, Nova Scotia. As the convoy entered the later stages of its voyage the slower vessels began to lag behind and *Kenordoc* was one of those stragglers. She made easy prey for Captain Kretschmer's U-boat.

He surfaced his vessel and ordered his crew to open fire with the deck gun. The location was 44 miles west-northwest of Rockall light and after a number of rounds from the gun the *Kenordoc* was clearly disabled and appeared to be in a sinking condition. Considering that it was broad daylight and there may be military escort vessels from the Royal Navy nearby, Captain Kretschmer elected to simply log the vessel as, "damaged" and re-submerge to wait for another target. In the gunfire Captain Brown and six of his crew were killed. The remaining 13 crew members were rescued by the *HMCS St. Laurent* under the command of Lt H.S. Rayner. In spite of her mortal wounds the *Kenordoc* continued to float as a derelict buoyed up by her lumber cargo. Being a hazard to navigation due to the fact that she was unlit and drifting in the shipping lanes used by the convoys the canaller was later scuttled by the *HMS Amazon*.

Three months and 10 days after the sinking of the canaller *Magog* another Great Lakes canaller was lost to U-boats. In the pre-dawn darkness 200 miles west of the Irish coast the canaller *Trevisa* was under the command of Captain Robert C. Stonehouse and hauling a lumber cargo just as the *Magog* and *Kenordoc* had been. She was a straggler from convoy SC-7 which was sailing the exact same route as convoy HX-52 and was also headed for Liverpool. About 10 minutes before four o'clock that morning U-124 commanded by Captain Georg-Wilhelm Schulz fired a torpedo that struck the canallers stern and the little lakeboat began to rapidly sink by her heels. Interestingly the U-124 had fired a previous torpedo at the *Trevisa* at 6:30 the previous evening, but the torpedo missed. When the stricken vessel finally did sink she took seven of her crew with her. Another 14 crewmembers survived and were picked up by the *HMS Bluebell*. Convoy SC-7 itself was a fairly disastrous outing with 20 of its ships being sunk by U-boats and another six damaged between October 17, when the *Trevisa* was sunk and October 19, when the final vessel was torpedoed. Captain Kretschmer of the U-99 sank six of those vessels and damaged one.

Known as the "lake class" steamer, these three island configured cargo vessels were produced for the first world war and were constructed to fit through the canals along the St. Lawrence River. For that emergency construction a number of shipyards along the lakes immediately turned to building these vessels. Most of them went to war with the moniker "lake" in their names. One such vessel was constructed at the Saginaw Shipbuilding Company and was launched sideways into the Saginaw River with the name *Lake Osweya* proudly painted on her bows. Belatedly joining the war effort, the *Lake Osweya* saw little action. Following the armistice, she found herself in layup along some Atlantic coast backwater. Together with 200 other "surplus" vessels she was purchased by the Ford Motor Company. In 1930 she was refitted with a diesel engine and entered coastal service for Ford. At the onset of World War II she was requisitioned by the federal government of the United States for defense shipping needs.

For the canallers built on the Great Lakes the year 1942 would bring the most carnage, suffering, and destruction of the war. It all began on February 19, as the *Lake Osweya* was bound for Halifax. Sailing unescorted she was in command of Captain Karl E. Prinz, her longtime master from before the war. Sailing in the company of the vessel *Empire Seal* the two vessels were 45 miles east southeast of Cape Sable Island, Nova Scotia when the U-96 under the command of Captain Heinrich Lehmann-Willenbrock fired a single torpedo that struck the *Empire Seal* at the bow; it was 11:30 in the evening. The vessel began to settle at the bow but apparently was not sinking. A second torpedo was fired 32 minutes later and struck the vessel amidships causing her to sink. All but one of her 44 crew members escaped in lifeboats. Witnessing this event Captain Prinz of the *Lake Osweya* took evasive action to try and avoid the lurking U-boat. Although the *Lake Osweya* was equipped with three-inch guns they were completely useless against a submerged U-boat. His only alternative was to alter course and begin zigzagging.

Zigzagging was a desperate and futile effort as the U-96 continued to stalk the *Lake Osweya*. At 7 minutes before five o'clock on the morning of February 20, Captain Lehmann-Willenbrock ordered a torpedo fired which struck the *Lake Osweya* just forward of amidships. The canaller broke in half and rapidly sank. The U-boat's commander reported seeing lifeboats successfully launched, but no survivors of the *Lake Osweya* were ever found.

Just three days later two Great Lakes canallers were lost on the same day, sunk by the same U-boat in different locations. The first to be struck was the *George L. Aoiran* which came into the sights of

WWII

U-129, 145 miles southeast of the island of Trinidad Tobago. Captain Asmus Nicolai Clausen was on his fourth patrol aboard the U-129 having been skunked on his first three patrols by sinking no vessels. Now he had the *Aoiran* in his periscope and was determined to sink her. Unfortunately, even though he had been tracking the freighter for four hours when he fired a torpedo at the bauxite laden canaller at the stroke of midnight, it missed her completely. Next, at 20 minutes after one in the morning, he fired another shot. The torpedo struck near the *Aoiran's* bow and the little canaller plunged to the bottom of the Atlantic in less than one minute. Captain John Allan and 14 of the *Aoiran's* crew never knew what hit them. Four survivors were later picked up by a United States Navy flying boat and taken to Trinidad.

With a confirmed kill in his logbook, Captain Clausen now continued his patrol looking for another ripe target. Just before three o'clock that afternoon, as the U-129 was running on the surface and recharging her batteries the deck watch sighted another vessel. U-129 was just 35 miles from where she had sunk the *Aoiran* and now through their binoculars the U-boat crew saw the silhouette of another vessel that looked exactly the same; she was the Great Lakes canaller *Lennox*. Coincidentally the *Aoiran* and the *Lennox* had loaded the same cargo at the same port, Paramaribo, Dutch Guiana, and both were headed for the Port of Spain in Trinidad. Once more Captain Clausen lined up the target in his periscope and fired a shot at the helpless freighter. She sank in almost the same way as the *Aoiran* and their graves are now just 35 miles apart. Only two of her 20 crewmembers perished in the sinking the rest were picked up by the tanker *Anthelrill* and dropped off at the Port of Spain. In the vastness of the Atlantic Captain Clausen had managed to sink two Great Lakes canallers carrying the same type of cargo, from the same port, with the same destination, on the same day and in nearly the exact same location.

It was just a little after two o'clock on the morning of March 14, 1942 as Captain William Darling was guiding the canal steamer *Sarniadoc* toward the port of Trinidad in the Caribbean. In her cargo hold was a full load of bauxite that she had loaded at Georgetown,

144

British Guiana three days earlier. British Guiana was a prime source of very high-grade bauxite during World War II. From bauxite is derived aluminum and from aluminum is derived aircraft the majority of whose components are made from that lightweight metal. Approximately 60% of raw aluminum that was produced for the allies during World War II came from British Guiana's bauxite docks. The tonnage of bauxite shipped from that country went from 476,000 tons in 1939 to 1,902,000 tons in 1943. Thus little canallers such as *Sarniadoc* were hauling a highly valued commodity. Her current load was destined for the port of St. Thomas in the Virgin Islands, but in the expanse of the Caribbean a loan periscope set its sights on a different destination for the little canaller.

Approximately 218 miles due west of Basse - Terre on the island of Guadeloupe, Captain Albrecht Achilles of the U-161 took his final sightings on the *Sarniadoc*. He fired a single torpedo that struck the vessel astern. Moments after the torpedo's detonation the relatively cool Caribbean waters washed into the hole the explosion had made in the canallers bottom and contacted her hot boilers. A moment later her boilers exploded and the *Sarniadoc* went to the bottom with all hands.

For Captain Achilles it was simply more tonnage added to his kill total in what the German submariners referred to as "the happy times." But the tables would soon turn on Captain Achilles, his crew, and the U-161. A year and a half later, on September 27, 1943, while on patrol a United States Navy Martian PBM Mariner flying boat spotted the U-161. A series of depth charges were dropped and the U-boat was destroyed taking Captain Achilles and his crew of 52 German sailors to the bottom of the South Atlantic, 217 miles east northeast of Salvador, Brazil.

At 40 minutes past three o'clock on the morning of April 3, 1942 the canaller *David H. Atwater* was steaming up the coast of Virginia en route to Fall River, Massachusetts with a load of 3,911 tons of coal. Unlike most of the canallers in this saga the *Atwater* was an American flagged vessel sailing strictly between United States coastal cities. Her primary duty was hauling coal for the Atwater Transportation Company. She had been built for World War I use, but by the time she was finished the war had been over for several

On September 27, 1943, while on patrol a United States Navy Martian PBM Mariner flying boat spotted the U-161. A series of depth charges were dropped and the U-boat was destroyed. Library of Congress

months. Constructed by the Great Lakes Engineering Works in 1919, she was purchased by her namesake coal company from the "mothball fleet" and pressed into service along the Atlantic coast.

Running just 7 miles offshore the *Atwater* was sighted by the U-552. The U-boat's commander, Captain Erich Topp, quickly realized that the *Atwater* was unarmed and unescorted and was a good target for his deck gun. He ordered the U-552 to surface and ordered his crew to man the deck gun. At a range of just 600 yards the U-boat's crew opened fire on the *Atwater*. In all they fired 93 rounds and the captain estimated about 50 rounds actually struck the vessel. The shelling caused the *Atwater* to catch fire and it was clear that she was mortally wounded. Additionally, the gunfire also damaged or destroyed her life boats. As the canaller began to rapidly sink her crewmembers had no choice but to jump overboard. Unfortunately, in this era a lot of merchant sailors who went to sea did not know how to swim. Nearly all of the *Atwater's* crew drowned including Captain William Keith Webster.

Gunfire from the U-552 not only sank the *Atwater*, but it also alerted the Coast Guard cutter *Legare* which immediately headed to the scene at full speed. They arrived in time to find the *Atwater* almost completely sunk with flotsam and three survivors clinging to the wreckage. Their final report stated that 24 mariners had been lost in the attack. Today, the *Atwater* rests on the bottom of the Atlantic 7.25 miles due east of Smith Hammocks and ten miles northeast of Little Tom's Cove, Virginia. The U-552 crept away completely unnoticed after the attack.

If there was ever a canaller that was not intended to sail the high seas, it was the motor vessel *Green Island*. Constructed by the Great Lakes Engineering Works for the Ford Motor Company the *Green Island* was specifically built to navigate the New York State Barge Canal. She had a pilothouse that could retract below her deck and masts that could be folded down so as to give her the low profile needed to allow her to fit under the bridges that span the Barge Canal. Her purpose was to carry massive loads of components such as axles, radiators, springs and other prefabricated automobile parts from the Ford plants in Detroit to their outlets in upstate New York. Upon her launching in 1937 there was a great deal of publicity and celebration. The *Green Island* was the first ship built on the United States Great Lakes in six years. It was a signal that the end of the Great Depression perhaps was at hand.

After three years of service to the Ford company the *Green Island* was requisitioned for saltwater use by the United States government. She was placed in service running about the Caribbean islands carrying assorted general cargo. The very low-profile that had been designed to go under the bridges of the Barge Canal quickly proved to be a major problem for her captain and crew while sailing the high seas. It wasn't the big ocean waves that threatened her, instead it was the fact that her low profile made her look very much like a surfaced U-boat. On the night of January 27th, 1942 the United States Navy minesweeper *Hamilton*, while performing escort duty for a convoy of troop ships heading from New York to the Panama Canal Zone, spotted the *Green Island* at five o'clock in the morning. Believing that they had found a surfaced U-boat the captain of the minesweeper ordered that a shot be fired over the bow of the *Green Island*. He then immediately turned the *Hamilton* toward what he believed to be a U-boat and commanded, "full speed ahead" with the intent to ram her. As the minesweeper closed in her captain suddenly realized that the vessel was not a U-boat and commanded, "full speed reverse" while at the same time ordering his helmsman to put the rudder hard over. It was too late, the minesweeper rammed the *Green Island* on her port side. Fortunately, the damage was not fatal and the little canaller was soon repaired.

Less than three months after her mistaken ramming by the *Hamilton*, the *Green Island* was back in service. On May 6, 1942 she was running unescorted from Mobile, Alabama to the island of Aruba. When she was 62 miles south of Grand Cayman Island the mistaken U-boat was spotted by a real U-boat. As the *Green Island* crawled slowly along her course Captain Ulrich Folkers of the U-125 drew a bead on the low-slung canaller. He fired a single torpedo that struck the *Green Island* nearly midships. The vessel subsequently broke in half, but remained afloat. Witnessing the 22 crew members taking to the lifeboats, Captain Folkers was satisfied that he had a successful kill. The U-125 remained on the scene without firing an additional shot. About an hour after the *Green Island* was torpedoed, her crew rowed their way back and re-boarded the vessel. Upon inspection it was clear to the crew that the vessel was a total loss and they returned to their lifeboats. Six hours after the initial torpedo hit the *Green Island* finally sank and the U-125 resumed her patrol. The following day all of the survivors were picked up by the British merchant vessel *Fort Qu'Appelle* and dropped off at Kingston, Jamaica. That same vessel would be torpedoed and sunk by the U-135 seven days later.

Exactly one year to the day after the sinking of the *Green Island*, the allies would take their revenge on U-125 and Captain Folkers. On the night of May 6, 1943 while patrolling in heavy fog the British destroyer *HMS Oribi* detected the signature of the U-boat on radar and rammed her. After the collision the U-boat became lost in the fog and was assumed to have been sunk. They were wrong, however, as Captain Folkers' U-boat was only crippled yet on the verge of sinking. He radioed for help, but the responding U-boats could not find U-125 in the fog. To make matters worse the area was crawling with British war ships. Only minutes before four o'clock on the morning of May 7, the corvette *HMS Snowflake* spotted the wounded U-125 on radar and closed to within 110 yards. Using their high intensity lights *HMS Snowflake* illuminated the U-boat and attempted to ram her. Captain Folkers used his boat's last bit of maneuvering and turned just in time to avoid being rammed by the corvette. Upon seeing that the U-boat was unable to continue the fight, the *HMS Snowflake* returned in an attempt to capture her, but Captain Folkers ordered the U-125 to be scuttled with explosives. Her crew went over the side as their boat went to the bottom of cold north Atlantic. *HMS Sunflower*, another corvette, arrived on the scene and requested permission to take the survivors aboard. The reply from the convoy commander said, "Not approved to pick up survivors" and the two corvettes sailed away into the night leaving the entire crew of the U-125 to perish in the bitter cold of the north Atlantic.

Do not feel too much pity for Captain Folkers as you read this. In his career as a U-boat commander he personally sent 203 men to their deaths in the waters of the Atlantic. He only once picked up two survivors as prisoners, a vessel's captain and chief engineer. He often surfaced the U-125 to photograph survivors floating in the wreckage caused by his torpedoes and deck guns before sailing away and leaving them to the Atlantic. On one occasion, October 8, 1942, while photographing the aftermath of the sinking of the *Glendene*, the survivors shouted to Captain Folkers that in his rush to see their vessel sink, the extra torpedoes he had pumped into her had killed five men! Captain Folkers simply replied that those were the last of his torpedoes and he was in a hurry to use them up so he could end his patrol and return home to Germany. Then he sailed away and left the survivors adrift in the Atlantic. Now, on May 7, 1943 Captain Folkers experienced first-hand what it was like to be left to die in those frigid waters. He and his 54 crewmen were all consumed by the sea.

WWII

On May 9, 1942, only three days after the *Green Island* had been attacked, the Great Lakes canaller *Mont Louis* under the command of Captain Walter Bowen slowly steamed directly into the crosshairs of the U-162. The canaller had a hold full of bauxite ore bound for Trinidad. Squinting through his periscope Captain Jürgen Wattenberg prepared to fire his first torpedo of the day and make an easy kill. The *Mont Louis* sank like a brick taking 13 of her crew with her. Seven crewmembers as well as Captain Bowen survived to be rescued the following day by the Canadian schooner *Mona Marie* which landed them at Georgetown.

Captain Wattenberg would later make a name for himself not by the amount of Allied tonnage he sank, but rather by his conduct upholding his sworn military duty to the utmost degree possible while he was in captivity and by making one of the most complex escape attempts as a POW.

Beginning his war career with the German Navy aboard the German battleship *Admiral Graf Spee*, Wattenberg served as a navigation officer. After that vessel was heavily damaged by the British in December 1939, it was then scuttled by a skeleton crew to prevent the British from capturing and examining it, the majority of the crew having remained ashore where they were interned in Montevideo, Uruguay. Wattenberg promptly escaped and made his way back to Germany in May of 1940. After a stint as a commander in training on the U-103 he took full command of the U-162 on February 7, 1942. Departing Germany on his way to prowl the Atlantic, Captain Wattenberg was one of the oldest U-boat commanders in the German Navy at age 41. His U-boat career, however, came to an end after just 163 days at sea and three patrols.

Depth charges from three British destroyers sealed the fate of U-162 on September 3, 1942. Captain Wattenberg and all but two of his crew were taken captive by the British. Wattenberg was shipped to the POW camp at Fort Hunt, Virginia where he was interrogated. Most German officers were fluent in English and in the terms of the Geneva Convention. So all interrogations were done strictly by the book and very little useful information was gained from the captive Germans. He was later sent to the Crossville, Tennessee POW camp arriving there on October 16, 1942. Wattenberg, however, quickly gained a reputation of being difficult and complaining. Prisoners who were not passive in their detention were often moved from one camp to another just to get rid of them. From his first taste of being a POW Wattenberg began to exercise the duty of every POW - which was escape. Before a good plan could be hatched, however, he was transferred again after camp after officials had discovered his plans to tunnel out of the camp to freedom. Exactly how he figured to get out of Tennessee without coming face to face with the business end of some citizen's hunting rifle, only Wattenberg knew. This time on January 27, 1944 he was sent to the desert POW camp at Papago Park, near Scottsdale, Arizona.

Believing, as did many of the German soldiers who were captured early in the war, that Germany was actually winning, Wattenberg began to organized an escape plan. Studying a contraband map of Arizona stolen from a gas station, the one-time U-boat commander began to formulate what may have well been one of the largest escapes ever attempted by German POWs.

Keep in mind that the German POWs had little or no geographic knowledge of the United States and especially of the areas where they were being held as captives. Few if any had traveled extensively in the United States and knew little of the vastness of the territory or the climate of the seasons. Wattenberg's plan was to tunnel out of camp and head for the Gila River, which was a wonderful and inviting blue line of water on the map. The Gila fed into the Colorado River, an even more inviting blue line of water on the map. The Colorado would take them floating all the way down to Mexico where they would somehow try to arrange to get home to Germany and back into the war. After all, Wattenberg had escaped and done it all before.

Using the excuse of building a volley ball court and garden to grow their own fresh vegetables, the POWs concealed the huge amount of dirt they were removing to make the 200-foot-long tunnel that was 16 feet underground. They were even allowed to use shovels given to them by camp officials for those projects. Using a camp uprising with prisoners clashing with guards as a distraction, 25

WWII

POWs including Wattenberg escaped through the tunnel under a road and into a gully. Their plan worked so well that no one noticed that they were gone until one escapee turned himself in after being lost in the Arizona scrub land for 17 hours! When the Wattenberg gang reached the Gila "River" they discovered that it was nothing more than a dry wash that was wet only in times of heavy rain. There would be no floating to Mexico for these Germans. Or course they were also cheated out of trying to float down the rapids of the Colorado River - people pay for that stuff these days.

All of Wattenberg's final command were soon rounded up and returned to camp. The former U-boat commander himself was the last to be apprehended after being spotted walking in downtown Phoenix 36 days after the escape. Throughout his career, Wattenberg was a dedicated officer in the highest tradition of the German Navy. He was repatriated to Germany in 1946 and later went into the brewing business.

Back out on the Atlantic two canallers from the same Great Lakes fleet were coincidentally lost on the same day, 1,160 miles apart in the Caribbean Sea. Both of these vessels belonged to the unlucky baker's dozen that went to war from Canada's N.M. Paterson Company. Of the 13 canallers from this fleet that departed the Great Lakes to serve their country, nine would not return with eight of those having been lost to enemy action.

At 7 minutes before the hour of eight o'clock on the morning of May 21, 1942 the Paterson steamer *Torondoc* was sailing toward the port of Trinidad with a cargo hold full of bauxite loaded at St. Thomas in the Virgin Islands. When she was 71 miles due west of the island of Martinique she came into the sight of U-69 and Captain Ulrich Gräf. Captain Gräf had already sunk three vessels during the month of May and was eager to claim his fourth. He fired a single torpedo that struck the *Torondoc* amidships.

Heavily laden with bauxite the *Torondoc* began to immediately sank. Her master, Captain Xavier Daneau, who had been in command of the boat both on the lakes and on the ocean, immediately ordered all hands to abandon ship. Everyone of the 22 crew members aboard the *Torondoc* made it safely to either the two lifeboats or two life rafts and successfully got away from the sinking vessel. The U-69 surfaced and Captain Gräf questioned the survivors to determine their cargo, departure point, and destination as well as any casualties. Once he had that information he sailed away leaving the shipwrecked crew to their fate. None of the *Torondoc's* crew were ever seen again.

Captain Gräf, after later sinking the abandoned tugboat *Letitia Porter*, would leave the Caribbean and commit one of the most daring raids on Canadian shipping during the war by taking the U-69 to the North Atlantic, up the Gulf of St. Lawrence and to within 170 miles of Quebec City! There he would sink the Canadian steamer *Carolus* on October 9, 1942. This was one of the closest excursions by any U-boat ever made toward the waters of the Great Lakes. Captain Gräf and the U-69 would be destroyed off of Newfoundland on February 17, 1943 during his next patrol.

A little more than 10 hours after the *Torondoc* had been sunk by the U-69, her Paterson fleet mate, the *Troisdoc* was about to meet a similar fate. Sailing from Mobile Alabama to Georgetown, British Columbia with a cargo of "general merchandise" the Paterson canaller was under the command of Captain René Cormier, a native of Québec. That evening at 22 minutes after six the *Troisdoc* came into view of Captain Günther Krech through the periscope of U-558. One of Germany's most experienced U-boat commanders, Captain Krech was on his sixth patrol. Since August of 1941 he had already sent to the bottom nine vessels and damaged a tenth. Now, with a keen eye, he carefully targeted his soon to be eleventh kill. Calculating the shot, he ordered the torpedo to be fired.

Aboard the *Troisdoc* Captain Cormier and his entire crew heard a loud metallic "THUD!" It was almost as if they had struck some submerged object, but they were 64 miles west of Jamaica, on the southern edge of the Cayman Trench - one of the deepest areas of the Caribbean Sea. There was no possibility of striking a submerged object. Perhaps something on the vessel had broken, or perhaps some huge piece of cargo had come loose. Just as Captain Cormier was scratching his head contemplating the possibilities the lookout shouted that he had spotted a U-boat surfacing nearby. The torpedo fired from the U-558 had been a dud.

WWII

If there had been any doubt as to what the crew of the U-boat intended to do next that doubt was soon erased as the U-558's deck gun began firing. Captain Cormier ordered his crew into lifeboats and they abandoned the *Troisdoc*. As the little canaller began to sink under the withering gunfire her crew noticed someone on the bridge of the U-boat gleefully taking photographs. A German war correspondent had been along for this cruise and was recording the final moments of the *Troisdoc*. The only high point in this bad day for the Paterson Company was the fact that all 18 persons aboard the *Troisdoc* escaped unharmed and were later picked up by the Corvette *HMS Clarkia* and dropped off safely at Mobile, Alabama.

Without doubt the most productive ship killer in the U-boat ranks was Captain Erwin Rostin commander of the U-158. He took command of his first U-boat on September 25, 1941 and set out on his first patrol on February 7, 1942. From that date onward through June 30, he sank 17 ships sending 101,321 tons to the bottom! Included in those 17 ships were three vessels of Great Lakes origin.

A German war correspondent aboard the U-558 photographed the sinking of the Troisdoc. *His photo became famous both during and after the war. Author's Collection*

154

First of the Lakers to be taken by Captain Rostin was the U.S. flagged *Caribsea*. Launched at Alexander Mcdougal's Duluth Ship Building Company in 1919 to support the Allies in World War I, she was originally named *Lake Flattery*. Once in salt water service, she never returned to the lakes. Built for one world war, she plied her trade until becoming the victim of the U-158 during a second world war. The canal sized "lake class" freighter was bound from Norfolk, Virginia to Baltimore, Maryland with a cargo of 3,600 tons of manganese ore when she met her end. Captain Rostin sank her with a single torpedo, 11 and three-quarter miles due east of the Cape Lookout lighthouse.

Second among the unlucky Lakers to fall into the sights of Captain Rostin's periscope was the Canadian canaller *Frank B. Baird*. Under the command of Captain Charles Tate, the little canaller was loaded with 2,457 tons of bauxite consigned to Sydney, Nova Scotia from British Guiana. Following the normal steamer track she was 456 miles southeast of Bermuda when Captain Rostin surfaced the U-158 and opened fire using the U-boat's deck gun. All 23 crew members managed to escape the *Baird* in lifeboats before she sank beneath them. Captain Rostin then sailed away leaving the *Baird's* crew surrounded by nothing but ocean. Fortunately, the Norwegian merchant vessel *Talisman* came upon the survivors and transported them to Pointe-Noire, Basse-Terre, Guadeloupe.

Another World War I "lake class" steamer that had been built at McDougall's Duluth Ship Building Company was sunk by Captain Rostin on June 5, 1942. Launched as the *Lake Flournoy* this canal sized steamer, like her sister ship *Lake Flattery*, passed through the locks along the St. Lawrence River, entered service on salt water and never returned to the Great Lakes. Built as part of the U.S. Shipping board contracts during the first World War, she had been launched in 1920 - too late for World War I service. After a short lay-up as surplus tonnage, she was purchased by the Lone Star Steamship Company in 1922 and renamed *Southseas*. In 1929 she was purchased by the Lykes Brothers Steamship Company and given her final name - *Velma Lykes*.

WWII

Bound for Cristobal, Panama from Galveston, Texas with a cargo of general merchandise the *Velma Lykes* was just over a dozen miles offshore from Cancun when a torpedo from the U-158 struck the vessel on her starboard side killing the three men who were on watch - it was just past 3:30 on the morning of June 10th. It took the ship about 60 seconds to sink by way of her stern and there was no time to launch lifeboats. The crew managed to scramble to safety on two life rafts that floated free as the vessel sank. The following morning the survivors were spotted by a Navy PBY patrol plane that had been escorting a convoy. Eventually they were picked up by the British motor vessel *Ardenvohr* while Captain Rostin continued his hunt for more victims. The U-boat commander probably never realized that he had bagged three Great Lakes built canallers in a row. Oddly, just five days later the *Ardenvohr* herself, with the *Velma Lykes'* survivors aboard, was torpedoed and sunk by the U-68! Fortunately, all of the *Velma Lykes'* crew rescued by the *Ardenvohr* survived their second sinking in five days!

On June 30, 1942 Captain Rostin's four-month rampage came to a sudden end 143 miles due west of Bermuda. The victim of one of her successes, the U-158, already out of torpedoes, recovered confidential papers belonging to the captain of the *Everalda* after sinking the Latvian steam ship with her deck gun. After taking the Captain of the *Everalda* and a Spanish seaman aboard, it is believed Rostin was heading to rendezvous with a German resupply submarine in order to reload torpedoes and provisions. After making a lengthy radio transmission back to base about the confidential routing documents U-158 had captured, allied listening posts were able to get a fix on the general vicinity of U-158 and that information was forwarded to the U.S. Navy flying boat squadron based on Bermuda. At that point a United States Navy Martian PBM Mariner flying boat discovered the U-158 on the surface with crewman on deck and dropped depth charges. Because of the men on deck the U-boat was unable to dive as quickly and one of the depth charges lodged in her deck as she submerged, exploding at depth and sealing her fate. The U-boat received her just deserts and went to the bottom with both prisoners and all 54 of her crew including Captain Rostin.

The PBY flying boat was the guardian angel to many a castaway from a torpedoed freighter - especially in the shark-infested waters of the Caribbean. Library of Congress, United States. Office for Emergency Management

Next on chopping block for the U-boats was another canaller that had been constructed on the Great Lakes. Although building of the steamer *Lake Fresco* had begun at the American Shipbuilding Company in Lorain, Ohio during the first world war, by the time she was finished in 1919 the war had been over for seven months. Like her sister ships she was laid up and declared surplus by the United States Shipping Board. In 1924 she was purchased by the Minnesota ñ Atlantic Transit Company of Duluth Minnesota and renamed *Jack*. She sailed the lakes carrying package freight until 1941 when she was requisitioned by the United States War Shipping Administration and sent to the Atlantic Ocean by way of the St. Lawrence River canal system.

Once on salt water the *Jack* worked for the United States Army and it was in their service that on May 27, 1942 she was hauling a very critical war cargo; 100 pound bags of pure sugar bound for New Orleans from Puerto Rico. Although equipment, bullets, and ammunition are critical in fighting a war, it is also true that an Army runs on its stomach. Sugar is a vital substance in the diet of every soldier and the *Jack's* load of 59,000 bags of the sweet crystals was to be put to good use meeting that need.

Reportedly "steaming 61 miles southwest of the Chieden lighthouse" in Haiti the *Jack* was hit by a torpedo fired by Captain Günther Krech of the U-558, who had sunk the *Troisdoc* six days earlier. At nine minutes before the hour of 11 o'clock on that morning Captain Krech fired a single torpedo at the *Jack* which hit her on the starboard quarter between hold number 2 and her forward mast. Detonation of the torpedo's warhead made a large hold in the vessel and blew her hatch covers off. It took only four minutes for her to sink, but that was enough time to launch her lifeboats. The starboard lifeboat was heavily damaged, but the port side lifeboat was intact - both were successfully launched. Unfortunately, the suction from the vessel's sinking took the *Jack's* port lifeboat and everyone aboard to the bottom with her. The two crewmen who had managed to get aboard the starboard lifeboat were able to pull 14 additional survivors into that lifeboat. Five other survivors took pieces of wreckage and assembled a makeshift raft upon which they floated. Meanwhile two of the vessel's armed guards along with five crew members got aboard one of the laker's life rafts. The crew of the U-boat logged the event and later radioed the details of their kill back to Germany as they departed the scene of the sinking.

For the next three days the *Jack's* survivors in the starboard lifeboat drifted helplessly in the Caribbean. Finally, on May 31, the United States Navy submarine *USS Grunion* discovered the damaged lifeboat and rescued all 14 aboard. The seven survivors afloat on the *Jack's* emergency life raft drifted in the Caribbean under the merciless sun for a total of 32 days before they were picked up and rescued. Unfortunately, the five people who were aboard the makeshift life raft were never seen again.

On June 1, 1942, the Gleaves class destroyer *USS Ludlow*, which had been escorting convoy AS-3, were alerted to wreckage and lifeboats floating near their location 215 miles southeast of Bermuda. In short order the *Ludlow's* crew came upon a crowded lifeboat and discovered 31 crewmen and one Army gunner aboard it. After rescuing them it was reported that the *USS Bernadou* had just plucked two gunners and two crewmen from an emergency raft. The survivors said they were from the steamship *Fred W. Green* and insisted that their vessel had been attacked by two or perhaps as many as three U-boats.

There seemed to be a run on the World War I era "lake class" canal freighters in the Caribbean during that summer of 1942. Exactly 5 days after the sinking of the *Jack* another lake class vessel, the *Green*, had been set upon by U-boats.

Constructed at the Great Lakes Engineering Works in Ecorse, Michigan in 1918 in response to urgent World War I needs, the steamer *Craycroft* was another vessel completed too late to serve in the war. It was purchased by the famous Great Lakes salvage wizard Captain John J. Roen in 1927. He added two large 30 ton cranes and 1000 tons of concrete ballast to the vessel and turned her into a salvage ship. She was rechristened *Fred W. Green* and saw active service on the lakes until 1932 when Captain Roen sold her for off lakes use. When World War II broke out in Europe the *Green* was taken over by the United States Maritime Commission and subsequently transferred to the British Ministry of War Transport.

A mixed cargo of military construction equipment, trucks and general military stores as well as a large quantity of beer, cigarettes and most importantly 48 bags of United States mail were in the cargo hold of the *Green* as she made her way from New York City to Bermuda and then on to Freetown. In command was Captain Arthur G. Sampson, it was May 31, 1942. At 2:52 that morning the first shell struck the freighter. Sighting with the aid of moonlight, U-506's Captain Erich Würdemann, one of the deadliest U-boat commanders had opened fire on the *Green* with his deck gun and anti aircraft guns. Tracer rounds were hitting the *Green's* steel hull and her steel deck house. As they hit they made sparks and ricocheted wildly in all directions. Responding to the attack the *Green's* Army gunner dashed aft to the vessel's 20mm gun and returned fire. That drew rounds from the U-boat's deck gun which hit the gun turret destroying it and killing the gunner. Next the U-506 began firing incendiary rounds and in short order the *Green's* upper hull was in flames. Her crew took to the lifeboats and abandon the vessel.

Seeing that the steamer was on fire and her crew had taken to the lifeboats Captain Würdemann ordered his crew to cease-fire. The last man to leave the *Green* was her captain who had been unable to reach a lifeboat and simply jumped off the bow. Although his crew searched for him, Captain Sampson was never seen again.

As soon as lifeboats were clear of the vessel the U-boat returned to firing rounds into the *Green's* hull until they could assure themselves that she was in a sinking condition. After confirming that their victim was indeed sinking, they maneuvered the U-boat over toward the lifeboats, questioned the occupants and then departed. Captain Würdemann had been forced to use his deck guns in the attack because the U-506 had already used all of its torpedoes. During the month of May, 1942 Captain Würdemann and the U-506 crew had damaged or destroyed 10 vessels and the sinking of the *Green* brought that total number to 11. She would be the last vessel that they would sink on this patrol as the U-boat and her crew would return to their base at Lorient, France to rest, reload torpedoes, and re-supply. U-506 would meet her demise 14 months later after being bombed by allied aircraft - she would take Captain Würdemann and his entire crew to the bottom of the ocean with her.

Thomas Maytham was a Great Lakes oreboat of the Victorian Era launched in 1892 at the Chicago Shipbuilding Company. In her prime she was a grand lake boat, but advances in material handling during the industrial revolution began to demand larger vessels that were configured and better suited to the newer shore-side unloading equipment which eventually made the *Maytham* outdated. The onset of the Great Depression found her laid up with no real future in the ore, grain, stone, or coal trades. Her owners came and went and it looked as if she was simply waiting for scrap prices to rise so she could be sold and melted down into razor blades.

Yet, in 1937 as the national economy began to look as if it may begin to grow a bit, the *Maytham* was towed to Rochester, New York and given a dramatic re-build. Her steam engine was torn out and replaced with twin diesels. Her hull was re-sized to fit the New York

State Barge Canal and she was converted into a tanker. Additionally, her name was changed to *Dolomite 2* and she went straight to work for the Rochester Shipbuilding Company. Her career in the canal, however, was shortened as the war in Europe erupted in September 1939. She was sold to the Seaboard Transportation Company in 1941, renamed *Motorex* and sent into coastal work on the Atlantic. With the British suffering huge tonnage losses due to U-boats, the United States Maritime Commission transferred the *Motorex* to them and they immediately sent her to work in the Caribbean.

Shortly before four in the morning on June 18, 1942 the *Motorex* was 75 miles off the coast of Panama headed for Cristóbal. No one on watch aboard the little tanker noticed as a telltale trail of bubbles whizzed just past her stern in the darkness. The torpedo had been launched by the U-172 but missed the *Motorex* completely. Undeterred, Captain Carl Emmermann decided to follow the little tanker until daylight and then sink her with his deck guns.

Surfacing at precisely five o'clock in the morning the U-172 fired the first round from her deck gun into the hull of the *Motorex*. That single shot was enough to cause the entire crew of the *Motorex* to abandon ship. It struck the bridge killing one crewman and convincing the others that the 20,000 barrels of diesel oil she carried in her hold could easily kill them all if ignited by the next round. Actually, it took another 39 rounds from the U-boat's deck gun to sink the tanker. Of her crew of 21, a total of 20 survived the sinking.

Throughout our tales of German U-boats and Great Lakes vessels we have listed accounts of some of the most successful U-boat commanders of the war. Logic however, dictates that somewhere out there must reside the least successful U-boat commander and that just may have been Captain Hans-Günther Kuhlmann of the U-166.

Arriving in the Caribbean on June 21, 1942 Captain Kuhlmann and his crew had been on station for nearly three full weeks and had yet to make a single kill. Technically, this was his third patrol as the German Navy would record it. The first patrol, although not considered a war patrol, was the two-day voyage from Kiel, Germany to Kristiansand, Norway in preparation for the U-166's first combat patrol west of the British Isles on her way to the U-boat base

WWII

at Lorient. The second was the ten-day voyage from Kristiansand to Lorient, France where U-166 took on additional supplies in preparation for the next patrol. The U-boat's dispatch from Lorient to the Caribbean was considered his third patrol. Now he was on station and eager to find targets. Captain Kuhlmann, however, didn't have nearly the luck of some of his counterparts. He and his crew sailed around and searched the empty horizon until July 11 when finally, something akin to a target was sighted. Just off the north coast of the Dominican Republic the U-166 set upon and attacked the 84 ton two masted sailing vessel *Carmen*. Using the U-boats deck gun, due to the small size of the schooner, the *Carmen* and her "vital" cargo of 400 pieces of cedar and mahogany wood as well as 2000 sacks of corn were sent to the bottom of the Caribbean. Undoubtedly frustrated, the crew of U-166 would finally get their first good target two days later - she was the World War I, lake class freighter *Oneida* of the Ford Motor Company.

Without question the largest consumer of the surplus lake class steamers built for the First World War was Henry Ford. Immediately after the end of the war the United States Shipping Board cancelled production of all their shipbuilding contracts. On the Great Lakes that left some vessels under construction and others finished with no place to go. On the Atlantic and Gulf coasts it left hundreds of ships in mothballs along the various rivers and back waters. To reduce much of this surplus tonnage, the board decided in 1924 to sell the vessels, some of which they paid as much as $875,000 per hull to have constructed. Ford purchased 150 of those lake class vessels plus 50 "sub class" submarine tenders for just over $8,000 each. The majority of these hulls were stripped down into barges and brought back to the Great Lakes through the St. Lawrence River system. The 50 "sub class" vessels would not fit through the locks along the St. Lawrence, so they were broken up and came to the lakes in the barges as scrap metal. That scrap metal was melted down in Ford's Detroit, River Rouge furnaces and used in automobile production. Two of the early arrivals for Ford were the lakers *Oneida* and *Onondaga*. Both lakers were refitted for salt water coastal use among Ford's east coast and gulf coast factories. On July 13, 1942 the *Oneida*, which had been chartered by the United States Maritime Commission was spotted by U-166 and at 10 minutes after six o'clock that evening Captain Kuhlmann gave the order to fire a torpedo at the little laker.

One lookout was stationed atop the *Oneida's* pilot house and there was a second one stationed on her port bridge. It was the lookout on top of her pilothouse who first saw the torpedo coming from the starboard side and shouted a warning down to Captain Walter Franklin Deal who reflexively ordered her wheel hard to port. The old boat moved too slowly and the torpedo struck her starboard aft quarter. She was running without cargo and the huge hole caused by the torpedo's warhead nearly tore her side off. The *Oneida* sank within minutes - she was just three miles off of Punta de Maisi, Cuba. Survivors from the sinking, 23 in all, used the vessel's emergency life rafts to stay afloat until they drifted ashore five miles north of Cape Maisi where they walked to the town of Punta de Maisi.

For Captain Kuhlmann it was his first big tonnage kill and he no doubt was certain that his U-boat's "happy times" were off to a great beginning; but he was wrong. Prowling northward toward the Gulf of Mexico he came upon the American flagged 16-ton motor fishing boat *Gertrude* three days later. Using the deck gun again he sent the little boat and her cargo of corn and 20 tons of onions to the bottom off the northern coast of Cuba. He then maneuvered the U-166 close to the U.S. mainland and positioned the U-boat 45 miles south of the mouth of the Mississippi River and the port of New Orleans. There just had to be easy pickings in that busy waterway and Captain Kuhlmann was likely desperate not to be known among his peers as the commander who sinks onions and corn.

On Thursday, July 30 Captain William Heath of the passenger and cargo vessel *Robert E. Lee* came into view of the U-166's periscope. Captain Kuhlmann fired a single torpedo and hit her a bit aft of her engine room. The *Lee* began to immediately sink - she had 404 souls onboard. Unfortunately for the U-166's commander and crew, their joy at having made this kill was short - as would be the remainder of their lives. The *Lee* was being escorted by the fast Navy patrol boat PC-566 which now had the U-boat on sonar and moved in to begin depth charging her. The crew of the PC-566 thought that they had destroyed the U-boat which was never heard from again. In 2001 an oil drilling contractor, C & C Technologies, was doing a bottom survey with a remote vehicle at a depth of 5,000 feet. They stumbled upon the resting place of the U-166 just one mile from the wreck of the *Lee*. There were 379 survivors from the *Lee*, Captain Kuhlmann's biggest and last kill. A check of the records, however, shows that surprisingly Captain Kuhlmann was actually not the least successful U-boat commander - he was just close to it. Numerous U-boat captains were commissioned during the war who never actually got to do a war patrol and many patrolled and never sunk a single vessel. At least Captain Kuhlmann deprived the allies of some onions and corn along with the *Robert E. Lee*.

Relatively shallow water makes a great breeding ground for sharks in the expanse of the Great Bahama Bank. It also makes for great shark fishing which the Carrillo family of Cuba had been doing as their livelihood for many years. One day in late July of 1942, while cleaning a catch, they discovered that the belly of one of their sharks contained human remains. Among the grisly find of lower torso bones were two rings sized for a man. One was made of ivory-like material and the other was a gold, fractured signet ring with the letters "G.D.H." inscribed on it. On the inner ring were the letters "E.R.G. 17." Considering the numbers of allied ships being sunk off the coast of Cuba the fisherman decided to turn the rings over to authorities. At the time they had no idea that the rings were directly related to the sinking of the steamer *Onondaga*.

Onondaga was a Ford fleet sister ship to the *Oneida*. On July 23, 1942 the *Onondaga* was running without escort along the Bahamas channel just north of the Cuban coast. With a speed of just over seven miles per hour and a belly full of magnesium she was an easy U-boat target. Captain Hans Witt of the U-129 torpedoed her at 22 minutes after 10 that evening. A single torpedo struck *Onondaga* amidships. The little vessel manufactured on the Great Lakes at the Detroit Shipbuilding Company went to the bottom in just over 1 minute. Although Captain Witt probably never gave much thought to it, this was his second Great Lakes vessel to be sunk during the month of July. The first had been the lake class steamer *Tachir*, built by

McDougall-Duluth Shipbuilding Company in 1920. He had torpedoed her 11 days earlier 74 miles south, southwest of Grand Cayman Island.

Onondaga had gone down so fast that her crew had no time to man lifeboats or launch the life rafts. Although the rafts had been designed to float free upon sinking, only 14 of her crew managed to make it to them. One of the 20 crew members lost in the sinking included Captain George Dewey Hodges, who was wearing the signet ring bearing his initials. Later the war administration showed the rings to Captain Hodges' widow who identified them as having been worn by her husband.

Some reports at the time stated that as *Onondaga* was loading at Nuevitas, Cuba, some of her crew were observed consuming alcohol causing very loose lips. Thus, the *Onondaga's* departure was common knowledge along the waterfront, as were her route and destination. The old war adage, "loose lips sink ships" was attached to her sinking. However, nothing in the German records indicate that this particular vessel was hunted down by the U-129 using such information. It is far more likely that the *Onondaga* was caught in the same way that the shark with the Captain's ring in its innards was netted. She simply happened to be in a heavily traveled area and became a target of opportunity. In other words, in the wrong place at the wrong time.

In one final twist to the *Onondaga's* story, along with her crew she had a single passenger on board. That passenger was Mellin Respess who had been the captain of the *Thomas McKean*. She had been torpedoed and sunk by the U-505 on June 29 and he was catching a ride to Havana to get another command. Thus, he had survived being torpedoed twice in less than one month. Of course he had also been the chief mate on the steamer *Okamar* which was torpedoed and sunk on March 20, so he was actually torpedoed three times in four months. There are no records of him having been torpedoed again during the war, but he may have had a tough time getting a ride to the mainland if anyone knew of his current streak.

The ashes of Captain Georg Lassen, a former U-boat commander, were scattered in late January of 2012 in the waters of Spain's Santa

WWII

PonÁa Bay. He had passed away of natural causes at the age of 96; proving that not all U-boat captains died young. In his career he sank 26 ships totaling more than 156,000 tons with one of those being the lake canaller *Prescodoc*.

Prescodoc had a fruitful career on the Great Lakes running through the Canadian canals and along the coasts of Canada. Launched at Swan, Hunter & Wigham, Sunderland, England in 1929 she carried whatever bulk cargoes could be loaded into her hold from grain to coal and everything in between. In 1941 she was sent from the fresh water seas to the salt water seas in order to aid the war effort. Her normal run, by 1942, was carrying bauxite around the Caribbean Sea. It was while performing that task that she sailed into view of Captain Lassen's periscope. The little canaller was riding high in the water with her cargo hold empty on the way to Trinidad when the U-160 hit her in the bow with a single torpedo. *Prescodoc* went down rapidly with only five members of her crew of 21 surviving. Captain Charles Prowse went down with his ship. The pilothouse clock showed 19 minutes past 10 on the morning of July 29, 1942.

Although a great deal of carnage was taking place in the Caribbean Sea as well as the Gulf of Mexico during 1942, the situation was just as bad in the North Atlantic. On the third of September, Captain Daniel Nolan was in the pilothouse of the *Donald Stewart* and not feeling at all good about the cargo he was assigned to carry. Instead of grain, coal, or iron ore that she had normally carried on the Great Lakes the needs of war now dictated that his little canaller be loaded with bulk cement topped off with drums filled with aviation gasoline. That cargo was critical in the construction of a new airfield at Goose Bay. As part of convoy LN-7 the *Donald Stewart* was U-boat bait looking for a place to happen. That place was 19 miles southeast of Mutton Bay in the Gulf of St. Lawrence - it was there that Captain Paul Hartwig of the U-517 torpedoed her. Captain Hartwig was on his first patrol as a U-boat commander and had already sunk two American flagged ships in the Gulf of St. Lawrence - the passenger liner *Chatham* on August 27, and the freighter *Arlyn* on August 28. Now, on September 3, he was

166

firing torpedoes at the lake canaller *Stewart*. Being unaware that the *Stewart* was carrying aviation gas, the intensity of her secondary explosion initially caused the U-boat captain to believe at first that he had hit two vessels simultaneously. As he watched through his periscope, however, the morning sun showed just one vessel going to the bottom.

HMCS Weyburn, the corvette which was doing escort duty, spotted the U-boat which had surfaced shortly after the attack. Coming at flank speed she charged in an attempt to ram the U-517. Captain Hartwig and his crew were able to crash-dive their U-boat in time to avoid being rammed.

A radio alert was flashed warning of the U-boat's presence and an RCAF Digby (which was essentially a Douglas B-18 Bolo) lumbered onto the scene. Flying just 150 feet off the water the Digby dropped depth charges. Unfortunately, the depth charges exploded on impact with the water and damaged the aircraft rather than the U-boat. Considering the chaos, it's amazing that only three lives were lost in the attack.

Yet all of that response did nothing to deter Captain Hartwig who then took the U-517 some 253 miles farther west in the Gulf of St. Lawrence and continued hunting. It did not take long as just three

A RCAF Digby was launched against the U-517, but did more harm than good. Brian Nicklas Collection

and a half days after he torpedoed the *Stewart*, the Great Lakes Canaller *Oakton* came into the U-517's cross hairs.

Unlike the other lakeboats in this chapter, which were hauling cargoes from one salt water port to another, *Oakton* had actually loaded her cargo in the heart of the Great Lakes. Sandusky, Ohio. During World War II, Sandusky was the prime outlet for the second most vital bulk commodity being shipped across the lakes - coal. *Oakton* had taken aboard 2,289 tons of the prized cargo at that port and then proceeded to do what the little canaller did best; haul it across Lake Erie, through the Welland Canal and the St. Lawrence canals to Quebec City. There the *Oakton* joined convoy QS-33. Her final destination was to be Corner Brook, Newfoundland, but Captain Hartwig would re-write that schedule.

Firing a spread of three torpedoes Captain Hartwig was trying to score a hat trick and get at least three of the four vessels in the convoy. His aim was deadly in its accuracy. Just 20 miles east of Cap-des-Rosiers he sunk the *Mount Taygetus*, *Mount Pindus* and the *Oakton*. The coal laden canaller was hit directly amidships and broke in half and sank within two minutes. Her crew managed to launch her lifeboats and all 20 escaped alive.

In even more brazen attacks, just four days later on September 11, Captain Hartwig attacked and sank the Canadian corvette *HMCS Charlottetown* in the mouth of the St. Lawrence only 260 miles out of Quebec City. Then he turned the U-517 around and headed back 120 miles to nearly the exact location where he had sunk the *Oakton*. On September 15 Captain Hartwig fired on convoy SQ-36. His four torpedo spread sank the Norwegian freighter *Inger Elisabeth* and the Dutch freighter *Saturnus*. Three crewmen were killed on the *Elisabeth* and one on the *Saturnus*. Being that the sinking's were just five and a half miles off shore, the survivors from both vessels rowed their lifeboats to safety.

With the sinking of the *Saturnus* Captain Hartwig was out of torpedoes. He and his crew had sunk 9 vessels in 19 days including two Great Lakes canallers. It was time to return to Lorient, France to reload and begin another devastating patrol or so he thought. After a month of rest, recreation, and re-fitting in France, Captain Hartwig

Albacore aircraft from the carrier HMS Victorious *spelled the end for the U-517. Aircraft, large or small were always the worst enemy of any submarine during World War II. United States Office for Emergency Management*

and the U-517 departed on November 17, 1942. Four days later they were engaged by Albacore aircraft from the carrier *HMS Victorious*. The aircraft dropped depth charges crippling the U-517 and left her in a sinking condition. The crew had no choice but to abandoning ship. Only one crewman was lost and the other 52 including the captain spent the rest of the war as POWs in custody of the British where they could do no more harm.

While Captain Hartwig was creating havoc in the Gulf of St. Lawrence, another U-boat commander was having far less luck down in the Caribbean. Captain Otto Fechner of the U-164 was on his first war patrol with his new command. Having arrived in the Caribbean Sea on July 18, 1942 the U-164 had so far claimed only one prize, the Dutch freighter *Stad Amsterdam*. Captain Fechner's crew had sunk her on August 25, and now as the first week of September expired they were hungry for another target. So 12 days after U-164's last kill, on September 6, the Great Lakes canaller *John A. Holloway* came crawling over the horizon like a snail.

WWII

Like her Canadian sister canallers the *Holloway* had been requisitioned to serve on the Atlantic at the beginning of the war. On one of her first ventures into the Atlantic her captain, J.V. Norris of the Upper Lakes Steamship Company got a quick lesson and how inadequate these little lake boats were when facing the high seas. Sailing from Halifax, Nova Scotia to the Caribbean the *Holloway* encountered a violent Atlantic storm. Captain Norris reported that the sea was "mountainous high," and all the way up in the pilot house the navigation charts had been washed from their drawers and floated in a foot of water. Soon they ran out of fresh water, and were forced to drink beer and fruit juice. For two long weeks the little lakeboat plowed its way through the hostile seas as her crew struggled to just keep her afloat. They had no idea if they were on course or heading off into the vast Atlantic never to be seen again. Finally, on the 14th day of their ordeal they spotted land! After putting into the unidentified port they saw that they were, "right on target," 1,100 miles from where they had started. Captain Norris said, "Like Columbus, I said a prayer."

Now, more than a year after her initial trial by saltwater and under the command of Captain James L. Holmes, the canaller *Holloway* was busy with a cargo of general freight. This trip took her from Mobile, Alabama to Key West, Florida then onto Guantánamo Bay, Cuba and finally to Trinidad. It was a route she would never complete as she steamed directly into the kill zone of the U-164. Considering the size of the vessel and wanting to conserve his torpedoes Captain Fechner elected to take a more gentlemanly path to the destruction of the little steamer.

Captain Holmes, unlike some of his crew, was an Englishman rather than a Canadian Great Lakes mariner. He was retired from the merchant marine, but had volunteered his services as a Master of Vessels when the war broke out. Among the Great Lakes men aboard the vessel was First Engineer William J. Collie of Toronto as well as four other men of the lakes. The crew, however, had been augmented by the addition of some native sons of Trinidad.

As a part of Convoy GAT-2 the *Holloway* did her best to keep up during the first day. Headwinds, however, slowed her pace and in the black-out conditions the rest of the convoy left her behind that night as she fell into the deadly position of a straggler. Now she was little more than U-boat bait.

Using their last torpedo, the U-164 scored a hit on the *Holloway's* stern, but it was apparently not a fatal blow as she continued to steam ahead. After issuing orders for the U-boat to surface, Captain Fechner ordered the U-boat's deck gun to be manned.

Aboard the *Holloway* the shout of "Torpedo!" from the lookout was nearly simultaneous with the explosion. Almost immediately the crew headed for the lifeboats. The starboard lifeboat had been blown overboard by the concussion of the torpedo and was being dragged along, swamped, but still moored with the aft davit line off the stern of the *Holloway* as she settled by her heels. Captain Holmes rushed to his cabin and grabbed the weighted bag of "secret documents" that every master was charged with. Scrambling to the deck he tossed the bag over the side into the sea. At that same moment he saw his crew had successfully launched the port lifeboat as well as the emergency life rafts. He then turned to see an ominous sight - the surfacing of the U-boat that had just torpedoed his vessel.

Using his binoculars Captain Fechner scanned the steamer. He could easily see that she was unarmed. Noting that, he set off on an intercept course and using his "loud hailer" he ordered the crew of the *Holloway* to immediately take to their lifeboats and abandon their vessel. It was an order that had already been carried out. With the little canaller still moving under power and almost sunk to her gunwale, Captain Holmes was the only man left aboard and he did as the U-boat commander ordered. Diving overboard Captain Holmes swam to the swamped starboard lifeboat and quickly released the line that was holding it to the *Holloway*. He floated clear as the steamer took her final plunge to the bottom of the Caribbean.

Like a hunter approaching a slain deer Captain Fechner eased the U-164 up among the survivors. The survivors of the *Holloway* were already gathering around the two lifeboats. Some bailing and the starboard boat would be just fine. Captain Fechner asked if there were any wounded among the survivors and how many had been killed. A quick headcount showed that there were no wounded and only one crewman, identified only as "one of the islanders" was missing. It was concluded that he was blown over the side when the torpedo hit. After questioning the survivors, the U-164 departed and Captain Holmes and his crew were left adrift, nearly in the middle of the Caribbean, and roughly 143 miles from the island of Aruba.

In modern times, people pay thousands of dollars to bask in the sun for a week on the decks of huge cruise ships in those same waters. In September of 1942, however, the crew of the *Holloway* spent six full days of hell drifting with the currents in that blue purgatory. Both lifeboats were equipped with sails and Captain Holmes took charge of one lifeboat and his first mate took charge of the other. Having been warned that the coast of Venezuela was infected with a plague of fever, Captain Holmes ordered the boats headed west southwest in order to land in Columbia. After the first night the two lifeboats became separated and the starboard boat sailed on alone. Although the crew begged him to just head toward shore the captain wanted nothing to do with the fever - so he held his course until he saw the snow-capped mountains of Columbia. Those snowcapped peaks told him that he was far enough west to head for shore. Finally, they landed near Santa Marta, Colombia. Once there the captain alerted local fishermen that there was still another boat out there. Meanwhile his crew were fed fish soup and turtle eggs. The following day their shipmates were brought in under tow of a motor fishing boat. The date was September 12, and the records show that during the entire ordeal only one man had perished and 23 survived.

Captain Fechner sank no more vessels on this patrol and headed back to Lorient, France having been out for a total of 82 days. Both he and the entire crew of the U-164 were killed off the coast of Brazil on their next patrol. They were spotted by a United States Navy PBY flying boat and depth charged on January 6, 1943.

Canada Steamship Lines sent a total of 15 canallers to war from their vast fleet at the outbreak of World War II - amazingly, they only lost three to the U-boats. Captain Thomas Edge was unlucky enough to have commanded one of those losses which quickly sank beneath his feet as one G7-e torpedo from the U-175 hit his vessel. That

The Consolidated PBY flying boat was the most widely used seaplane in World War II. It could do reconnaissance, rescue downed flyers, transport wounded or supplies and it could kill U-boats. Library of Congress

canaller was the *Norfolk*, hit amidships on her starboard side. Bound from Paramaribo, French Guiana to the Port of Spain on the island of Trinidad with 3055 tons of bauxite in her hold, the little canaller broke in half and plunged to the bottom of the Caribbean in less than 2 minutes. Captain Edge and five of his crew went to the bottom with their vessel. Fortunately, the war service refit of the *Norfolk*, like all of the other vessels converted for war service, included four life rafts designed to float free when the vessel sank. Thirteen of her crew scurried aboard those rafts. Just four hours after her sinking the survivors were picked up by the Spanish merchant vessel *Indauchu*. That vessel in turn delivered them safely to the Port of Spain - the date was September 18, 1942.

Entering the kill into his logbook that day aboard the U-175, Captain Heinrich Bruns dutifully noted the longitude and latitude of 8°36'N, 59°20'W, some 342 miles north, northwest of Paramaribo. Although he had done his duty, Captain Burns was not a U-boat man as such, but rather he was a true sailor in the greatest sense of the word. He loved sailing the German tall ships and in war he much preferred commanding fast destroyers. When no destroyer commands were available, he volunteered for U-boat duty. That decision would ultimately lead to his demise on April 17, 1943 in the North Atlantic south-west of Ireland where the U-175 would be attacked by the United States Coast Guard. Using depth charges to force the U-boat to the surface and deck guns to finish her off the Coast Guard cutter *USCGC Spencer* ended the career of the U-175 as well as her captain and 12 of her crew. The 41 survivors spent the rest of the war as allied POWs.

One fact that few people realize when it comes to World War II is that very high on the list of critical materials needed to keep the war effort going was paper. Aside from the paper used to keep

Seen here the U-175 sinking after being depth charged by the USCG cutter Spencer. *We know this is the U-175 because the* Spencer *only killed two U-boats during the war; the U-633, which had no survivors and never surfaced, and the U-175 which did surface after depth charging and had 41 survivors. The date was April 17, 1943. Library of Congress*

records and transmit communications more than 700,000 different items were either made of or contained in paper products used by the Allies during the war. As the war dragged on paper would become very scarce.

Sunday, October 11, 1942 found the Great Lakes canaller *Waterton* under the command of Master William Lutjens on her way from Corner Brook, Newfoundland sailing west toward the Great Lakes. Considering how valuable paper products were during the war, it's amazing that the Germans didn't set out to first bomb Corner Brook into the stone age. It was one of the key producers of raw pulpwood and paper products in the north east Atlantic area. On that October morning *Waterton* had a hold filled with 2,000 tons of newsprint and wood sulfate. Unlike most of the canallers in this chapter, she was headed from a saltwater port to a freshwater port. She was scheduled to do exactly what she had been designed originally to do, navigate the locks along the St. Lawrence River, cross Lake Ontario, transit the Welland Canal and sail across Lake Erie to Cleveland, Ohio where she would deliver her war critical product.

As the *Waterton's* course was set to enter the Gulf of St. Lawrence as a part of convoy BS-31 she was hit by two torpedoes fired by the U-106. Just 12 and a half miles southeast of St. Paul Island she sank by the stern. All 27 of her crew were picked up by the *HMCS Vison* and only the *Waterton* and her paper products were lost.

A dramatic shift in U-boat activity took place in 1943 and it proved to be a very good thing for the fleet of Great Lakes vessels still working in the war zone. To illustrate the point, consider that theater-wide 142 U-boat attacks took place in November of 1942, but only 16 took place in November of 1943. In fact, during several months of 1943 the number of attacks by U-boats on allied shipping was lower than the totals that some U-boat captains had for a single patrol in 1942. None of the Great Lakes canallers in service during 1943 were attacked or sunk by U-boats. Much of this decline had to do with the equipment used to detect U-boats by the allied forces as it became more technically advanced and more available beginning in 1943. "The Happy Times" as the U-boat crews referred to the years between 1940 through 1942 had come to an end.

WWII

This July 1943 photo shows an unidentified U-boat under attack by allied aircraft. Note her crewmembers near the coning tower running for their lives. The "Happy Times" for the U-boat crews had come to an end. Library of Congress

On September 3, 1944, almost two years after the *Waterton* was sunk, another Great Lakes canaller, the *Livingston*, which like *Waterton*, (owned and operated by the Bowater¥s Newfoundland Pulp & Paper Mills company in Corner Brook,) was torpedoed by the U-541. She was on her way from Boston to Halifax with general cargo. 13 of her crew went down with the little steamer.

U-541's commander was Captain Kurt Petersen and what makes this sinking of the Great Lakes canaller *Livingston* somewhat unique is that she was the one and only ship sunk by the U-541 and her commander after four patrols and 316 days at sea. The U-boat itself was surrendered to the allied forces on May 12, 1945 at Gibraltar,

Spain and later scuttled in the north Atlantic off the coast of Ireland.

Perhaps the last of the Great Lakes canallers to become a U-boat victim was the little steamer *Soreldoc*. She had started her career in the war trade by running bauxite cargoes. The lake canallers were especially well suited for this because they all had a shallow draft and flat bottoms which allowed them to run in the many rivers and shallow inlets along the Caribbean shores. Unlike many of her unlucky sister canallers from fresh water, she actually managed to avoid being targeted by U-boats prowling the Caribbean. Eventually, *Soreldoc* was reassigned to coastal service in the islands of Great Brittan. Being so close to the fighting there, upon her arrival she was armed with a 50 caliber machine gun on each bridge wing and a 12-pound cannon on her stern.

All of that armament did nothing to deter the U-boats lurking around the British Isles. On February 28, 1945 the U-775 was in St. George's Strait between Ireland and England. Nearby to the south was the U-1302 as both waited for a handy target. U-775's commander, 24-year-old Captain Erich Taschenmacher sighted the *Soreldoc* just after 10 in the morning and fired a single torpedo. It struck the canaller amidships and broke her completely in half. Her bow section rolled over in less than a minute and most of the crew on that part of the boat had no chance to escape. The stern took about six minutes to sink, but was threatening to go down much faster. The crew on the stern section simply jumped overboard. The survivors were picked up by a local fishing boat and taken safely to dry land. Captain John Hamilton, the *Soreldoc's* master was one of those lost with the vessel.

Although one Great Lakes source states that it was U-1302 that torpedoed the *Soreldoc*, that U-boat actually torpedoed the steamer *Norfolk Coast* on the same day that the U-775 torpedoed the *Soreldoc*. The two sinking's were just 20 miles apart in the St. George's Strait.

During World War II more than 90 canallers went to war from the Great Lakes. Although I may have missed a few, what you have just finished reading is an accounting of most of those who were lost during the conflict. Although sending those slow vessels into U-boat

WWII

infested waters may seem like insanity to us today, it is important to remember that war IS insanity. Yet, for their individual countries and for the restoration of freedom in nations that their crews could most likely not point to on a globe, the crews of the Merchant Marine saw the need, answered the call, went to war, sacrificed, and paid a high price while doing their part to achieve final victory.

WHERE WAS CAMP FREELAND?

In the fall of 1973 my family moved from the east side of Saginaw, Michigan to the tiny farm town of Freeland, Michigan. This move was a desperate effort to escape the nonsense of the Saginaw public schools on the east side of town where their eldest son, me, had just squandered three years in what could loosely be called the seventh eighth and ninth grades. Entering Freeland high school, I discovered, refreshingly, that education actually took place there. Part of that education involved a class known as "Comm. 1" taught by a longtime Freeland educator the late Mrs. Mary K. DeLano. She was one of the people who actually inspired me to become a writer. One day while sitting in her class she began to tell the students an anecdote about the days of World War II and a German prisoner of war camp called "Camp Freeland." Although most of the other students gave the subject a yawning "so what," I was fascinated.

As time went by I attempted to do my own research and find out where this Camp Freeland had been located and see if there were any remnants of the POW camp remaining. Now for those of you reading this who may not know much about the town of Freeland it was, in 1973, a classic Midwestern farm town. We had a small grocery store called "Pat's", a tiny drugstore, a tiny post office, a volunteer fire department, one or sometimes two police officers and a single traffic light. The county roads stretching north, south, east and west allowed me to get on my bicycle and ride in any direction for hours and often see nothing more than farmland and barns. I graduated in a class of

179

WWII

Mrs. DeLano, my high school writing teacher - who not only told the story of Camp Freeland to our class, but also was the person who inspired me to become a writer. Considering this is my 24th title as an author, I guess it's only fitting that I include her picture. The "Victorian," Freeland High School's yearbook, 1975.

120 students. The most prominent feature in town was Tri-City Airport (known today as MBS International Airport). The new house that my folks moved into was just 1,412 feet from the airport fence. Almost in my back yard! Aircraft landing on runway 5 approached practically over our house. My mother never had a straight picture hanging on the wall because they always vibrated out of position from the jets passing overhead. We loved living there.

Many times during my high school years I took to my bicycle and headed out on the country roads looking for the fabled Camp Freeland. Mrs. DeLano had told us odds and ends about the camp yet never told us its exact location. I reasoned that during World War II a prisoner of war camp had to be located out in the countryside away from the main part of town. Certainly you wouldn't want escaping

Where Was Camp Freeland?

prisoners housed near the railroad tracks that bisected Freeland. It would be so easy for an escapee to hop a train and make their getaway. So with that in mind I made excursions out onto Carter Road, Brooks Road, Vasold Road, 7-mile Road, Buck Road and so on - yet never finding anything that looked even vaguely like the remains of a World War II POW camp. "Where was Camp Freeland"?

As World War II progressed and the fight against Nazi Germany began to turn in the allies' favor, hundreds of thousands of German soldiers surrendered. By November of 1944, the number of Italian prisoners residing at camps in the USA reached its peak at 51,156. In May of 1945 the number of German POWs in the states reached its peak at 371,683. Of course this was the same month in which Nazi Germany unconditionally surrendered ending the war in Europe. It is worth noting here that although the number of prisoners being shipped to US soil were largely German and Italian, the number of Japanese prisoners were significantly smaller. In August of 1945, the same month in which the Japanese unconditionally surrendered and World War II came to an end, the number of Japanese POWs on US soil peaked at 5,413. This is a stunning example of the fact that the Japanese chose to fight to the death rather than surrender. In 1942 exactly 52 Japanese POWs were interned on US soil. In 1943 the total number rose to 116 and in 1944 the total number had risen to 2,629. The combined total of POWs held on United States soil reached its zenith in May 1945 at 425,871.

Early in the war the relatively few axis prisoners captured were kept behind the lines in the theatre of operations, however, as the war progressed and more and more POW's began to be taken, the problem became what to do with them all.

It was expected that the Articles of the Geneva Convention were to be followed by all of the signatory countries including the United States. It was further expected that all prisoners of war were to be treated humanely, quartered in an environment similar to their native environment and could not be used as "forced" labor. With the first allied victories of World War II POW camps in England were soon overcrowded. The only solution was to begin shipping POWs to the United States. POW camps suddenly sprang up all across America.

WWII

Masses of German and Italian solders surrender in the North African desert and march off to Allied POW camps. Library of Congress

At first there were a few camps in the Midwestern region where the environment was similar to that in Germany. Those camps, however, were rapidly overcrowded and smaller camp annexes had to be established across the country with many being established in the Great Lakes region.

It is very important to note here that the POWs were not criminals. They were soldiers who were fighting for their nation under the orders of their superiors. They had surrendered and in order to comply with the Geneva Convention they were brought here to the United States and Canada to await the outcome of the war. Although many in the US War Department had feared that the POWs would act as blood-thirsty combatants and do whatever they could to continue to fight in America after their arrival with escape and sabotage, their fears were unfounded. The German POWs were so well disciplined as soldiers that they continued to maintain respect for rank and order while in captivity. For the most part their officers obeyed the camp authority and ensured that their men conducted

182

Where Was Camp Freeland?

themselves in a military manner. Very few German POWs broke US law. When they did it was always during failed escape attempts. Such isolated incidents often involved the stealing of vehicles or property in order to further their escape efforts. In those cases, they were given a military court martial and sentenced to a US military prison. The Italian POWs had no desire to fight for "Il Duce" Mussolini, and were quite content in the USA. It was only during repatriation after the end of the war that many of the POWs gave their Army captors difficulty - many of the German and Italians did not want to leave the USA and return to their home countries.

Few German POWs were actual members of the Nazi party. In fact, it was against military policy in Germany for soldiers, sailors, or members of the air force to join any political party. Although it was mandatory for German citizens to join the Nazi party the military was not a part Hitler's party - they simply followed his orders. The armed wing of the Nazi party, however, was the Waffen SS. They acted as an army and were fanatically faithful to Hitler. They were also responsible for a very large portion, but not all, of the war crimes committed in the name of Hitler during the war. At their peak, they numbered an estimated 900,000 which consisted of both volunteers and conscripts. If they asked you to join, you either did so or you were arrested and sent to a concentration camp. Few POWs were SS members as the SS fighters often fought to the death and following the invasion of Europe by the Allies, SS members were shot on sight because they often booby-trapped themselves when surrendering. Those who did come to the camps in the United States were universal trouble makers and were some of the few POWs moved from camp to camp during their internment.

Life in the camps was quite orderly and relatively peaceful aside from an occasional SS fanatic. The POWs performed whatever work the local region facilitated and were paid in camp script that allowed them to buy items from the camp store. Cigarettes and beer as well as materials for arts and crafts were commonly purchased. Recreational activities such as volley ball, soccer and even ice hockey were used to pass the time in the camps and help keep the prisoners active. Nearly every camp had a soccer field of some sort that had been constructed by the prisoners. Additionally, POWs formed glee clubs and produced stage plays. Of course escape planning was also a pass-time. Every POWs duty was to escape, so when such events took place the guards and camp commanders knew that the POWs involved were simply doing their duty. Of course dishing out a punishment of 28 days' solitary confinement for an escape attempt was also the duty of the camp commander and in line with the restrictions of the Geneva Convention. Many of the guards felt that they were there to protect the POWs from angry and vengeful US citizens rather than the other way around. That protection was specifically outlined in Article 13 of the Geneva Convention. In the later years of the war, exhausted and starved POWs arrived at the camps and got their first hot showers in many months and their first hot meals in recent memory.

By 1944 America was peppered with some 155 "main camps" designed to hold between 4,000 and 2,000 POWs. The Great Lakes region had approximately 18 main camps. I use the term "approximately" because during 1943 the total overall number of POWs, both German and Italian ballooned from 2,300 in January of that year to more than 172,000 in December! To this day some confusion still exists as to exactly how many POW "camps" were established in the United States. The tally tends to vary depending on one's definition of the term "camp." Sometimes "camp" was a word that described as few as two POWs in one location for a protracted period. The War Department was scrambling to house and secure those POWs who were flooding into the United States. It didn't take a brilliant strategist to figure out that the more crowded the camps became, the more likely there may be trouble. Those fears ranged from a SS instigated ruckus, to worse, a mass escape. The War Department initially focused their efforts on minimizing the risk of trained enemy soldiers escaping and proceeding to loot, rape and sabotage their way across the United States.

Guards were scarce as able bodied manpower was being sent to fight overseas. Often, American soldiers who had been wounded and returned home to recover, but due to the severity of their wounds could not return to combat, were assigned to duty as camp guards.

Where Was Camp Freeland?

On a good day the War Department was happy when they had a total of 1 guard for every 10 POWs, but that was not always the case. The solution was to spread the POW ranks thinner through the nation. More and smaller camps would mean less chance of a mass uprising of prisoners storming the wire and escaping. As a result, the camps were branched out into annexes of smaller camps that peppered the 48 states.

Around the Great lakes area, a large number of these small POW camps sprung up in such places as the depression era Civilian Conservation Corps or "CCC" camps which were converted into POW camps. Additionally, local race tracks, sports fields, and other similar sites which could be easily fenced off and guarded were utilized. Sometimes just open farm land where tarpaper buildings could quickly be erected were taken over and nearly overnight a POW camp sprung up. The town of Sidnaw in Upper Michigan saw its population literally double overnight as about 250 Germans arrived in the darkness and populated the new POW camp that was nearby. Even Fort Niagara and Fort Henry, Ontario were converted for use as POW camps. Just as an example of how many small camps popped up in the Great Lakes area, Wisconsin alone had 38 camps by VJ day and Michigan had 32 - one of which was Camp Freeland.

POW camps were one of the lesser publicized war efforts taking place in America. Often, little official notice was given to local residents before the camps were set up and when the prisoners arrived it was with little or no public announcement. The reason for this low key operation was twofold. First the Geneva Convention forbade POWs from being made into public spectacles. Secondly, there was the concern that angry local residents who had lost loved ones in the war my attempt to retaliate against the prisoners. However, on many occasions the small-town residents of a nearby camp heard that the POW train was coming and gathered near the station just out of curiosity. They were kept at a distance by heavily armed Army guards. Of course the local folks always went back to their normal routines after the POWs were trucked away to the camp. There was never a case of any organized revenge against POWs in America. In fact, when the first POWs arrived in the Upper Michigan town of Wetmore on February 12, 1944 a crowd of locals gathered at the train depot to gawk. What they saw were 262 Germans, disembarking from the train and piling into Army trucks, laughing, smiling and joking in German as they went off to nearby Camp Evelyn. When the trucks went through town, the POWs smiled and waved at the local folks.

In the Great Lakes region, the POWs provided badly needed labor in agriculture. The industrial, high-paying jobs in the war plants had drawn away all of the migrant workers who normally picked crops such as cherries, beans and apples. In 1942 and 1943 many Wisconsin farmers left their cherry crops to rot on the trees because they had no one to pick them. Yet at that same time fruits and vegetables were being rationed across the nation. The simple answer to that dilemma was to hire the POWs to do the picking as well as the tending of crops such as onions, grapes, carrots and potatoes, just to name a few.

At Camp Freeland the common toil was the harvesting of the sugar beet crop. Interestingly, in order to harvest the beets each POW needed to be equipped with a knife. The combination of a prisoner and a knife may seem to go together like a sparkler and gasoline, but the German POWs were so well behaved that it never caused trouble. In fact, as the lady who brought the daily bucket of beer out into the field for the prisoners, each POW would dutifully stow his knife behind his back in his belt so the beer lady didn't feel threatened. POWs were paid 80 cents per day when they were working and 10 cents per day when they were off.

Peas were a major crop in Wisconsin and local canning and shipping was a good business until the start of the war - then it became a war-time necessity. Once again, however, the universal problem of migrant workers being siphoned away to work in the down-state war plants popped up. So once again the solution was POW labor. Farmers were eager to get the prisoners into their fields to help harvest the crops. The canning factories found the Germans to be efficient hard workers with an inherent desire for perfection and efficiency as well as a fine eye for detail.

One of the "odder" camps sprung up as a result of the needs of the Bayfield, Wisconsin Canning Company. In late August of 1945,

Where Was Camp Freeland?

more than three months after the surrender of Germany and VE day, the Army set up Camp Bayfield near the shore of Lake Superior. At first there was no barbed wire or guard towers - because the entire camp was inside the Bayfield County Courthouse and Community Center! Cooking and eating accommodations were established on the first floor as were the guard's quarters while POWs slept on the second floor in the gymnasium. Showers were located in the basement. All of the prisoners were there to service the Bayfield Canning Company.

In the forests of Michigan's Upper Peninsula five annex camps of about 200 to 400 POWs were established between February of 1944 and January of 1945. Those camps were established to support the harvesting of a critically needed war product; wood. Believe it or not, one of the most valued materials on both sides in World War II was paper. In Germany and Japan wasting paper could actually get you shot. Here in America there were penalties, although not as extreme as in the Axis countries, for wasting critical war commodities yet paper products were still sorely needed. In order to make paper you need pulpwood and with the labor force so depleted there was almost no one to harvest the trees for pulping. As with other agricultural products, the POWs were used to harvest pulp wood as well as wood for other purposes such as cedar posts for fences, wood for railroad ties, and wood for chemical processing. The POW crews who cut the wood were given axes and two-man hand saws that were issued in the morning and returned in the evening. The pulpwood "sticks" were actually tree trunks measuring up to 12 inches in diameter and eight feet in length. When production slowed the pulpwood foreman smuggled in bottles of beer. The hardest workers were rewarded with a bottle of suds, which sent a message to the others and production increased. By the end of the war the five upper peninsula camps, Evelyn, Sidnaw, Au Train, Pori and Raco had produced 800,000 sticks of pulpwood, 45,000 railroad ties, 197,000 cedar fence posts and 225,000 cords of chemical wood valued at $716,000.

Not all POWs in the Great Lakes were held in one camp. A good example of migrating POWs was Door County, Wisconsin on Lake

WWII

Michigan. There, in the summer of 1945, POWs were brought in by train from camps in the northwestern US where they had been harvesting sugar beets. The first 80 arrived just about the time that Germany surrendered. They were needed to harvest cherries as the summer ripening began. The prisoners, however, were not held in a single camp and trucked out to the orchards. Instead they literally camped in the fields by using the cabins that in pre-war normally housed the Mexican migrant workers. There was no barbed wire and no guard towers.

Of course there was some real worry in the local community that the prisoners could cause problems by simply walking away from the farm. Additionally, a number of rumors about POWs were floating around among local residents. On May 25, 1945 the army went public and allowed the "Door County Advocate" newspaper to visit the ex-

When the word got out that German POWs were working in the fields of Door County without any fences or barbed wire, fear and rumors spread around the area. Thus, the Door County Advocate *newspaper was allowed into the work area to do a photo essay and freely ask questions.* Door County Advocate

Where Was Camp Freeland?

tended camp and do an in depth photo essay to help dispel the rumors. The point that we were no longer at war with Germany and the prisoners were simply waiting to be processed in order to be sent back home was emphasized. Before the harvest was too far along, the farmers were asking for more POWs to help bring in the crops. The concept of a POW camp without barbed wire worked quite well.

Canada had gotten its first POWs long before the United States was drawn into the war. Entering the conflict on September 10, 1939 Canada, as a Commonwealth Country, would fight side by side with England. On the night of June 18, 1940 German bombers conducted the first of many night bombing raids on English ports, factories, and airfields and on July 1, daytime bombing was commenced. As casualties on both sides began to mount, German air crews forced to bail out of their damaged aircraft were captured and imprisoned. Additionally, the prospect of a German invasion of Britain loomed. Having German prisoners in the country as it tried to fight off an invasion was a problem that the British simply did not want to have on their hands. Then, on July 10, the aerial "Battle of Britain" began in earnest and soon enemy pilots were being shot down and captured in droves. By the end of the war Canada would find itself hosting more than 33,000 POWs.

Yet in June of 1940, before the Battle of Britain had actually started, Winston Churchill's government had approximately 15,000 German POWs in custody. The fear was that if Italy entered the war that number would increase by 40% overnight. The British at first asked the Canadians to import 7,000 POWs. As those Germans were being settled in Canada another 1,000 Luftwaffe flight crews were added to the list. Soon the fighting in North Africa opened the flood gates and thousands more POWs were sent to Canada. All the while the USA remained a neutral country just to the south.

Securing the POW camps in Canada fell largely on members of the Veterans Home Guard - later known as the Veterans Guard of Canada or "Veterans Guard." These were soldiers who had fought in World War I and who, now in their 40s, because of age, were turned away from re-enlisting in the regular army. As a group, they were persistent in their desire to help protect their country and their nation soon recognized their value. At their peak in 1943 they had 9,806 regulars and 451 officers and one of their primary tasks was guarding POW camps.

Of the more than two dozen main POW camps in Canada, 13 were located near the shores of the Great Lakes and the St. Lawrence River. For those prisoners who were being held on the shores of Lake Superior or Georgian Bay escaping would almost guarantee the escapee that they would be eaten by a bear or a pack of wolves. But, to some of the POWs on the banks of the Detroit, Niagara, and St. Lawrence rivers that location meant that freedom from imprisonment was just across the river. That posed some interesting problems for the Veterans Guard and U.S. Border Patrol in the months before the United States joined the war.

One famous case involved Franz von Werra a Luftwaffe pilot who was shot down over Kent in England on September 12, 1940. A lucky hit from a British anti-aircraft round disabled his aircraft's engine and he was forced to glide onto a field. Von Werra was quickly captured by locals and turned over to the proper authorities. After his interrogation von Werra was sent to a POW camp and while there was placed with a group of other POWs and marched off on an "exercise" outing or so they thought. He escaped during the march by jumping a stone wall and crouching down behind it as the whole POW parade marched on. He was captured six days later when a local farmer recognized him as the missing prisoner and called the police. He was given 28 days in solitary but before he could serve his full sentence he was transferred to another camp. Six weeks later, as members of the camp gathered and sang a wonderful and loud choral that entertained and distracted the guards, von Werra and four other prisoners crawled through a tunnel and escaped. This time the crafty pilot had planned his escape a bit better and walked onto the Royal Air Force base at Hucknall. Posing as a Dutch pilot who had run out of gas on a cargo flight and was forced to bail out von Werra managed to get the security staff to take him into their offices for questioning. The offices were close enough to the flight line for the German pilot's next move. As one of the security officers was busy making phone calls to confirm von Werra's story, the Luftwaffe pilot

Where Was Camp Freeland?

There are very few photos of POWs at Camp Freeland, but I was given two from the Fletcher Collection. This one shows POWs in the early days of the camp, before the wood and tarpaper cabins were constructed. Photo courtesy of Don Boothe

made a dash for the flight line, scrambled into a Hawker Hurricane and attempted to take off. While he was trying to figure out how to start the aircraft's engine base personnel grabbed him and pulled him from the cockpit. He smugly thanked them and wished them luck for when the Germans over-ran their country. He said that they then would be the ones going to prison.

That was the end of von Werra's war in England as the British promptly loaded him aboard a POW ship and sent him to Canada - following another 28 days in "the cooler" of course. On the voyage to the Great Lakes von Werra was among nearly 1,000 other POWs on the former passenger liner *Duchess Of York* en-route to Halifax. She had been shuttling Canadian troops to England and POWs back to Canada. During that trip von Werra constructively used his time to befriend the ship's crew, especially the deckhands and galley staff. He sold his combat ribbons in order to obtain Canadian cash and learned Canadian slang as well as the geography of the eastern portion of the country. He also worked hard on becoming more fluent in speaking English. All of his preparation on the voyage to Canada would aid in his next escape attempt.

Simplicity is always the best way to thwart security. When I worked as a retail loss prevention agent I always said that the best way to steal from a big retail store was to simply walk in, pick up what you want and walk out. It is the people with the most complex plans that are easily caught. In von Werra's next escape attempt his method was very simple. As the POWs were aboard a train that ran along the St Lawrence River, he simply opened a window and jumped out. At the time the train had slowed as it passed through a railroad yard at Smiths Falls, Ontario and von Werra and another German pilot, Otto Hollman, were able to hit the ground uninjured. Railroad employees saw Hollman go out the window and alerted police who quickly nabbed him, but no one saw von Werra and so the cops thought they had caught the one and only escapee.

Smith's Falls was the last opportunity before the POW train headed deep into Canada's great white north bound for Nyes, Ontario on the shore of Lake Superior - from which there would be no escape for the Germans. The rail yard where von Werra hit the ground was about 27 miles from the St. Lawrence River and within hitch hiking distance of the United States. Unfortunately for the Luftwaffe pilot it was late January, bitter cold outside, and a heavy snow was falling. Still, he managed to make his way to the shore of the St. Lawrence River after two days of hiding in barns and hitching rides at night. Somewhere between Prescott and Johnstown, Ontario von Werra, waiting until darkness, stepped onto the river's ice. He had assumed that the St. Lawrence was frozen all the way across to the US shore. After all it was unbelievably cold; the only thing that seemed to be able to move that night was his feet and they were numb.

Unfortunately, the one piece of information that he didn't learn about the Great Lakes and the St. Lawrence River on his voyage over was that it rarely froze completely that far upstream. At the point where he had decided to cross, the river was about one-mile-wide and as he got about half that distance he discovered rapidly flowing open water about 300 feet wide. Von Werra knew too well that if he tried to swim for it, the cold would sap the life out of his body in minutes. He had no choice other than to retreat back to shore. Most escapees would have simply given up - but not von Werra. Instead he went looking for a small boat of some sort. Luckily, he found one and with a plank from a nearby fence acting as an oar, he could now paddle his way to freedom. With amazing effort, the benumbed pilot managed to drag the boat to open water and launch it and himself. Of course he lost his makeshift oar in the process and found himself drifting with the swift current - headed back toward Montreal instead of rowing happily to the United States.

Von Werra's luck, however, had not run out as his little rowboat suddenly slammed into some large ice slabs and stopped. He was able to climb out and walk the rest of the way across the St. Lawrence to freedom in the United States. He made landfall on the grounds of the New York State Mental Hospital. After a short walk he found a

Here we see the tents that made up the early shelter for POWs at Camp Freeland. Photos of Camp Freeland are very scarce and this one is from the Fletcher Collection. Photo courtesy of Don Boothe

193

car with a driver, Al Crites, and once in it asked him if he could get a ride down to Ogdensburg, New York. Crites, a Canadian citizen who happened to be working in the US, gave the disheveled, half frozen man a ride to downtown Ogdensburg. Along the way von Werra, mistakenly thinking he was riding with a neutral American, bragged of his escape unaware that he was riding with a Canadian. After dropping the wayward POW off in downtown Ogdensburg, Crites found the nearest phone and called the police. Von Werra was immediately arrested by a police department that had no idea what to do with an escaped POW.

Eventually the US Border Patrol was contacted and they took custody of von Werra. They also contacted the German Consul in New York City who wasted little time travelling to Ogdensburg to pick up their escaped pilot. Now the entire affair entered the diplomatic web of red tape between Canada, the United States, and Germany. After all, the US was officially a neutral country - but Canada wanted their POW back, yet in Germany he was a hero and of great propaganda value to the Third Reich. Von Werra had committed no crime in the US other than vagrancy for which he officially was being held. The Canadians wanted to charge him with stealing a boat and the Germans wanted to pin a medal on him. While everyone was pondering what to do, the German consulate quickly paid the $5,000 bond to get their pilot out of the Ogdensburg jail and then just as quickly smuggled him down to Mexico where he was transported south through Central America and later South America and finally ending up in Rio de Janeiro. From there he was sent back to Germany to do what he most desired - rejoin the Luftwaffe and Hitler's war. Von Werra was killed on a routine air patrol off the coast of Holland just six months after he left Rio.

Nearly two months to the day after von Werra's successful escape two more German POWs escaped from the old Fort Henry POW camp. Located on the far eastern end of Lake Ontario Fort Henry was originally constructed to guard the mouth of the St. Lawrence River. It's gray stone walls were imposing and depressing - the POWs hated the place. Having mistaken a late March thaw for the end of winter Heinz Rottmann and Bernhardt Gohlke squeezed through a gun port in the 1838 era fort's stone wall. To their glee they found that, unlike von Werra's attempt, the water was frozen solid all the way across to Wolfe Island and then on to the US shore. To their dismay however, after their escape, they saw the March thaw end and the weather suddenly turn bitter cold. In the night they trekked on across the farmlands of the island and followed the shore to an area where the US mainland looked to be closest, which was probably Point Alexandria. From there it was just 4,800 feet across the solid ice to the lights of Cape Vincent, New York as they made their final march to freedom. Upon reaching the shore they both nearly collapsed. They found some bushes and covered themselves with white bed sheets they had brought along as camouflage.

Shortly after the two escapees reached their hiding spot, officer Graham Thompson of the Veterans Guard in the company of a US Border patrol agent took up station on the Cape Vincent breakwater sheltering from the wind under the lee of the lighthouse. While the two officers waited and scanned the area with their flashlights they heard a rustling sound across the harbor ice in the scrub brush. Venturing over they found the two POWs huddled under the fallen snow waiting for daylight and spring to return. This time their custody was short and not as sweet as von Werra's. At first the Veterans Guard was sent back to Canada as the POWs were now in US hands. But in short order the Veterans Guard was asked to return and the POWs were handed over with little discussion. The US Border Patrol had learned a hard lesson from the highly publicized von Werra debacle. No longer was it safe for German POW's to escape from Canada and seek refuge in the United States.

Much the same as would later take place in the United States, many Canadian held German POWs were sent out and paid to aid in farming. Canadian farmers often treated their POWs as a part of the family and in turn the POWs fell in love with the beauty and open spaces of Canada - which is not a hard thing to do. Following repatriation to Germany at the end of the war large numbers of POWs wanted to immigrate back to Canada and their host farmers often sponsored them. Some of the immigrant former POWs actually married the farmer's daughter.

WWII

Lessons from the Canadian POW camps were quickly adopted in the United states as it amassed large numbers of prisoners. For example, in Canada the only thing that marked a POW on their clothing was a huge red dot painted on the back of their shirt. Many joked that it was a target but the penalty for a guard shooting a POW was quite stiff, so no one was going to use them for target practice. Yet almost none of the general public were aware that the symbol of the big red dot indicated a POW who may also be an escapee. This policy provided opportunity for POWs who did escape to walk the streets of towns and cities unnoticed because it was unlikely that most of the people they encountered knew what the red dot meant. So, in the United States POWs were marked with "PW" in large letters printed on their shirts and pant legs.

Although the camps in the United States Great Lakes region were quite peaceful it was still the duty of every POW to escape. There were a total of 1,073 German escapes from POW camps in the United States between November of 1942 and February of 1945. Of that total, 947 were recaptured in three days or less. Only 25 POWs were on the loose when the war ended and only six of those remained at large by the late 1950s. The last escaped German POW gave himself up in 1985 after reading the definitive book "Nazi Prisoners of War in America" written by Arnold Krammer. Georg Gaertner contacted the author of the book by telephone and surrendered to him.

One of the more unusual escape attempts took place in Michigan and failed as a direct result of the POWs not knowing United States geography or the actual vastness of the Great Lakes. I personally witnessed a modern illustration of that lack of understanding. In the early part of my flying career I was working with a group of flight instructors who were visiting from overseas in Holland. Two of them were tasked to ferry an aircraft that my company had sold. That trip took them from Maryland to Iowa. When they got back they expressed their astonishment at just how large the United States is. It was a similar lack of geographic knowledge that led to a fairly comical incident at Camp Allegan located 28 miles north, northwest of Kalamazoo in Michigan's lower Peninsula. Some of Camp Allegan's German prisoners decided to mount an escape attempt and thought

Where Was Camp Freeland?

their plan was quite fool-proof. Having gained knowledge that Wisconsin, across Lake Michigan, had a large population of German immigrants, they decided to escape to that state in the hope of finding sympathetic expatriates of the Father Land. After a protracted amount of time gazing upon Lake Allegan, which was, located adjacent to the camp a couple of POWs decided that it was Lake Michigan and they could escape by swimming across it. The tiny lake is, at the most, 3 miles long and 1 mile. After successfully getting out of the camp they dove into the lake and succeeded in swimming all the way across. They were quickly captured and no doubt educated on the difference between tiny Lake Allegan and the much larger Lake Michigan. Additionally, they learned that on the other side of Lake Michigan there was not another country, but just more of the United States and their chances of being shot by armed Americans was far greater than locating anyone sympathetic to Germany.

There were also cases were some Americans decided that they loved the POWs more than they loved their own country. Such was the case in the Camp Owosso escape. Located six miles due west of the town of Owosso, Michigan near the intersection of Catland Road and M-21 in the lower peninsula, the camp was established in 1944. POWs were there to work on the local farms as well as a local canning company which resulted in some fraternization between the POWs and the local farm families. Mid-day meals were often supplied by the farm families and although "fraternization" was strictly forbidden, human factors led to an escape.

In July, 1944 two local girls who worked at the canning company, ages 18 and 20, sneaked out to the camp with bolt cutters. Snipping the barbed wire, they freed POWs Eric Classen and Gottfried Hobel, both age 20. The escape was supposedly motivated by love but the tryst didn't last very long. Reportedly Shiawassee County Sheriff's deputies and troopers from the Michigan State Police took just 12 hours to find the four lovers. They were discovered huddled in some bushes near Colby Lake more than 40 miles northwest of Camp Owosso. All four were arrested; the Germans were returned to the camp to serve 28 days in solitary confinement. The two girls, however, went on trial in Bay City facing conspiracy charges. They stated to the jury that they thought they were pulling a prank and the escape was a "joke." One of the girls also stated that she was in love with one of the Germans. Yeah, in 1944 at the peak of World War II that statement probably helped her a lot with the jury. When convicted the two girls found that their affair of the heart cost them each more than one year in prison. Classen and Hobel each later made individual escape attempts by walking away from different farms and were quickly captured again. It's doubtful that they were on their way to visit the girls. The escapes were more a matter of opportunity than of love.

A few months after the surrender of Japan, around the Great Lakes and across the nation the POWs were being repatriated to their native countries. As camps around the Great Lakes region closed they were often torn down nearly as fast as they had appeared. Farmers across the Midwest urged the War Department to allow them to keep their POW workers at least until the normal groups of migrant workers had returned. Unfortunately for them there would be no exceptions and every last POW would be removed from United States soil and shipped back to their homelands with the greatest of haste. The small annex camps, such as Camp Freeland, were the first to be vacated. Many of the POWs did not want to leave North America. Some were disillusioned with their homeland as they suddenly saw the propaganda that had been fed them for half of their lifetime was little more than a tool to get them to do the bidding of the lunatics who had run their homelands into ruin. Others knew that their loved ones were dead and there was nothing left for them to return to but the wreckage of a lost cause. Many Germans also knew that their home towns were in Soviet occupied zones and they could face starvation, enslavement, and even death simply by returning to where they had been born.

July 23, 1946 saw the last German POW depart United States soil from Camp Shanks, New York and board the transport ship *Texarkana* or so the Army stated publically. There still were 141 Germans serving terms in civilian prisons, 134 in assorted hospitals and 25 escapees at large in the United States.

So, where was Camp Freeland?

Where Was Camp Freeland?

The only building remaining from Camp Freeland immediately after the war. It was converted into a snack bar. Midland Daily News

Well, as it turned out all of my long distance bike rides in search of Camp Freeland were for naught and were just good exercise. Camp Freeland could easily have been seen right through our dining room window! The Tittabawassee Township property that had been requisitioned for Camp Freeland from the Ballien, Myers, Wagner, Meilke and Luts families (all of whose kin I attended high school with) was where today's MBS International Airport now resides - just 1,412 feet from my back yard when I was in high school. Without even knowing it, sometimes history can be found in your own backyard.

THE FOG OF WAR

As World War II reached its midpoint in 1943 the allied troops were massing on the English Isles in preparation for a June 1944 invasion of the European continent as the Eighth Air Force was being fed into the Nazi air defense meat grinder. The island hopping campaign in the Pacific was beginning and the allied fleet of warships made of Great Lakes steel was finally beginning to grow. That growth, however, was given life mainly through the steady

Railroad cars filled with red iron ore at Allouez, Wisconsin waiting to be shipped down the lakes in 1941. Library of Congress

movement of iron ore shipped from the upper lakes to the mills in the southeast. That meant that shipments had to continue at an emergency war time level.

By 1943 nearly every vessel that could carry a load of ore had been pressed into service on the lakes. Outdated ore boats that had been laid up in the depth of the depression with their useful careers considered to be at an end were freed from the lay-up wall, dusted off, oiled, greased up and returned to service. Anyone with experience in lakes shipping was now considered to be critical to the war effort and rather than be sent to fight were instead assigned to sail the Great Lakes. Every licensed crewman from captains and mates to chief engineers and second and third engineers were now officially Coast Guard reserve officers and required to wear the uniform. Vessels were duty bound to run as quickly as possible and carry as much ore as their draft would allow. Every hour of delay was considered to be of aid to the enemy, every pound of ore left behind equated to war material not manufactured that may have been used to save the life of someone's son. Urgency was not in the air - urgency was a fact of life. All of that meant that the fleet of ore carriers had to keep moving through storms, snow, ice, gales and fog - keep going toward victory - that was the mindset.

On June 15, 1943 Allied troops prepared for the invasion of Sicily while on the Great Lakes the movement of ore pressed ahead. In the first few hours of that Tuesday morning Captain Arliagh H. Dennis was standing watch in the darkness of the blacked-out pilothouse of the 600-foot-long oreboat *George M. Humphrey*. Sailing for the Kinsman Transit Company with a belly full of 13,992 tons of iron ore scheduled for delivery to the steel mills at South Chicago. Captain Dennis' biggest problem that night was not Nazi U-boats, Japanese dive bombers, or even harbor mines that his salt water counter parts in the merchant marine service had to contend with in this time of war. Instead, the captain was up against an old foe; fog. A heavy rain was falling and accompanied by fog so thick that it was hard to see the stern lights from the pilothouse.

Radar during the war was something afforded only to the military. Captain Dennis had only his ears and his instincts to help

The Fog Of War

On a dark and rainy night the steamer George M. Humphrey *was feeling her way through the fog in the Straits of Mackinaw when fate singled her out. Ralph Roberts Collection*

him grope his way through the fog as he entered the Straits of Mackinac. Lakeboats of every sort crowded the waterway and each was required to blow the standard three blast whistle signal required of vessels moving in fog. That meant that each captain was forced to listen through a thicket of vessel whistles and try and decide which of them may be coming toward him and may pose a hazard. Vessel masters had been using this method for more than a century and collisions in the fog have been common for just as long.

Heading upbound in the same murk was the Pittsburg Steamship Company's 600-foot ore carrier *D.M. Clemson* under the command of Captain Chris Johnson. His boat was running light and on its way up for another hold full of red iron ore. Like Captain Dennis, Captain Johnson had all of the pilothouse windows wide open and his ears tuned toward the vessels blowing their fog signals. Each pilothouse on every vessel was a world onto itself and although the sounds of war were far from the Straits of Mackinac, on upper Lake Huron the moans of those steam whistles carried their own sense of danger and dread.

WWII

At 2:50 that night the glow from the lights of a huge steel steamer suddenly loomed in the fog on the *Humphrey's* starboard side. There was no time to react and Captain Dennis barely had time to cuss before the inevitable collision took place. The inertia of the two vessels alone doomed them to collide and there was nothing that any human could do to stop it. With the thundering groan of tortured steel plates, the oncoming lakeboat crushed into the side of the *Humphrey*. In her pilothouse, the *Humphrey's* navigation crew were nearly knocked from their feet. Then, for a few moments there was silence and stillness. The on-coming lakeboat's captain had instinctively rung "reverse" on her chadburn and soon she began to back away. In the pea soup fog there was just enough visibility to read the opposing boat's nameplate, "*D.M. Clemson.*" Now the *Humphrey* rolled back onto an even keel. In her pilothouse her navigation crew quickly realized that their job of actually navigating the *Humphrey* was now over - forever.

Under his feet the *Humphrey's* captain felt that his boat was rapidly sinking. He rang the general alarm, woke the off duty crew and gave the order to abandon ship. As the crew quickly lowered the life boats and went over the *Humphrey's* rail she rapidly began to settle beneath them. In just 15 minutes she plunged into 78 feet of water. Meanwhile the *Clemson* hove up alongside to help rescue the *Humphrey's* crew. Every member of the crew had been able to escape the sinking vessel without as much as a bruise. It appeared to Captain Dennis that as he looked up at the bow of the vessel that collided with him, the *Humphrey's* part in the war effort had come to an end as her wrecked hull rested on the lake bottom with just the tips of her two masts sticking above the waves. But, in the most amazing salvage effort in Great Lakes history, the *Humphrey* would soon return to the fight.

Enveloped in the same soggy weather on the same date as the *Clemson* and *Humphrey* - the brand new oreboat *Frank Armstrong* was on her way downbound in the upper St. Marys River. Having just come off of Lake Superior the *Armstrong* was on her second trip since having left Ashtabula, Ohio where she was launched just 11 days earlier. As a part of the war effort she was one of a special breed of huge ore carriers known as the "Maritime Class" which had been rapidly designed and constructed. Overall the United Sates Maritime commission had contracted for a total of 16 new steamers to be built on the Great Lakes and the *Armstrong* was one of those new boats. Measuring 620 feet long, 60 feet in beam and 35 feet in depth each of the "Maritimers" was able to carry more than 16,000 tons of badly needed iron ore each trip in support of the war effort.

On June 15, 1943 the *Armstrong* was under the command of Captain H. Chesley Inches. Captain Inches would later gain fame as one of the most well-known Great Lakes maritime historians and in his retirement would serve as the curator of the Great Lakes Historical Society - but on this foggy date in the middle of World War II, he was only concerned with getting his cargo down the lakes. As he carefully guided his boat toward the Soo Locks, the 500-foot Canadian steamer *Goderich* appeared through the fog and collided with the *Armstrong*! Fortunately, it was only a glancing blow and both vessels managed to remain afloat. The collision took place off of Point Iroquois in some of the deepest water of any river on the Great Lakes and had the blow been anything near what had been inflicted on the *Humphrey* the brand new *Armstrong* would have ended up as little more than a footnote in Captain Inches' later research.

Earlier that foggy week there had been other collisions on Lake Superior. Departing Fort William, Ontario with 215,000 bushels of grain in her belly was the Paterson Line steamer *Prindoc*. In command of the 363 foot lakeboat, Captain Richard A. Simpell was doing his part to aid in the war effort by instinctively groping his way through the dense fog. Unfortunately, Captain Dyer of the Canada Steamship Lines' 250-foot canal steamer *Battleford*, was of the same mind, but headed in the opposite direction. The two boats collided with the *Battleford* receiving the lesser damage in the accident. The *Prindoc*, however, was mortally wounded and began to rapidly sink. Fortunately, there was enough time for her crew to man their lifeboats and escape the sinking vessel. She went to the bottom near Passage Island at the mouth of Thunder Bay.

The day after the *Prindoc* found her eternal resting place at the bottom of Lake Superior, the fog got in the way of two more vessels on White Fish Bay. This time it was the Oglebay Norton steamer *W. W. Holloway* colliding with the Buckeye Steamship Company's *Harry W. Hosford*. Although the 552 foot *Holloway* was heavily damaged, she was well able to stay afloat and make some headway. The 530 foot *Hosford*, however, was so badly wounded that she had to be run aground at Point Iroquois to keep her from going down in deep water. Both boats were quickly repaired and returned to service hauling war-time iron ore.

Late April of 1944 saw US troops in the South Pacific landing in northern New Guinea as a part of operations "Persecution" and "Reckless." At that same time across the planet in England troops and equipment were massing for the invasion of Europe. Meanwhile, on Lake Erie perhaps the most horrific Great Lakes fog-induced collision took place near the beginning of the opening of navigation the following season. Temperatures along the shores of the lake were in the mid-50s on April 26, 1944, yet dipped toward the 30's that night. The lake water was still bitter cold at just 42 degrees and the result of the temperature swing over the cold water created a thick blanket of fog. Suddenly at the port city of Ashtabula, Ohio maritime radios began to crackle with urgent messages from out on the lake. The atmospheric conditions were awful that morning and greatly interfered with radio reception, but anyone listening at half past five o'clock could tell that something dreadful had happened and a lakeboat by the name of *Reed* had been involved. Throughout the day additional reports came in by way of radio. Finally, 11 hours after those initial reports a huge lake freighter emerged from the fog outside of the Ashtabula harbor entrance. Her bow was ripped open and mangled as if yawning with a jagged steel mouth. Local boat watchers and marine men strained to read the name painted upon her bow as she slowly emerged from the gray blanket that hung so low over the lake as well as the shore.

A half day earlier the whole disaster began with the 468-foot ore carrier *James H. Reed* easing her way through the fog in the pre-dawn darkness. In command of the *Reed* was Captain Burt Brightstone and standing at the boat's helm was wheelsman Fred Preston. Captain Brightstone had left the pilothouse in charge of the third mate with instructions to call him immediately if the mate felt that another vessel may be near. Just minutes past 5:00 am the mate heard what he thought may be the fog whistles of a nearby vessel. Rushing down to the captain's cabin he alerted the *Reed's* master who in turn hustled to the pilothouse. Heading up the gangway Captain Brightstone could hear the whistle that had concerned the mate. It was a vessel, and it was close - too close! Entering the pilothouse, the captain rang "Stop" on the engine chadburn and then grabbed the *Reed's* whistle pull and blew the fog signal. The *Reed's* signal was matched by another vessel's whistle that seemed to come from right on top of them!

Captain Brightstone's first instinct was to get the crew out of their bunks and he ordered the mate to activate the general alarm. Throughout the vessel large bells rang with a shrill tone loud enough to wake even the soundest sleeper. At that same instant the captain and his wheelsman, who had both been rapidly scanning all of the pilothouse windows in search of some clue as to which direction the

Thanks to a thick blanket of spring-time fog on Lake Erie the James H. Reed *went from being a Great Lakes workhorse to a menace to navigation in a matter of minutes. Ralph Roberts Collection*

approaching vessel may be coming from, were frozen by the glow of lights as a monster loomed off the starboard bow. With a cargo hold full of 7,500 tons of iron ore the *Reed* was low in the water and the approaching boat, which was running without cargo, towered high overhead. Instinctively, Captain Brightstone knew that his boat was finished. He told his pilothouse crew to grab their lifejackets as he snatched his own. Both he and his wheelsman burst from the pilothouse. At that same instant the two steel giants crashed together.

Cutting deep into the *Reed's* heavily weighted hull the collision nearly cut her in half. She began to sink so quickly that before the captain and wheelsman could step farther than the pilothouse, the frigid lake water was already at their knees! A heartbeat later a wave of ice water smashed both men up against the pilothouse as the *Reed* began to plunge into Lake Erie and take them with her. Both men found themselves floundering in the icy water. By luck alone they bumped into the *Reed's* life raft and managed to struggle aboard. They were so benumbed that when they tried to paddle the raft, they simply could not - so they simply laid there waiting to be rescued, or slip away to the great beyond.

So rapidly did the bow sink that the watchmen who were quartered in the forward fo'c'sle, off duty in their rooms, had no chance to escape. Back in the stern quarters the crew had a bit more time. John Laucks, a 17-year-old deckhand, having been alerted by the general alarm, emerged from his room only to find that the boat's steam lines leading to the forward cabins, had been ruptured in the collision and the deck was enveloped in a cloud of live steam. He had to dash through it in order to make his way toward the lifeboats which were stored atop the aft deckhouse. Reaching the starboard side lifeboat, he found that he was unable to unlash it and launch it by himself. Fearing that the quickly sinking vessel would pull him down with it, Laucks simply jumped overboard. The instant that he hit the water his body went numb from the cold. On the port side, Chief Engineer R.O. Fletcher found 18-year-old deckhand Leonard Dzieweczynski and another crewman attempting to launch that boat. Chief Fletcher shouted that there was no time for that and ordered them to just unhook the davits and let it float free. A moment later the *Reed* suddenly

The Fog Of War

No one aboard the Ashcroft *or the* Reed *could have done anything to avoid the collision. Theirs was an era before radar and GPS when only the ears and instincts of their captains could be used to make their way through the fog.* Author's Collection

plunged to the bottom. Dzieweczynski was sucked down with the boat and found himself clawing at the frigid water in a desperate struggle to reach the surface. Fortunately, he had his life jacket on and it helped him float to the surface. He took a breath and was sucked under again. For a second time he clawed his way to the surface, took a breath and was again pulled under. Finally, he bobbed to the surface and was dragged safely aboard one of the *Reed's* life rafts.

In the galley of the *Reed* the end of a true love story was tragically taking place. Chief Cook Ray Losey and his wife Camille had been working on breakfast for an hour when the collision happened. Within the relationship of this sailing couple there was only one true fear; Camille could not swim and was dreadfully afraid of the water. As the *Reed* went down, 19-year-old deckhand Marlon Godschalk saw the two cooks go down with the boat - locked in each other's arms.

WWII

In the pre-dawn darkness and fog those who had survived the *Reed's* sinking found themselves benumbed by the lake among a mass of wreckage. Not a moment too soon the lifeboats from the Canada Steamship Lines 560 foot lakeboat *Ashcroft*, the vessel that had struck the *Reed*, came rowing into the wreckage field. Soon anyone living was plucked from cold lake. Among those picked up by the *Ashcroft's* lifeboats was wheelsman Preston and Captain Brightstone.

As the *Ashcroft* entered Ashtabula harbor and tied up at the Pennsylvania Railroad coal dock the onlookers were amazed at the tremendous gash in her bow - it was now 5:15 in the evening. Police had been stationed there since 2:00 pm as the word got out that she was coming there. More than 1,000 people had gathered to meet her and gasp at her damage. She would, however, be quickly repaired and returned to service - after all, there was a war on. Yet the *Reed* would remain forever where she sank. Since she was directly in the navigation channel, her remains were considered a menace to navigation. A contract was made with the Johnson & Shockley Company of Lewis, Delaware to dynamite the forward and aft cabins of the wreck in order to provide a 36-foot depth clearance for vessel traffic. In all the *Reed* took 12 members of her crew to a frigid death with her.

Just three hours and 45 minutes after the *Ashcroft* and the *Reed* collided, the thick spring fog that hovered over Lake Erie caused another wartime casualty. Exactly 33 miles west - southwest of the *Reed's* final resting place, Columbia Transportation Company's 432-foot steamer *Frank E. Vigor* was hauling a capacity load of raw sulfur. Used to make gun powder, explosives, vulcanized rubber and other badly needed wartime products, sulfur was one of the unglamorous and easily overlooked critical wartime commodities. It was also unglamorous to load and unload. The yellow cloud of sulfur dust that came from the loading and unloading process stung the eyes of the crew and got into everything from their underwear to the cook's food. Crews hated carrying sulfur more than any other product on the lakes. To make matters worse that same nasty dust that came with the rocks of mined sulfur was also quite flammable. Crews were often restricted from smoking while hauling sulfur - and that really bothered them almost as much as having it in their underwear.

210

The Fog Of War

To facilitate the loading and unloading of assorted cargoes from scrap metal to sulfur the *Vigor* had been equipped with two deck-mounted cranes in 1941. These diesel-powered cranes were of the same type used by railroad construction crews and sat on bogies that traveled upon two standard railroad rails that were welded length wise to her spar deck just outside of her hatch combings. This allowed the cranes to travel and have access to her open hatchways. Their clamshell buckets could then scoop out the cargo, or, in the case of cargoes such as scrap metal, they could lower electro-magnets down and pull the cargo out then whirl around and drop it onto the dock or into waiting railroad cars. This ability to load and unload almost anywhere she could be moored made her a very valuable asset in the war effort.

Although most poorly researched accounts put the *Vigor* "inside the confines of the treacherous Pelee Passage" they are incorrect. At the moment that she collided in the fog with another vessel that April morning in 1944, she was, in fact, just over 25 miles east of the Southeast Shoal light that marks the eastern end of that passage and thus a considerable distance out in the open lake. Yet, at that point

After steaming more than two dozen miles clear of the "...confines of the treacherous Pelee Passage" the Frank E. Vigor *was safe from the shoals, but dangerously off course in Lake Erie's fog. Ralph Roberts Collection*

the distance between the upbound and downbound courses on Lake Erie are only about 6,000 feet apart. Unfortunately, the *Vigor* had strayed more than half that distance toward the oncoming shipping lane. There the 500-foot ore carrier *Phillip Minch* had also strayed toward the *Vigor's* lane. Running blind in the fog with nothing to revealing their positions other than the repeated blasts of their steam whistles, the two lakeboats slammed together - it was 8:50 in the morning.

At that moment 26-year-old third engineer Fred Bernatowicz was on duty in the *Vigor's* engine room giving loving care to her triple expansion 1896 steam engine. Even though he and the boat's chief engineer were both deep in the engine room, they knew in an instant that their boat had been hit by another vessel as they were nearly knocked off their feet. The chief instinctively ordered his engine stopped and Bernatowicz dashed for his life jacket.

As the bow of the *Minch* cut into the side of the *Vigor* the electrical conduits leading from the stern to the bow were severed and began sparking wildly. Additionally, the friction of the two steel vessel ramming together created sparks that when combined with the sparking severed electrical wiring ignited the yellow sulfur dust. In a matter of seconds, the cargo of the *Vigor* was set afire. The result was a cloud of noxious smoke that swept over the stern. It prevented Bernatowicz from reaching one of the lifeboats and as he dashed toward the other lifeboat, he felt the deck of the *Vigor* beginning to roll under him - she was capsizing!

There was only one safe refuge in Bernatowicz's reach and he scrambled toward it. Nearly at deck level was the huge anchor of the *Minch* and there were already two of his fellow crewmen standing on it. They beckoned to the oncoming engineer and then gave him a hand-up onto the supposed safety of the anchor. Just then the *Minch* began to back away and as she did the *Vigor* suddenly rolled over. As the sinking steamer went over, her deck cranes, which were held down on their rails by nothing other than gravity, toppled into the lake. As the aft crane came loose its boom swung around and knocked Bernatowicz from his perch on the anchor and into the frigid lake. Fortunately, he was kept afloat by his life jacket and managed to stay alive until the *Minch's* lifeboat came along and two of her crewmen plucked him from the icy water. All of the *Vigor's* 32 crewmen survived the wreck.

These were just two of the worst collisions that took place in that single fog. Several additional fender-bender type of collisions also took place. Yet while the *Reed* and *Vigor* went to the bottom of the lake to remain there forever - up in the Straits of Mackinac a very different story was taking place as one man with a unique vision and skill was executing a plan that would recover a giant oreboat from the grasp of the lake waters. Captain John Roen was about to do the impossible as well as his part to help win the war. He was going to raise the wreck of the *George M. Humphrey*.

When the *Humphrey* went to the bottom of Lake Huron in the Straits of Mackinac her value was listed by her owners, the Kinsman Transit Company, as $1,600,000. Considering that in 1943 she was the largest vessel ever to sink on the Great Lakes and absolutely nothing of her size had ever been refloated from that depth, her owners gave her up as a total loss. With her two mast tips sticking up just above the surface in a very busy waterway the wreck was considered to be a hazard to navigation and the government began taking bids to clear away the masts. Enter Great Lakes salvage wizard Captain John Roen.

Captain Roen signed the contract to clear the *Humphrey's* wreck with an amazing side-deal. His deal was that instead of just clearing the masts, he would buy the entire boat and her ore cargo for a single dollar! Additionally, rather than scrapping the boat he would attempt to raise her. Traditionally, on the Great Lakes, the laws of salvage are far different from those of salt water. Any wreck on the lake bottom remains the property of the original owner or the original insurance underwriter. On salt water, for the most part, it is finders-keepers when someone salvages a wreck. Captain Roen's deal was that if he raised the *Humphrey*, he would own her - for a dollar. Either way, he would clear her away and she would no longer be a menace to navigation. The insurance underwriters and the U.S. Government happily agreed to the deal and probably thought that the good captain had a screw loose somewhere.

WWII

In September of 1943 Captain Roen began work on the *Humphrey*. The first task involved the un-dogging and opening all of the oreboat's 17 hatches. Each of the hatches consisted of a series of over-lapping heavy steel leafs held in place by clamps. These leafs were normally opened by having the boat's steam-powered winches attaching a steel cable which was used to pull back the leafs. Unfortunately, when you are more than 70 feet under water, it is really hard to get steam up. Hardhat divers had to be lowered down and they opened each hatch by hand. The currents in the Straits of Mackinac are strong and each diver needed to fight to keep their position as well as to get the hatches open. To make matters worse, not only was the work being done in the middle of one of the busiest waterways on the Great Lakes, the weather on the lakes during that time of the year can turn notoriously bad, often on very short notice.

Once the hatchways were cleared a buoy was attached to each hatch. These would allow the clamshell buckets that were lowered from a crane on a barge floating above the wreck to correctly target the open hatch. Once in the cargo hold the clamshell could then take a bite out of the iron ore and raise it to the surface. The soaked ore was then placed into another waiting barge. By the time that the 1943 winter weather forced Captain Roen's crew off of the *Humphrey*, they had recovered about 8,000 tons of iron ore from the wreck; more than half of her cargo.

During the winter months of 1943-44 the British began night bombing raids on Germany's capitol city of Berlin. On one of those raids was famed American radio broadcaster Edward R. Murrow who was aboard a Lancaster bomber as an observer. Additionally, the first "victory" class ship, the *United States*, was launched at the Oregon Shipbuilding Corporation shipyard. Troops of the United States invaded Majuro and Kwajalein in the Pacific and US submarines built on the Great Lakes began scoring their first victories against the Japanese. Perhaps most importantly, the P-51 fighter made its debut in the European air war. This forever spelled the end of air superiority for the Germans as the P-51 was now able to protect the bombers all the way to and from their targets. During those same winter months, Captain Roen spent the cold dark days in his office at Sturgeon Bay,

Wisconsin planning a spring offensive of his own. He would not be battling the Axis powers directly, but instead would continue to battle the Straits of Mackinac in his fight to raise the *Humphrey*.

The project to raise the sunken ore boat required procedures never tried before at these depths along with special tools that had to be designed and constructed from scratch. Huge steel rigs and special towing equipment had to be made in a time when materials for such items were quite scarce. Blueprints and action diagrams had to be produced, reviewed by the crews and the divers, tested and changed over and over. A special model representing a 140-foot section of the oreboat's hull was also constructed so that tests could be carried out. A plan for re-sealing the boat's damaged ballast tanks while under water was devised as well as a plan for pumping air into the repaired tanks and expelling the water trapped inside. A team of four hard hat divers were hand-picked by Captain Roen to do the highly hazardous under water work. The final plan consisted of a series of small lifts and tows where the patched up wreck would be lifted slightly and then dragged into shallower water. This would be repeated over and over until the boat was not only clear of the shipping lane, but her decks were at the surface. All the while three of Captain Roen's barges, the *Maitland*, a former railroad car ferry, the *Industry*, and the *Hilda* would hover overhead. Then the water would be fully pumped from her hold and the *Humphrey* would be towed to Captain Roen's shipyard for repairs in order to put her back into service as an operational ore carrier. Great Lakes marine men quietly smirked at the effort - Captain Roen was attempting the impossible.

In May of 1944 the ice was finally completely clear of the straits and the work on the *Humphrey* began once more. As the Japanese were being slaughtered at the Admiralty Islands, off New Guinea and the Germans were forced out of Anzio, Captain Roen's divers began the work of making the *Humphrey* somewhat floatable. The 18 by 24-foot hole in her side was sealed up with timbers and canvas. Next some 15,000 feet of 7/8-inch steel cable was attached to the wreck and the *Maitland*. Once the wreck was ready to begin lifting, the actual lifting was accomplished by flooding the *Maitland's* ballast tanks and sinking her down a depth of eight feet. The slack was then taken up on the cable and the *Maitland*'s tanks were pumped dry. Next the *Maitland* and the *Humphrey* were towed a short distance into shallower water where the process was repeated. Finally, on September 10, 1944, the same day that Luxembourg was liberated by the U.S. First Army, the decks of the *Humphrey* surfaced.

Amazingly, the wreck was completely repaired and refitted to re-enter service in the iron ore trade for the Great Lakes 1945 shipping season. Once again she was supplying the steel mills before the end of World War II. Having been renamed *Captain John Roen* she was a part of the Roen Transportation Company. Captain Roen sold her in 1947 for 950,999 times more than he had paid for her. She ended her days on the lakes when she entered winter lay-up at Erie, Pennsylvania on December 6, 1985 and never left the lay-up wall again as an active vessel. She was towed off for scrapping on May 2, 1988 arriving at Kaohsiung, Taiwan on October 2, 1988.

LAKEBOATS OF WAR

Iron ore fed the Arsenal of Democracy during World War II. Yet even with every lake freighter that could carry ore pressed into emergency war-time service the shipping capacity was still not enough to meet the need. As early as the winter of 1940-1941, a survey conducted by the United States Maritime Commission showed that iron ore demand would increase by 20% during the 1941 Great Lakes shipping season. That estimate was made under the assumption that the United States would remain out of the current global conflict. If the nation entered the war, the need would drastically increase. Additionally, when the overseas conflict was factored in, grain export shipments would also spike as well. The total fleet of US bulk carriers on the lakes at that time consisted of 363 powered boats and 21 barges with a total capacity of 3 million long tons. If the US entered the war the Commission estimated that an additional 7.5 million more tons of capacity may be needed.

Although the isolationist sentiment appeared strong from sea to shining sea that winter, it was clear to anyone willing to face reality that a neutral United States could be doomed to go the way of neutral Belgium if the Axis powers decided to come ashore. War was looming on the horizon - like it or not. Thus, the Maritime Commission approached the Lake Carriers Association which represented nearly all of the vessel owners operating on the inland seas, and urged them to come up with a private ship-building program that would fill the foreseen gap in carrying capacity. Assistant Chairman of the Commission, Commander Howard

WWII

Vickery found, to his disappointment, that the members of the Lake Carriers Association were highly doubtful that the United States would enter the war. For that reason, they refused to invest their own money in something that may ultimately result in excess vessel tonnage. On October 7, 1941 Commander Vickery was officially notified that the Association could not come to terms - it was exactly two months before the Japanese attack on Pearl Harbor.

Left with no choice, the Maritime Commission would have to act within the framework of the government in order to produce the needed capacity for hauling iron ore. An order was placed on October 11, 1941 with the American Shipbuilding Company for the construction of six steam-powered ore carriers at a price of $1,972,000 per vessel. That same day a similar order was placed for 10 ore boats at a cost of $2,200,000 each to be built by the Great Lakes Engineering Works. All of the vessels were to be delivered by the middle of 1943. Unlike the members of the Lake Carriers Association, the shipyard owners were more than happy to take the orders and immediately began hiring additional workers - many of whom would soon be drafted away to fight the war that in 1941 most American's were against getting involved in. Each of the new "Maritime Class" lakeboats was to be 620 feet in overall length, 60 feet in beam and 35 feet in depth. For their time they had cavernous cargo holds and were able to carry 16,000 tons of cargo.

Perhaps more motivated by happenstance than Hitler the Pittsburgh Steam Ship Company had been planning the construction of five new boats as early as March of 1938. At that time, they owned the largest fleet of Great Lakes ore carriers and had an eye toward the future. They saw an increase in demand for ore as America began to pull out of the depths of the Great Depression and placed orders for vessels to meet their future needs. The five new steamers would be a whopping 639 feet 6 inches long, 67 feet in beam and 35 feet in depth. Each would be powered by a steam turbine engine that would produce 4,000 shaft horse power. The "Shipmasters Association Directory" lists a cargo capacity of 16,800 tons for all five steamers. Each had 18 hatches on 24 foot centers. Due to their large size and capacity the five new vessels were nick-named "The Supers."

Lakeboats Of War

War-time meant the urgent need for larger ore boats and fulfilling that need came quickly as the first of the "Supers" the Leon Frasier *splashed into the water launching on February 28, 1942. Ralph Roberts Collection*

Launching on February 28, 1942 at the Great Lakes Engineering Works in River Rouge, Michigan the first of the Supers was Christened the *"Leon Frasier."* She slid sideways into the water as the British RAF bombed Lübeck and destroyed more than 30% of the city throwing Hitler into a rage. The *Frasier's* keel had been laid on June 5, 1941 just nine months' shy of her launching while the United States was officially still a neutral country. Now, with World War II fully engulfing the entire globe the new lakeboat was part of the massive build up to victory.

Sisters to the *Frasier* followed in rapid succession. On July 1, 1941 the keel for the *Enders M. Voorhees*, which was identical to the *Frasier*, was laid down and she was launched April 11, 1942 at the River Rouge shipyard. Just 14 days later another identical Super, the *Benjamin F. Fairless*, slid down the builder's ways at the American

WWII

Shipbuilding Company at Lorain, Ohio. Her keel had been laid down on July 7, 1941. The final two Supers were launched on the same day. The *Irving S. Olds* and the *A.H. Ferbert* splashed their way onto the Great Lakes at Lorain and River Rouge respectively on May 22, 1942. This was the first U.S. National Maritime Day. The ability of the Great Lakes fleet to ship iron ore had been increased by a total of 84,000 tons as the five Supers went to work. Unfortunately, the *Ferbert* ran aground on the bolder-laced bottom of the St. Marys River near Sault Saint Marie on her maiden upbound trip. She had to return to the shipyard for repairs.

As the Supers were being finished the first of the Maritime Class of ore boats were being started. On February 2, 1942, the keel for the *Pilot Knob* was laid down. She, however, would not be considered as the first of her class because a month and a week after her keel was laid, the keel for the *Adirondack* was laid down and that vessel would be finished first and launched on September 9, 1942 - more than a month ahead of the *Pilot Knob*. Both boats were given names selected by the Maritime Commission as both were launched

The five Supers went straight to work, able to ship 84,000 tons of iron ore in total. Ralph Roberts Collection

under government contracts. The first eight Maritime Class ore boats were launched with Maritime Commission names; *Lake Angeline*, *Belle Isle*, *Hill Annex*, *McIntyre*, *Pilot Knob II*, *Lincolnshire* and *Mesabi*. The names selected all had their origins derived from iron ore ports, locations, or the mines where the ore originated. All were changed shortly after the vessel's commissioning as private owners took charge of each vessel. *Adirondack* was renamed *Richard J. Reiss* as she went to work for the Reiss Steam Ship company. *Pilot Knob* became the *Frank Armstrong* when she joined the Interlake Steam ship company. *Lake Angeline* was painted black with pea-green cabins and white trim and became the queen of the Cleveland Cliffs Iron Company fleet under the name *Cadillac*. *Belle Isle* shared the pea-green cabins look and the spotlight as an assistant queen of the Cleveland Cliffs fleet under the name *Champlain*. *Hill Annex* joined the Supers in the Pittsburgh Steam Ship Company fleet with her new name *George A. Sloan*. The *McIntyre* found a home with the *Frank Armstrong* at the Interlake Steam Ship Company under the name *Frank Purnell*. *Pilot Knob II* went to the Bethlehem Transportation Company under a name board that read *Steelton*. She had been proceeded to that fleet by 10 days by the *Mesabi* which had been renamed *Lehigh*. Only the *Lincolnshire* had not tasted fresh water under a Maritime Commission moniker. She had been acquired by the Interlake fleet while she was still on the builder's ways and was renamed *E.G. Grace*. Yet she would have been the second Maritime Class boat to be named *Lincolnshire*, the first having been launched on November 28, 1942 and subsequently renamed *Sewell Avery* and acquired by the Pittsburgh Steam Ship Company.

This flurry of vessel acquisitions did not arise out of war-time patriotism on the part of the vessel owners or the Lake Carriers Association. What happened was that the Maritime Commission had announced that they were beginning a program by which they would buy "equivalent tonnage" from every fleet who bought a Maritime Class vessel. This was a plan where the companies who bought the new vessels could continue to run their out-dated vessels until the war was won. At that point the Commission would take the obsolete lakeboats out of service and leave the fleets with their new boats.

This eliminated the worry that vessel owners had about being stuck with excess capacity after the war. At the end of the war, 36 outdated ore boats were turned over to the War Shipping Administration through this process. In turn the War Shipping Administration chartered back 34 of the old boats to their original fleets in order to keep the movement of iron ore flowing at the highest levels possible. The two boats that were not chartered back, the *S.B. Coolidge* and the *Amazon* had been used as partial payment to the Maritime Commission for the purchase of the Maritime Class vessel *Clarence B. Randall*. As property of the Maritime Commission they were transferred to the Gartland Steamship Company to replace the canallers *Black Bay*, *Bennington*, *Brockton* and *Covalt*. Those vessels had been requisitioned by the Maritime Commission and sent to salt water as a part of the war effort - all were lost at sea.

VJ Day and the end of World War II brought a wave of excesses across the United States. From returning planes and service personnel to millions of tons of war production that had been stockpiled and awaiting deployment, for example, P-40 fighter planes were so plentiful that they were stacked on their noses like vertical files in the aircraft bone yards. Likewise, foods intended for overseas were stocked in huge warehouses that were soon opened to the public. Until the early 1960s my maternal grandmother went to, "the surplus store" once a month to buy cheap canned goods. Jeeps and trucks built for the war in Great Lakes area factories could be purchased at bargain basement rates. The ride wasn't smooth, but you could go anywhere. It was not uncommon in the 1960s to find that the tow truck at your local gas station was a former World War II surplus vehicle. Yet the one place that didn't suffer from surplus tonnage was the Great Lakes ore fleet. In fact, the Maritime Commission's eye to the future ensured that the boats that were running in 1945 pretty much kept running during the following post-war shipping seasons.

All of the Supers and the Maritime Class lakeboats went on to have long careers. Yet, what the Germans and Japanese could not do to slow the flow of iron ore across the lakes during World War II, other foreign nations accomplished in the decades following the war by dumping cheap steel on US shores. The cheap steel that flooded

Lakeboats Of War

US markets combined with the failure of American steel and automobile companies to modernize and adopt new materials and manufacturing processes led to a steep down-turn in Great Lakes heavy industry in the early 1980s. Additionally, the introduction of the huge 1,000 - foot ore carriers with their massive cargo capacity and improved engines at about the same time meant that the days of the Maritime Class vessels were numbered. The final nail in the coffin for many of those carriers indeed turned out to be their engines. The decade of the 1980s saw a steady parade of 600-foot class ore boats going from lay-up to the scrap yards.

The first of the Maritime Class boats to see her career suddenly end was the *Thomas Wilson*. She finished her final season at Toledo, Ohio on December 16, 1979 while sailing under the Columbia Transportation Division of the Oglebay Norton Company. There she would remain as the sun bleached out her vibrant "Columbia cream" superstructure and iron ore red hull colors for the next eight years. In December of 1987 she was sold for overseas scrapping departing the Great Lakes on December 18, 1987.

Three days after the *Wilson* entered Toledo, the *Clarence B. Randall* entered that same port and tied up for the last time. She also sported those elegant Columbia colors and she too would sit and fade for seven long years. The *Randall* would depart Toledo in the same tow as the *Wilson* as both headed for the same scrap yard in Taiwan.

Only one Maritime Class lakeboat was taken out of service in the 1980 season. The *Steelton* was taken to Toledo on May 9, 1980 and laid up awaiting the scrapper's torch. She had an odd relationship with her sister Maritime Class boat *Frank Purnell*. The Interlake Steam Ship Company had taken all three of their Maritime Class boats and given each a cargo hold refurbishment prior to 1966. But at the end of the 1965 season they had decided to convert one of their World War II Maritime boats to a self-unloader. That rebuild would almost totally scrap the new cargo hold. Not wanting to throw away that investment completely they entered into a one-on-one swap of vessels with the Bethlehem Transportation Corporation for their boat *Steelton*. That vessel was sorely in need of a new cargo hold bottom. Thus the two boats were swapped and the *Steelton* became the self-unloader *Frank Purnell* in Interlake colors and the *Frank Purnell* became the *Steelton* in Bethlehem colors. It was the *Purnell* that was laid up in Toledo in May of 1980 and just to make things more confusing for boat watchers she was in Columbia Transportation colors having sailed for that fleet since 1974 as the *Robert C. Norton*. She withered at the lay-up dock the better part of 14 years before finally being towed overseas to the scrap yard in India in late 1994.

The Cleveland Cliffs Iron Company had been one of the legacy shipping companies for nearly a century with a fleet of two dozen ore boats after World War II. Yet the onset of the 1980s recession hit them hard and 1981 saw two of their Maritime Class boats put into their final lay-up. On September 7, 1981 the *Cadillac* went to the place where lakers went to die in the 1980s - Toledo. She was joined there at the end of the 1981 season by her fleet mate *Champlain*. Both vessels sat idle there as "deals" for their sale came and went as did deals for their scrapping. *Cadillac* and *Champlain* were finally towed overseas clearing Quebec on September 8, 1987 with both meeting the scrapper's torch in Aliaga, Turkey.

1981 was a bad year for the Maritime and Super classes of lakeboats with a total of eight being taken out of service - one quarter of the entire class in a single year. All but one found their fate at the end of the scrappers cutting torch. The one that escaped the torch went on to an even more degrading demise - she was the *Sewell Avery*. A member of the Pittsburgh Steam Ship Company and garnished with their tall silver smokestack the *Avery* was in the business of long-haul iron ore transportation from the day she had been delivered, May 26, 1943 until she was tied to the lay-up wall at Superior, Wisconsin - September 30, 1981. The fleet had recently taken possession of its second "footer" the 1,004-foot long *Edgar B. Speer* making the company top heavy with older, less efficient, smaller tonnage capacity vessels. With ore demand in a steep decline it was time to radically thin the fleet. There was no future at all in their business model for a World War II era vessel that was not a self-unloader. The steel mills along the lower lake shores were on the verge of collapse and the shore-side unloading rigs were rapidly becoming out-dated. Even the price for scrap metals was depressed.

Although many of Maritime Class of ore boats ended being cut up by the scrappers torch, the Sewell Avery *met a more degrading fate. She was sunk as a dock-face and eventually covered with fill dirt. DJ Story Collection*

The best use for the *Avery* in a depressed economy was to sell her by any means possible. Thus in 1986 the A.B. McLean company of Sault Saint Marie, Ontario bought the idle steamer and towed her up to the Soo and sank her as a dock face at the end of Old Vessel Point.

Launched as *Pilot Knob*, Maritime Class hull number 522 was re-Christened the *Frank Armstrong* before she sailed her first trip for the Interlake Steamship Company on June 4, 1943. She was the second Maritime Class vessel to be launched. The *Armstrong* served Interlake well until the recession of the 1980s when she too was found to be out-dated and not worth the cost of operating. On November 3, 1981 she was laid up at DeTour, Michigan. Among lakeboat fans hopes were high that she would return to service when the economy improved. Many pointed out that when boats were laid up on the St. Marys River it often meant that they would be back out and running later. Of course those opinions were based on times when the industrial heartland was not crumbling into ruin. She waited at her dock until late 1987 when she was towed away for overseas scrapping.

Allied bombers targeted Rome, Italy for the first time on June 19, 1943. On that same day the *Robert C. Stanley* splashed sideways into the muddy water of the River Rouge, Michigan shipyard of the Great Lakes Engineering Works. It had taken just seven months and two weeks to construct the new lakeboat. She would depart the Detroit River upbound for Two Harbors Minnesota for her first of many loads of iron ore to fight the Axis forces on September 30, 1943. On November 10, 1943 she would come about as close to foundering in a storm as a lakeboat can get without actually going to the bottom. While heading westbound across Lake Superior in a savage storm her hull suddenly cracked! The crack ran across her deck and more than a dozen feet down both sides. The crack was more than 3 inches wide and the boat was threatening to break in two and sink into Lake Superior's frigid depths. Working in desperation her crew ran steel cables from her forward winches to her aft winches on both sides and then cranked them as tight as possible. A distress call was put out and two nearby lakeboats came to her aid. Together the three made it safely into Whitefish Bay and then on to the Soo. Once there a makeshift patching of her hull was applied and she sailed on to Duluth for her load. She made a second round trip before laying up at her winter quarters in Toledo on December 8, 1943. What is amazing is that this vessel brought down two cargoes of iron ore with her hull kluged together in the depth of winter! This clearly shows the urgency of ore movement across the Great Lakes during World War II. She was finally given a permanent repair in March of 1944. All of that drama was far behind her as she sailed into Duluth for the final time on November 25, 1981 where she went into layup. She was sold for scrap seven years later and departed the lakes for Aliaga, Turkey in a tandem tow with her fleet mate, the 614 foot *Ralph H. Watson* on May 16, 1989.

Perhaps the most reluctant to leave the lakes was the first of the "Supers" to go into final lay-up; the *A.H. Ferbert*. Finishing her final season on the Great Lakes the Super Class oreboat passed under the Duluth aerial lift bridge for the final time under her own power on

November 30, 1981. She had spent her entire career hauling ore for the Pittsburgh Steam Ship Company, which merged into the United States Steel Corporation in 1951 and then became the United States Steel Great Lakes Fleet in 1967. To the *Ferbert* all of that meant nothing other than a few minor changes in her paint scheme. By 1981 her useful life as an ore carrier for that company was over and they laid her up. After six years the once proud steamer was sold for scrap. She was towed out of Duluth on September 15, 1987 but seemed to want to avoid the trip. First she got into heavy weather on Lake Superior and became more than the tug *Glenada* could handle. A second tug, the *W.J. Ivan Purvis* came out and assisted the tow to the Soo. After successfully navigating the locks and the lower St. Marys River, the *Ferbert* broke her tow line at DeTour. As she drifted with the strong current she went aground and punched a hole in her bottom. Once her tugs had gotten her free and her flooding was contained the tow headed down Lake Huron. This time she decided to snap her tow line in the St. Clair Cutoff Channel. It took six tugs to free her this time. When she arrived at the Welland Canal, she got wind-bound for the better part of a week before she could finally be towed off the lakes. The *Ferbert* made it only as far as Sydney, Nova Scotia where the winter forced her tow to tie up until spring. She arrived in Turkey on June 20, 1988 - nine months and five days after she had left Duluth.

Duluth was sort of a final stop for four of the five World War II Supers. At the end of the 1981 shipping season three Supers made their final mooring after passing through the Duluth Ship Canal. Following the *Ferbert's* lay-up on the final day of November, the *Irving S. Olds* entered the harbor at Duluth on December 3, 1981 and 23 days later the *Enders M. Voorhees* shut her engines down for the final time there. Less than a year later, on October 4, 1982 the *Benjamin F. Fairless* was laid up with her sister ships at Duluth. Considering that the fifth Super, the *Leon Fraser* had been laid up at Lorain on December 20, 1981 it appeared that the World War II Supers were finished.

Although some sources report that the *John T. Hutchinson* never came out for the 1981 season, I stood on the bank of the Saginaw

WWII

River in the middle of the night in June of that year and watched her come in and unload. Factually, she laid up in Cleveland at the end of the 1981 season. There was a scheme cooked up by her owners at the time, American Steamship Company, to replace the *Hutchinson's* stern with that of her fleet-mate the *Saginaw Bay*. The reasoning was that the Lentz Compound steam engine that had been installed in the *Hutchinson*, and several other Maritime Class lakeboats was (as reported to me personally by Chief Russell Pank of the American Steamship Company) "A real pain, a mechanical nightmare." The *Saginaw Bay*, however, had been converted to a diesel power plant during her 1963-1964 winter lay-up. Since the 1917 vintage *Saginaw Bay* was already taken out of service, her entire stern, plus her propulsion equipment could simply be put on the *Hutchinson*, problem solved! Unfortunately, the United States Coast Guard didn't see it that way and refused to approve the plan. The *Hutchinson* departed the lakes for scrapping in Taiwan on October 2, 1988.

Lehigh, the next to last Maritime Class boat to enter service was laid-up at the close of the 1979 season. She got a temporary stay of execution when she was purchased by the fledgling Canadian vessel operators Pierson Steamships Limited, also known as the Soo River Company, in late 1981. She was the first World War II Maritime Class oreboat to sail under the Canadian flag. She ran for a single season under her new owners as the *Joseph X. Robert*. In 1982 she was transferred to the P&H Shipping Company and renamed *Willowglen*. Ten years later she was sold again - this time to Goderich Elevators Limited where she served as a grain storage barge until 2005 when she was sold for overseas scrapping.

One of the oddest post-war paths for a Maritime Class vessel to find herself on was that of the *J.H. Hillman Jr*. She sailed for the Great Lakes Steamship Company during World War II and thereafter until 1957 when she was sold to the Northwestern Mutual Life Insurance Company who in turn chartered her to Oglebay Norton Company from 1960 to 1965. In 1966 she went to the Wilson Marine Transit line and then to Kinsman Marine Transit in 1973 and back to the Oglebay Norton Company in 1974 who converted her into a self-unloader that same year and re-named her *Crispin Oglebay*. She too

228

Lehigh, *the next to last Maritime Class boat to enter service, was laid-up at the close of the 1979 season. She was later sold to the Canadian Soo River Company and ran as* Joseph X. Robert. *Eventually she was transferred to the P&H Shipping Company and renamed* Willowglen. *Pete Merlin photo*

was swept up in the economic down-turn of the early 1980s and laid up at Toledo. She did come out to sail again in 1989 but was returned to lay-up in 1991. Just when it looked like her time was done, she was purchased by Upper Lakes Limited, a Canadian firm, for use as a transfer barge and that's where her story got strange. After one season as a barge under the name *Canadian Transfer*, the folks at Upper Lakes cut the stern off of their diesel-powered vessel *Canadian Explorer* and used it to replace the steam-powered stern of the *Canadian Transfer*. That diesel power plant was now going to provide propulsion to its third bow section! It had previously been launched as the stern of the salt water vessel *Cabot*, then went onto the *Canadian Explorer* and now onto the *Canadian Transfer*. Yet the changes in identity for the Maritime Class boat were not yet finished - she was sold another time to the Algoma Central Corporation and re-named *Algoma Transfer*. Her identity crisis was finally resolved when she was towed away for scrapping at Port Colborne, Ontario in May of 2014.

After reading all of that you may get the impression that all of the World War II Maritime Class and Supers are gone from the Great Lakes. In fact, as of this writing in 2017, that would be an incorrect assumption as several of those boats that helped to win the war are still in existence on the lakes. If you look closely on your next visit to the fresh water seas, you just may see one.

Of all the World War II Maritime Class and Super Class vessels only one resisted the lay-up wall during the dark days of 1981-1982. That vessel is the *George A. Sloan* which after conversion in 1967 to a self-unloader, was able to work efficiently in the stone trade. Then, after dodging the recession of the early 1980s she had her steam power plant replaced by a diesel system in 1985 which gave her a new lease on life. In 2001 she was purchased by the Canadian

The J. Burton Ayers *was given a new lease on life when Lower Lakes Towing rescued the World War II Maritime Class boat in 1995 and re-named her* Cuyahoga. *DJ Story photo*

Grand River Navigation Company purchased the Richard Reiss *in 2004 and operated her as the* Manistee. *DJ Story photo*

company Lower Lakes Towing which has the reputation of rejuvenating and operating classic old lakeboats. As of this writing, she can be seen tramping around assorted ports all across the Great Lakes as the *Mississagi*.

Prior to the purchase of the *Sloan*, and much to the delight of lakeboat watchers, Lower Lakes Towing rescued the world War II Maritime Class *J. Burton Ayers* in 1995 and re-named her *Cuyahoga*. She too is working hard continuing to move cargos to ports around the Great Lakes.

Grand River Navigation Company, an affiliate of Lower Lakes Towing, purchased the *Richard Reiss* in 2004 and operated her as the *Manistee*. She, however, was placed in long term lay-up at Toledo since Christmas Day, 2015 - her future is unknown as of this writing.

Perhaps the luckiest of the World War II constructed freighters is the Super *Leon Fraser*. Like all but one of her breed, the *Fraser* was laid-up during the dark days of the 1980s recession. Her lines

WWII

Steaming proudly from the McArthur Lock the Alpena *continues to carry cargo across the lakes. DJ Story photo*

were cast ashore, supposedly for the last time, at Lorain, Ohio on December 20, 1981. A dark shadow was then cast over her in 1986. The American Shipbuilding Company yard at Lorain, where the boat was sitting idle, was bought by Elyria, Ohio's Spitzer Management and scheduled for "redevelopment" into what today is known as the elegant community of "Harbor Walk on the Black River." Spitzer stated that they expected to incorporate the *Fraser* into the ambiance of their development. Many in the depressed Great Lakes boat-watching community cheered as it looked like 44-year-old Super would be spared from the scrapper's torch. Yet, those who were more familiar with how developers actually operate feared that this could mean as little as cutting off her pilothouse and sticking it in the parking lot of their marina. Contrary to the original announcement, no effort was made to integrate the *Fraser* into the development and in the autumn of 1989 the old Super was towed to Lake Superior and converted into a cement carrier. She was reduced in length to 519 feet and returned to service during the 1990s with the name *Alpena* under Inland Lakes Management which had previously bought the lakes legacy cement shipper Huron Cement. After another 15 years of service in the powdered cement trade what should have been her death stroke occurred on December 11, 2015. As she rested in dry dock at Bay Shipbuilding in Wisconsin a fire broke out in her engine room and quickly spread to her upper deck cabins. Firefighters from all of Door County responded and in seven hours had the situation under control. The outer paint on the old boat was scorched and considering her age and the fact that vessel owners on the lakes are eager to scrap old vessels and replace them with cheaper tug and barge units many of us thought that her days were done. Amazingly, she was repainted just 16 days later and headed off for repairs. The last of the World War II Supers sails on at the time of this writing, and perhaps you may one day see her classic "Huron Cement off-white" colored hull out on the horizon. May she ply the Great Lakes as she did in the war, for many years to come.

In the end these vessels were built in haste to win a war. They served that purpose very well and then went on to continue transporting the raw materials needed by a developing super power; the United States. Much of what we see today as the foundation of this country was constructed with the ore hauled in these vessels. Yet their time came and went and now, like all World War II veterans, only a few remain.

MIGHTY MAC

Anyone familiar with the history of World War II has heard of "Rosie the Riveter" the female icon of the Arsenal of Democracy. Yet, in the summer or 1943 in the Great Lakes city of Toledo, Ohio a slightly different version of that lady stepped forward in order to build one of the most formidable machines of the war. From the kitchens and living rooms of that city a small army of determined and patriotic ladies of the lakes picked up tools that they had never before set their hands upon and turned themselves into "Rosie the Welder" at the Toledo Shipbuilding Company's yard and began the task of building a Great Lakes vessel that would become a legend over the next six decades.

In the vast expanse that encompasses the Great Lakes there is only one force that can choke off the annual flow of raw materials across the inland seas. That force is the unstoppable annual arrival of winter and the frigid temperatures that turn the beautiful blue waters into a mass of white ice. Since the beginning of navigation on the lakes the extent of the shipping season has always been dictated by the cold grip of winter. Once the channels and ports are locked by ice, the big freighters are simply tied up at their assigned winter docks until the coming of spring. Normally the shipping season comes to an end when the water begins to freeze up in the latter part of December and doesn't release its grip and allow the movement of ships until sometime in March and, on occasion, April. With Japan's attack on Pearl Harbor followed shortly after by a declaration of war by Germany's Adolph Hitler on the United States,

WWII

During World War II the ladies of the lakes picked up their tools and went to work. They were instrumental in building the most powerful icebreaker in the world at that time - the Coast Guard Icebreaker Mackinaw. *Office of War Information Collection*

the arsenal of democracy suddenly needed ever day that it could squeeze out of the annual shipping season.

On December 17, 1941, exactly ten days after Pearl Harbor, the United States Congress authorized the funding of a new vessel specifically intended for service on the lakes. She was officially known as "hull 188" and she was to be an icebreaker. The new vessel would belong to the United States Coast Guard and was to be the most powerful boat to ever serve on the Great Lakes. Built similar to the Wind Class icebreakers that the US was lend-leasing to the Soviets for Arctic service during the war, Wind Class icebreakers were some of the strongest vessels afloat at that time. The icebreaker being constructed in Toledo was to be similar to her salt water kin, yet unique in her own right. Coast Guard Admiral Edward Thiele, the father of the Wind Class design, described hull 188 as, "a Wind Class ship that was squished down and pushed out and extended to meet the requirements of the lakes."

Designed to be 290 feet in length and 74 feet in width hull 188 would be 21 feet longer and 11 feet wider than her salt water counterparts. She would also be land-locked during the war as she could not fit through the St. Lawrence River system's locks. Her diesel-electric power system consisted of six 2000 horsepower Fairbanks-Morse diesel engines which drove her two stern screws and one bow screw. Her stern screws were able to propel her forward with enough force to ram through ice 11 feet thick or to simply move ahead and continuously break ice two and one half feet thick. The bow propeller aided her ice breaking by sucking the water out from under the ice ahead of the ship. She also had the ability to roll from side to side and wiggle her way out of any ice entrapment. She did that by way of "heeling pumps" that could transfer water from one side to the other in her lower hull at a rate of 160 tons in just 90 seconds! Hers was a design that would become legendary on the Great Lakes.

Keel laying for hull 188 took place on March 20, 1943 as General Montgomery's troops struck the Mareth line in Tunisia and finally began to break out. It was a time when the outcome of the war was still very much in doubt. The United States military had inducted 3,033,361 individuals in the year before hull 188 had her keel laid down and they would induct another 4,915,912 men and women while the vessel was being constructed - with the overwhelming majority being men. Like every other type of war-time production, able bodies and hands were needed to build the icebreaker; enter "Rosie the Welder."

Since 1906 the Toledo Shipbuilding Company had been constructing lakeboats. Everything from huge steel ore boats, and car ferries, to passenger vessels were side-launched down the builders' ways into the Maumee River's muddy water. A total of more than 180 assorted vessels had been produced by the yard prior to 1942, but the hands doing that work had always been those of men. As the newly laid keel of hull 188 was blessed by a local clergyman,

WWII

Shipyard Superintendent Joe Rawlinson looked on knowing that there was not enough man power to complete the job and he would have to begin to hire and train female staff to build the ship. As women began to go to work in the shipyard, the news media across the entire region took notice. Photographers arrived and took group pictures of the ladies in their over-sized men's work clothing. With sleeves and pant legs rolled up to give some semblance of actually fitting, the women with their ever present bandanas on their heads posed holding their torches, wrenches and work gloves. They were an inspiration for other women to break free of the household and do their part in the war effort.

Often federal programs other than those that simply provided funding for construction went a long way toward aiding in building vessels such as hull 188. A good example is The 1940 Community Facilities Act also known as the Lanham Act. It provided funds to communities that were swamped by the influx of workers seeking jobs in the war plants. It also provided funds for day-care facilities. This allowed women who went to work in places such as the Toledo shipyard to have a safe place that watched and fed their children while mom was at work and dad was at war. Soon, the structure that was hull 188 began to grow as the ladies of the lakes built her from the keel up.

Of course every vessel has to have a name and so it was decided that hull 188 would become the icebreaker *Manitowoc*. There was just one problem with that name and it became apparent on November 30, 1943. It was on that date a Tacoma Class patrol frigate was side-launched at the Duluth Globe Shipbuilding Company yard. Their hull number 115 had been christened *Manitowoc*. Wanting to avoid confusion the Maritime Commission, the same people who had launched one oreboat named *Pilot Knob* and then seven months later launched another oreboat of the same class also named *Pilot Knob*, decided that they could not have two vessels during the war by the same name. Thus, the *Manitowoc* being constructed at Toledo was renamed *Mackinaw*.

Launching of the icebreaker *Mackinaw* took place on March 4, 1944. In her launch photo a legion of shipyard workers can be seen gathered on the gantry in the background. Scores of Rosie the Welders watched with pride as the magnificent monster that they helped create with their own hands slipped into the water with a massive splash. She would spend the next eight months in the fit out slip being made ready to go out and fight the ice. Even before she was completely outfitted the news media of the day boasted that she was the largest, strongest and most powerful icebreaker in the entire world.

Although it may be argued that in some aspects the salt water Wind Class icebreakers could outmatch her, the *Mackinaw* was indeed the greatest icebreaker ever to sail the Great Lakes. Prior to her creation icebreaking had traditionally been little more than a part-time seasonal job for lake vessels. Called "bucking ice" the task was one that certain lakeboats found to be a side benefit to their original

The history of ice breaking before the Mackinaw *was littered with disaster. On March 8, 1920, following in the path of the big steel car ferry* Pere Marquette 18 *the wooden "ice-crusher" break-bulk carrier* Pere Marquette *became trapped along with the car ferry just short of Ludington, Michigan. As the ice shifted it crushed her hull and she sank becoming a total loss. Author's Collection*

design. A good example of this would be the use of the whaleback steamers. Their spoon-shaped bow allowed them to ride up onto the ice allowing their own weight to then crush the frozen lake surface. Of course since these vessels were not designed for icebreaking, they paid a price in broken propeller blades and rudders.

Some captains of standard lakers, determined to buck the ice, pumped ballast aft and thus raised their bow nearly out of the water in order to have a similar result as the whalebacks but they too often ended up with broken blades, rudders, and sometimes hull plates. Other vessels, such as car ferries, were actually quite efficient at icebreaking. In most cases they had been designed for year-round navigation across the rivers and lakes. Yet their very purpose of supporting the railroads and the movement of rail cars and their cargoes across the lakes generally prevented the ferries from making long trips to clear channels for the bulk carriers. Eventually icebreaking tugs were entered into service, often with good results. But, no matter what the tugs, ferries, or any other method used to buck the ice - the ice always won in the end and nothing, other than the occasional mild winter, was able to extend the shipping season. Now, as the winter of 1944-1945 set in, the *Mackinaw* was poised to change all that.

During late November of 1944 the *Mackinaw* did her sea trials and then went straight to work. Her first mission was to spearhead a convoy of smaller icebreakers and three salt water freighters that had been constructed at Duluth-Superior. The three C1-M-AV1 motor vessels were the *Pemiscot*, *Hidlago* and the *William N. Nelson* all of which had left Duluth-Superior on Friday January 5, 1945 downbound for Sault Saint Marie and the frozen St. Marys River. These three cargo vessels were considered to be so vital to the war effort that they would be helped through the ice-covered river by three United States Coast Guard icebreakers. The Coast Guard icebreaker *Woodrush* aided the three motor vessels in getting out of Duluth harbor at the head of the lakes and all three then crossed Lake Superior unescorted. On station waiting for the convoy were the icebreakers *Sundew*, *Chaparral* and the brand new $10,000,000 *Mackinaw*.

Mighty Mac

Three newly constructed C1-M-AV1 cargo vessels, like the one shown here, were so urgently needed in the war effort that they were ordered to start downbound from Duluth in January of 1945. They were the first escort mission for the ice breaker Mackinaw. *US Navy image*

Sundew met the three new freighters at the northern rim of Whitefish Bay's ice field and began breaking a path to the locks at Sault Saint Marie. The three cargo vessels were not designed for working in ice of any sort. They were general cargo carriers built to serve the coast lines and islands that the allied forces had recently taken from the enemy. Each was 388 feet long, 50 feet in beam, and had a depth of 21 feet. Their diesel engines provided 1,700 horsepower to a single screw allowing them to reach a maximum speed of just over 13 miles per hour. Each, when placed into commission, would have a crew of 85 including officers. Their route to salt water would be by way of the Chicago Sanitary and Ship Canal and along the Mississippi to the Gulf of Mexico where each would be officially commissioned into the United States Navy. This trip would be the first time that any movement of this sort had been attempted between Lake Superior and the Gulf of Mexico in the winter months and could only be attempted because of the *Mackinaw's* entry into service.

Approaching the locks, the convoy found that the icebreaker *Chaparral* had been busy breaking up the ice around the canal. That little icebreaker had originally entered service as the *Halcyon* working for the Detroit Ferry Company. In 1941 she was taken over by the government and moved to Toledo to be rebuilt as a Coast Guard buoy tender and ice breaker. Her 134-foot length was just right for service around the locks at Sault Saint Marie. *Chaparral* led the way into the lock followed by *Pemiscot* and then *Hidlago*. All three vessels locked down together. Next down came the *Sundew* leading the *Nelson* - the entire process took just over an hour. As the convoy reached the lower level they found the *Mackinaw* waiting for them. All but the *Chaparral* would tie up below the locks and wait for daylight.

Dawn found the *Mackinaw, Sundew, Pemiscot, Hidlago* and the *William N. Nelson* casting off their lines and preparing for the run down the frozen Saint Marys River - it was January 8, 1945. The ice along the river was only eight to 12 inches thick and was of little challenge to the *Mackinaw*. It must have been somewhat amazing for the crews aboard the three C1-M-AV1 motor vessels to watch - the *Mackinaw* was able to run through the ice almost effortlessly at a speed that was near "full ahead" on their chadburn. They simply followed along in her wake headed for Lake Huron. Once in the Straits of Mackinac some of the ever-present windrows of ice sheets stacked upon themselves were encountered. There the ice was as much as 10 feet thick and the big icebreaker had to back and ram a few times. Eventually the open water of Lake Michigan was reached and the *Mackinaw's* spearhead duty was done. The three motor vessels sailed on to Chicago and then the Gulf of Mexico. The *Mackinaw* turned around and headed for her namesake city on the Lake Huron shore. There reporters were allowed to come aboard and capture her story. Not since 1904 had such a late season passage down the Saint Marys River occurred.

Although the *Pemiscot, Hidlago* and *Nelson* successfully left the lakes as scheduled, all three vessels got caught in a log-jam of war materials being manufactured faster than they could be commissioned and crewed. The only one of the three to enter service before the war was over was the *Hidlago* and she only stuck her toe into the conflict. After waiting on the Mississippi until August of 1945, she was towed to Galveston, Texas for her final fit out. During

Mackinaw *shown escorting the three C1-M-AV1 motor vessels* Pemiscot, Hidlago *and the* William N. Nelson *in the St. Marys River on January 8, 1945. Office of War Information Collection*

that tow she was commissioned into the Navy on August 4, 1945 and placed under the command of Lt. John W. Thompson. After a brief shake-down cruise was taken along the Texas coast, the vessel was officially ready to enter the war. Ordered to the Pacific the *Hidlago* headed out toward the Panama Canal Zone on September 5, 1945 - three days after Japan signed the formal surrender papers. She subsequently was ordered back to Norfolk, Virginia after the surrender and never saw any additional operational service after that before being sold off for scrap.

The *Mackinaw*, however, would continue to win her battles with the winter ice around the Great Lakes and make those Rosie the Welders proud of their work for more than six decades. Routinely she would come to the rescue of lakeboats snared in the ice. No matter how badly a vessel was stuck the term, "The *Mackinaw* is on her way," always meant that the boat would soon be on the move once again. Some of her greatest moments came in the 1970s when the concept of year-round navigation on the lakes was tested. The idea came out of the "Rivers and Harbors Act of 1970." The original concept was that for every dollar that the federal government invested in winter navigation on the lakes seven dollars would be returned to the US national economy. In fact, it turned out to be more like three dollars for every one dollar spent. But, with an asset like the *Mackinaw* used to its fullest potential as well as other Coast Guard icebreakers, the concept actually seemed to work. From 1973 to the end of the decade, winter navigation seemed to become the normal way of doing business rather than the exception. Then came the collapse of heavy industry around the lakes and the sagging market for raw materials as the 1980 recession took hold. That spelled the end of year-round navigation.

On June 10, 2006 the World War II icebreaker *Mackinaw* was officially decommissioned. On that same day a new vessel by the same name was commissioned to replace her. Smaller and less powerful than her predecessor the new *Mackinaw* has state-of-the-

Placed 16 inches apart, about half the distance of most ships, the Mackinaw's *bow ribs help support her thick bow plating against the sheets of ice. Library of Congress*

In her native environment, the Mackinaw *cruises in the vastness of Great Lakes ice. A closer look shows her decks crowded the families and friends of Coast Guardsmen. Library of Congress*

art electronics and propulsion yet will always work in the shadow of the war-built veteran that she replaced. Today the original *Mackinaw* is moored at its namesake port of Mackinaw City, Michigan. Converted into a museum ship the vessel is a unique tourist attraction in that you can actually purchase a ticket to do a sleep-over aboard the icebreaker! Of course you have to bring your own food, bedding and water as well as being comfortable with using a porta potty, but still - you're aboard the *Mackinaw*!

VICTORY

On May 7, 1945 General Alfred Jodl of the German High Command signed the first of many unconditional surrender papers followed by a flurry of surrender documents being signed by assorted German commanders. On May 8, it was announced officially, the war in Europe was over. Although celebrations broke out across half of the globe there still remained the Japanese enemy fighting in the Pacific. Like zealots they were savagely fighting to the last man.

General Alfred Jodl of the German High Command signs the first of many unconditional surrender papers. Library of Congress

WWII

At precisely noon Tokyo time on August 15, 1945 NHK radio announced a broadcast "of the gravest importance." All Japanese people were ordered to stand and listen. "His Majesty the Emperor," the announcement continued, "will now read his imperial rescript to the people of Japan." With that, a recorded message from Emperor Hirohito was played informing the people of Japan that he was ending the war. He never used the word "kofuko" which means surrender. Up until that moment the estimated 3,000,000 Japanese who were still scattered around the Pacific had been told nothing other than Japan was winning the war and the words of their divine leader came as a shock. Unlike the Germans, who surrendered completely, many in the Japanese military went on a rampage and slaughtered allied POWs. Hours after the Emperor's broadcast Admiral Matome Ugaki led a flight of 11 kamikaze torpedo bombers in a strike against allied ships off Okinawa. At the Oita airfield remaining kamikaze pilots were bragging that they would sink any American ship that entered Tokyo Bay. Upon hearing this the Emperor sent his younger brother, Prince Takamatsu, to ensure that the Imperial orders were obeyed. In the end the propellers were removed from all kamikaze aircraft. It would take more than a month before the idea of Imperial forces achieving victory faded and they finally accepted that Japan was now a defeated nation and would soon be under allied occupation.

Meanwhile in the United States, the euphoric celebration on V-J day had also faded. After four long years of all-out war, blackouts, rationing, shortages of basic staples, and dealing with the loss and maiming of loved ones, people were wondering what was next. Americans looked around and saw that with peace came quiet - the quiet that a war production line makes when it stops. Mountains of parts needed for war product manufacturing were stockpiled. Likewise, the tooling needed to make those parts into the weapons of war now sat unneeded. Many of the tanks, ships, submarines, and aircraft that used those parts now sat idle and the soldiers, sailors, and airmen who used them were now being discharged and heading back home. After nearly full employment, the war-time economy that had driven a feeble United States industrial base roaring out of the Great Depression had suddenly evaporated. Everything used to fight

Admiral Chester Nimitz signs for the United States Navy the surrender document that ended World War II. Library of Congress

the war from the tons of ammunition to the legion of Rosie the Riveters was now "surplus."

From 1940 through 1945, war materials were produced in astounding quantities. A few examples - produced were 12.5 billion rounds of small arms ammunition, 5.15 million bombs, 87% of which were manufactured by the auto industry, 2.48 million mines, 58.5 million rifle clips, 981,350 aviation drop tanks, 315 million cartridge cases, 2.620 billion ammunition belt links, 20.87 million helmets of which 85% were produced by the auto industry. The list runs on longer than I'm willing to type, but the point is that as the war drew to an end the pipeline of those finished materials as well as the parts coming from subcontractors needed to be full at all times. The Automotive Council for War Production stated that because of the massive flow of materials in the supply chain, there was no way to accurately list the total amount of surplus. The materials never stayed in one place long enough for a complete inventory to be made.

Most of the aircraft, tanks, jeeps, trucks and assorted armored vehicles that became surplus were stored outdoors in the deserts of the American southwest. The parts to make them, however, were left where they were delivered. Following V-J Day there were still supply ships heading out into the Pacific as others were unloading their cargos at the hundreds of outposts and bases around the region. Additionally, hundreds of thousands of soldiers and sailors that were deployed not only in the Pacific theater, but also throughout Europe still had to be supplied. At that same time, a flood of unneeded war materials was being returned to US ports. It was a logistics nightmare.

Managing spare parts alone had been a never ending problem for the Army Ordnance Department throughout the war. As an example, the spare parts to maintain 100 medium tanks for one year took up twenty railroad box cars - and while they may have had the parts in the system, it didn't mean that everything was in the right place at

Surplus B-17 bombers waiting to be scrapped. Library of Congress

the right time, in the right quantities due to the amount of handling and the distance many of these parts had to travel. When it came to the jeeps being produced in places such as Toledo, Ohio the Army Ordnance Department estimated that in 1940 it would take 1,006 different spare parts to keep one going. That estimate was woefully off as it turned out that the number of parts needed would be 2,500. Each and every part had to be correctly identified and stored. To make matters more complicated, it took more than 9,000 pieces to make up one jeep. When the war ended those huge stockpiles were declared as surplus. Some surplus was made available to the public at bargain rates but, fortunately most was retained and used post-war to support jeeps in use by the military. Yet after V-J day, it all looked like a mountain of surplus.

A concerted effort was made to repurpose what may be useful, but parts to assemble aircraft or tanks as well as the tools to make those machines are only good for making aircraft or tanks. The rest was simply scrap metal to be sold for whatever the scrap market may be willing to pay. Often the stock piles of war material awaiting disposition were taking up needed space and hindering the auto makers as they tried to convert back to the peacetime production of automobiles.

A good example of what happens when a plant is in high production mode making military equipment and then the contract is suddenly terminated is that of the Ford tank plant. They had been building tanks to meet a pre-Pearl Harbor contract for 7,000 model M3s. That contract was terminated when the War Department decided to switch to the M4 tank. Ford estimated that there were more than 25,000 surplus M3 parts and tools, excluding raw materials. The cost of the surplus materials and tooling was set at over $80 million. Raw materials such as the 17,000 tons of raw steel that Ford had purchased for $55 per ton were put up for bid by the Ordinance Board. The highest bid was for $20 per ton. Unhappy with that result, the Ordinance Board started selling the steel piece-by-piece and managed to liquidate 11,000 tons at an average of $48 per ton. In addition, 2,100 manufactured parts worth more than $4 million were deemed to be unusable and were classified as scrap.

WWII

1,400 metal dies that had cost $2.5 million went directly to the scrap yard at a value of less than $1 per die. More than 3,000 custom jigs and fixtures used to assemble tank components were removed from the factory floor.

In an attempt to see if disassembling a $4,250 fixture and recovering the usable parts would be practical, the Ordinance Board had one dismantled as they tracked the cost vs benefit. The value of the usable parts came to $9. What remained was worth $11.70 as scrap. That brought the total value of the fixture to $20.70, but the cost in labor to dismantle the fixture was $30. This would prove to be representative of what every war materials producer would experience after the war.

Most of the unions in the manufacturing industry preserved the seniority numbers of the men who left to serve in the military. For the returning veterans this softened their transition back to civilian life. They could simply report back to their old job and pick up where they left off. Since most of their job experience had been in peace-time manufacturing and the factories were now changing back over to peacetime production, no large scale retraining was required. Also, since their pre-war seniority numbers put them ahead of the workers who had replaced them during the war, they could displace lower seniority employee's from those jobs. Although this was great news for the veterans returning to the Great Lakes region, it was very bad news for those Rosie the Riveters and Welders. Females were unceremoniously pink-slipped from the plants and shipyards and sent back to what was considered in the late forties as "their proper place" at home.

Perhaps the most cheated by victory was the WASPs - the members of the Woman Airforce Service Pilots. These female pilots had demonstrated their ability and competence in high performance complex aircraft countless times as they ferried a total of 77 different types of aircraft in the service of our nation. From 1942 to December 20, 1944 the WASPs flew a total of 12,652 aircraft from the assembly locations. A total of 1,102 women pilots served as WASPs and 38 of those died during that service. A WASP camp was located at the Romulus, Michigan Army Air Base near the Willow Run facility. In the end the Army refused to acknowledge the WASPs as members of the military. It was not until 1977 that an act of Congress officially declared that the WASPs were indeed military veterans.

After V-J Day the folks at Ford's River Rouge facility found themselves with a fairly interesting surplus item - rocket engines for buzz bombs! You read that right folks. Following D-Day in Europe the allied forces swept across France and soon took control of the most of the sites where the Germans had been launching their V-1 pilotless flying bomb also known as the "buzz bomb." The V-1, "V" standing for Vergeltungswaffen or "revenge weapon" had been developed at the same Peenemunde facility as the famous V-2 rocket. Launched on a rail by a powerful rocket charge, the V-1 used a pulse-jet engine that gave it a range of about 160 miles while flying at an altitude of between 2,000 and 4,000 feet. Upon running out of fuel, the pulse-jet,

The American version of the buzz bomb, officially called the Army Air Corp LTV-N-2, or the Navy's JB-2 Loon. Brian Nicklas photo - Udvar Hazy, National Air and Space Museum

which made a loud buzzing sound, would quit and the V-1 would then simply spin to the ground where its 1,800-pound warhead would explode. These weapons were intended to terrorize civilian populations as much as they were intended to destroy property.

The V-1 possessed several serious flaws. First it had a limited range which meant that it could only be launched from sites within 160 miles of its targets. Secondly, it had a very limited guidance system that basically only controlled heading and altitude, so it wasn't able to hit specific targets. Third, it flew at low altitudes and within the speed envelope of the Allied fighter planes and could easily be shot down. The British took full advantage of these flaws and Allied bombing raids on the production facilities as well as the launch sites soon limited the number of V-1 launched. Even with most of the launch sites eventually being overrun by the allied ground advance, the Germans did manage to keep launching them until a month before they surrendered.

Allied forces began gathering components from crashed V-1s as well as dud vehicles nearly as soon as the first V-1s began dropping on England. Many of those parts ended up back in the United States for evaluation. Back home, beginning in June of 1944, the buzz bombs were back-engineered for American use against the Japanese. In short order the Ford Rouge plant was not only making truck and aircraft engines, but also the PJ31 pulsejet engine for an American version of the buzz bomb officially called the Army Air Corp LTV-N-2, or the Navy's JB-2 Loon. Those engines were then shipped to Republic Aircraft in Long Island, New York where the airframes for the Loon were being assembled. This was no small undertaking - the JB-2 Loon went into mass production and 1,292 of the buzz bombs were constructed. Intended to be fired from ships and aircraft during the invasion of the Japanese mainland, the buzz bombs were never used in combat as V-J Day sent them into the war surplus category. The Army Air Corp, later to become the United States Air Force, and Navy continued to use the Loon for guidance and launch testing through the end of the decade. But, Ford ended up with 1,100 buzz bomb engines in stock at their River Rouge facility. It is doubtful that Paul Schmidt, the German inventor who fathered the pulsejet engine, ever imagined his brainchild would end up in a pile of surplus junk behind the Ford plant in River Rouge, Michigan.

Along with the materials used in combat there was a surplus of other hardware that many a Great Lakes boat-watcher have bemoaned since V-J Day. By late 1944 the delivery of iron ore was beginning to exceed the amount needed for war-time steel production. Seeing that trend the United States Maritime Commission, which had increased the capacity of ore transportation across the Great Lakes by scooping up older and smaller ore boats from shipping companies in exchange for underwriting the building of newer and larger vessels, began to release the old lakeboats back to their original owners to dispose of as they pleased. A total of 36 classic lakeboats had been involved in the deal and were managed by the War Shipping Administration. The oldest of these ore boats had been launched in 1892 and the newest had been launched in 1907. Through 1945 they were being returned, one-by-one. At the close of the 1944 navigation season 29 of the historic lakeboats were laid up in the bay off Erie, Pennsylvania. Not wanting to have excess shipping capacity, the original owners of those vessels allowed the War Shipping Administration to declare them as surplus and in November of 1945 all 29 were sold to the Steel Company of Canada Limited, or "Stelco" and eventually cut up and melted down as scrap in that company's Hamilton, Ontario furnaces. The remaining seven vessels that did return to their original owners were all scrapped by 1953. They had done their part to win the war and then they did their part to feed the demands of a post-war economy.

Returning service personnel came back to the Great Lakes region much in the same manner as all allied veterans of World War II. Many participated in the victory parades while others who didn't have enough "points" to return home remained as part of the occupation forces and came back long after the parades were over. Those who missed the victory parades often made up for it by marching in their communities annual Fourth of July and Veteran's day parades where they were warmly welcomed back by their friends and family.

WWII

My Mom tells the story of the return of her big brother, my Uncle Jack and his homecoming from the Pacific. He had been in the service from the beginning of the war to the end and saw action in the worst jungle fighting in New Guinea and the Philippines. On the night of his return home he gathered the entire family around the table at the McGarrity family household. Mom, then age 10 and her cousin Jacquelyn, then age 8 were ordered to leave the room. Being curious kids, of course, they snuck back in and hid under a table that was draped with a floor-length cloth. There they listened all night long as Uncle Jack told his story in graphic, horrifying detail. Mom said it was the first time she ever heard the "F" word - and it was used often especially in reference to the Japanese. When he finished telling what he had been through he firmly said, "There, now don't any of you ever ask me about it again."

No one ever did.

He returned to work in a local Saginaw industry, raised two daughters, and was well known as the fun-loving rascal of the family. Although he probably always carried a disdain for his former enemy, he never showed any animosity when two of his nephews, one of whom was me, both married women of Japanese descent.

There was a high monetary price for victory in the cost of equipment, parts, labor, raw material, and logistics, a debt with which the people of the United States found themselves burdened. That would be paid off over time. Yet there was still a higher cost that will never be repaid. It was the cost of those who made the ultimate sacrifice, those who died and those who were wounded both physically and emotionally during the conflict. It is a burden that those who fought and survived will carry until their final day.

AUTHOR'S NOTE:

Considering how the war ended with the dropping of both atomic bombs on Japan, I often hear revisionists protest that dropping those bombs was unnecessary. I have a different perspective, let me explain. I was born into a family where I had 19 cousins. Four of my uncles were in uniform during the war. Uncle Jack was serving in the Pacific and would have been part of the invasion forces attacking the Japanese home islands had it been necessary - it would have been his third invasion. Uncle Tom was at a forward staging area as a member of the Army Signal Corps and Uncle Bill was state-side waiting to be deployed with the Marine invasion force. Uncle Buck was serving in North Africa and would likely not have been part of the invasion of Japan. If the first three of my uncles aimed at Japan had been in that invasion, where allied casualties were estimated to be, at a minimum, 250,000 and over the length of the campaign as high at 1,000,000 - the odds are that none of them would likely have survived. Additionally, Japanese civilian casualties were estimated to be perhaps 10 to 20 times that amount due to the suicidal indoctrination of the population as demonstrated on Saipan and Okinawa where civilians leaped from cliffs to avoid the "Devil Americans", or who were sent to their deaths by Japanese soldiers. In the home islands of Japan, it would have been far worse as women and children would likely choose suicide over capture. A heavy toll of civilians killed in collateral damage from bombing and shelling would have been experienced as well. My own mother-in-law may likely have been one of them – she was Japanese, born in 1941. If the atomic bombings had not happened, I would likely have had only nine cousins and I may not have my wonderful wife. The revisionists can speculate all they wish, but I prefer history the way that it actually happened.

WWII

BUY BONDS!

Every World War II era movie that I ever watched always ended with a message for the audience to buy war bonds.

So, I figured this book had to end with: BUY BONDS!

SOURCES

BLACK-OUT!

References:

Robert Forsyth, "Messerschmitt Me 264 America Bomber: The Luftwaffe's Lost Transatlantic Bomber."

James P. Duffy, "Target America: Hitler's Plan to Attack the United States."

Steve Horn, "The Second Attack on Pearl Harbor: Operation K and Other Japanese Attempts to Bomb America in World War II."

René J. Francillon, Ph.D., "Japanese Aircraft of the Pacific War."

Justin Engel "Leaders Ponder Saginaw Malleable Foundry's Fate" Mlive January 24, 2010

"Air Raid Warning" Castle Films, 1942

"Wacky Blackout" Warner Brothers, Looney Tunes, 1942

"February 26th Midnight Curfew into Effect" 1942

"Civil Defense Training: What to Do in a Gas Attack of the World War II Era" 1942

"The Civilian Serves" 1942

"This is the Story of Our Part in the War" Saginaw Malleable Iron, 1944, found at www.usautoindustryworldwartwo.com

davistownmuseum.org/bioLufkin.html

j-aircraft.org/xplanes/hikoki_files/g10.htm

digital.ncdcr.gov

fulton.nygenweb.net

usautoindustryworldwartwo.com

WWII

CAUGHT OFF GUARD?

References:

"The Second World War," Winston Churchill

"The Forked Road: Canada 1939-1957," Donald Creighton, McClelland and Stewart

"No Ordinary Time," Doris Kearns Goodwin

"Lend-Lease, Weapons for Victory," Edward R. Stettinius Jr.

"Erie, Link to the Great Lakes," Carl B. Lenchner

"Saginaw's Changeable Past," Jeremy W. Kilar

"War in the Pacific," Brigadier General Jerome T. Hagen

"The Huron Heritage 1907-1957," George W. Stark

"The Great Depression and World War II," Rodney P. Carlisle

"No Ordinary Time," Doris Kearns Godwin

Dylan Lettinga, MHUGL; ss.sites.mtu.edu, "The Dow Chemical Company, Midland, MI,"

Multilateral Agreements 1918-1830; Naval Armament Limitation Treaty

Brooks Scrapbook, 1940, 1941

history.army.mil, "A Brief History of the U.S. Army in World War II"

MICHIGAN'S HEAVY BOMBER

References:

"Consolidated B-24 Liberator," Graham M. Simons

"The Arsenal of Democracy, FDR, Detroit and an Epic Quest to Arm an America at War," A.J. Baime

"The Great Depression and World War II," Rodney P. Carlisle

"No Ordinary Time," Doris Kearns Godwin

"Willow Run," Randy Hotton and Michael W.R. Davis

"On Silver Wings," Marianne Verges

"Woman Pilots of World War II," Jean Hascall Cole

"Yankee Doodle Gals," Amy Nathan

"Selfridge and Collins," Dan Heaton

"Detroit in World War II," Gregory D. Sumner

Movie short; "Woman on the Warpath," 1943, Ford Motor Company.

Movie short; "The Story of Willow Run," 1945, Ford Motor Company.

Movie short; "Razing the Bomber Plant," 2017 Yankee Air Museum.

"United States Army in World War 2, Special Studies, Buying Aircraft: Material Procurement for Army Air Forces," Irving Brinton Holly Jr.

Austin Weber, "A Historical Perspective" (The B-24 Bomber), assemblymag.com, August 1, 2001

Ted R. Bromund "Up from the Ashes a Museum of the Arsenal of Democracy Takes Shape at Willow Run," The Weekly Standard, Volume 20, Number 11, November 24, 2014.

R.J. King, "Aim High," business, "Detroit Business Magazine", February 23, 2016

WWII

"Two Ton Tessie: The Story of a Willow Run B-24 Bomber," June 27, 2017, savethebomberplant.org

thisdayinaviation.com

airplanesofthepast.com

A PROUD CANADIAN VETERAN

References:

"Namesakes 1930-1955," John Greenwood

"Great Lakes Ships We Remember," Peter J. Van der Linden

"Fresh Water Whales"," Richard Wright

Lillian Roemer, "Biography of the Beautiful Northwest," "Inland Seas," Volume 51, Number 3, Fall 1995

"Buffalo Examiner", February 2, 1894, February 6, 1894

"Detroit Free Press", August 8, 1894, August 19, 1894

"Buffalo Evening News", June 3, 1911, June 6, 1911, June 16, 1911

Merchant Vessel List, US, 1898

uboat.net

Brooks Scrapbook, 1940, 1941

Rand McNally's Indexed Atlas, Buffalo, New York, 1911

WWII

FORTRESS SOO

References:

"Ship Master's Directory," Great Lakes, 1948

"Iron Fleet," George J. Joachim

"Tin Stackers," Al Miller

"War in the Pacific, Vol. I" Brig. Gen. Jerome T. Hagen

"The Great Depression and World War II, 1929-1949," Rodney P. Carlisle

"Great Northern Railway Ore Docks of Lake Superior Photo Archive," Douglass D. Addison, Sr.

"City of Rapids: Sault Ste. Marie's Heritage," Bernie Arbic

"Locks and Ships" Soo Locks Boat Tours guidebook, 1989

"Pictorial History of the Great Lakes," Harlan Hatcher and Erich A. Walters

"Lore of the Lakes," David Thomas Bowen

"Detroit Free Press", August 4, 1940

E-mail correspondence with Brian Nicklas, aviation archivist, National Air and Space Museum, September 16, 2016

Johnna Rizzo, "Japan's Secret WWII Weapon: Balloon Bombs," National Geographic.

Johnna Rizzo, "The Japanese harnessed air currents to create the first intercontinental weaponsóballoons," National Geographic.

Michigan Aviation Archeology website, mi-aviationarchaeology.com

Michigan's Internet Railroad History Museum web site, michigan-railroads.com/RRHX/Ports-CarFerries/DocksPortsMenu

Sources

Wisconsin Central web site, wisconsincentral.net/Culture/Culture/AshlandOreDocks

Ben Pletcher, MHUGL, ss.sites.mtu.edu/mhugl/2016/10/16/3312/, "Lockdown: The Story of the Soo Locks and WWII," October 16, 2016

lre.usace.army.mil/Missions/Recreation/Soo-Locks-Visitor-Center/Soo-Locks-History/

WWII

FLAT TOPS ON FRESH WATER

References:

"Freshwater Whales," Richard J. Wright

"Great Lakes Car Ferries," George W. Hilton

"Great Lakes Ships We Remember," Peter J. Van der Linden

"Great Lakes Ships We Remember II," Peter J. Van der Linden

"Great Lakes Ships We Remember III," Peter J. Van der Linden

"Lake Michigan's Aircraft Carriers," Paul M. Somers

"Navy Pier, A Chicago Landmark," Douglas Bukowski

Gordon P. Bugbee, "The Nightboat Lines of Lake Erie" The Telescope, XXVI, No.1, January-February, 1987

Captain John J. Manley, "Great Lakes Lady Bares Her Fangs," "Inland Seas," Number 14, Spring 1958

Brian Higgins, "Fresh Water Flat Tops," "Inland Seas," Number 43, Winter 1987

Jack McKillop; "United States Navy Aircraft Carriers December 07, 1941," bluejacket.com

David O'Mally; "Paddle Wheel Flattops of the Great Lakes," vintagewings.ca

"Japanese Carriers of World War II." ww2pacific.com

Bill Lee; "PADDLEWHEEL AIRCRAFT CARRIERS, A Prime Example of Necessity Being the Mother of Invention" nnapprentice.com

Phone conversation with Cdr. Jim Brady USN Ret. December 17, 2015

E-mail communications with David Brady, December 16, 2015

Sources

Author's NOTE: Several modern sources show Commander Richard Whitehead as having originated the concept of the Great Lakes aircraft carrier. I found the 1958's "Inland Seas" account of Captain Manley who, unlike contemporary authors, was actually there, to be the most credible and it is his account that is referenced in this chapter.

Author's NOTE: It has been published that the car ferry City Of Midland *was also considered for carrier conversion along with the* Seeandbee. *This is incorrect because the only* City Of Midland *to sail the lakes prior to World War II was a wooden-hulled break-bulk and passenger vessel that burned to a wreck in 1916. The next vessel to carry a similar name was launched more than a decade after the war.*

WWII

MYTHS AND HAIR-BRAINED IDEAS

References:

"Seaway," Jacques LesStrang

"Lake Carriers," Jacques LesStrang

"Graveyard of the Lakes, Mark L. Thompson

"Shipwrecks of Sanilac," Pat Stayer

"Lake Ontario," Authur Pound

Stephen Weir, "The Mysterious Sinking of the *Charles S. Price*,"

"Inland Seas," Volume 42, Number 2, Summer 1986

"Inland Seas," Volume 42, Number 2, Summer 1986

Brooks Scrapbook, 1940, 1941

uboats.net

uboataces.com

SILENT KILLERS

References:

"Fresh Water Submarines, The *Manitowoc* Story," Rear Admiral William T. Nelson.

"Know Your Lakers of World War I," Rev. Edward J. Dowling, S.J.

"Slide Rules and Submarines," Montgomery C. Meigs

E-mail correspondence with Brian Nicklas, WWII U-boat researcher, June 29, 2017

combinedfleet.com, Imperial Japanese Navy Page

ibiblio.org/hyperwar/USN/rep/Midway/Midway-Interrogations.

uboats.net

ussjallao.com

Pogy SS-266 World War II Patrol File, Division of Naval History, Ships History Section, US Naval Department

Jallao SS-368 World War II Patrol File, Division of Naval History, Ships History Section, US Naval Department

Kete SS-369 World War II Patrol File, Division of Naval History, Ships History Section, US Naval Department

CINCPAC File: A8/ (37) JAP/ (26), Serial 01753, From; Commander-in-Chief, United States Pacific Fleet Admiral Chester Nimitz, JUNE 21 1942, "Interrogation of Japanese Prisoners taken after Midway Action 9 June 1942."

Correspondence with Wells Chapin, 05/21/2017, former lead radio man and cryptology officer *USS Jallao* as well as the publisher of this book.

WWII

TANKS ALOT

References:

"United States Army in World War II, The Technical Services, Ordnance Department: Procurement and Supply," Harry C. Thomson and Linda Mayo

"World War Two Tanks," George Forty

"War Assets Report - Industrial Plants," September 1946

"LIFE Magazine," February, 16, 1942, "US Auto Plants Are Cleared for War"

"Buick at its Battle Stations," 1944, pamphlet, usautoindustry-worldwartwo.com

"Cadillac From Peace to War," pamphlet, usautoindustryworld-wartwo.com

"On the Job Chevrolet, Volume Production for the Nation's Need," September 19, 1944, pamphlet, usautoindustryworldwartwo.com

"Detroit Diesel Fights," 1943, pamphlet, usautoindustryworld-wartwo.com

"This is the Story of Our Part in the War - Saginaw Malleable Iron Division General Motors Corporation," 1944, book displayed at usautoindustryworldwartwo.com

C. Peter Chen, "Detroit Arsenal Tank Plant" ww2db.com

Jodi McFarland. "Saginaw Metal Castings Operations timeline" mlive.com

usautoindustryworldwartwo.com, David Jackson

Communication with David Jackson, November 27, 2017

U-BOAT BAIT

References:

"Namesakes 1930-1955," John O. Greenwood

"Know Your Lakers of World War I," Rev. Edward J. Dowling, S.J.

"The Ships of the Paterson Fleet," Gene Onchulenko and Skip Gillham

"The Ford Fleet, (1923 ñ 1989)," Clare J Snyder and Michael W. R. Davis

"Upper Lakes,1932-1982," Wally Macht

"An Honorable German," Charles McCain

"Freshwater Whales," Richard J. Wright

"Great Lakes Ships We Remember," Peter J. Van der Linden

"Great Lakes Ships We Remember II," Peter J. Van der Linden

"Great Lakes Ships We Remember III," Peter J. Van der Linden

"Fresh Water Submarines, The *Manitowoc* Story," Rear Admiral William T. Nelson.

uboats.net Web Site

Paul Collins, "Sinking of the CARIBOU," Newfoundland and Labrador Heritage Web Site, 2006.

Author's note: Without the aid of the fantastic U-boats dot net web site this chapter would not have 60% of the detail that I was able to construct. If you are at all interested in U-boats, please visit that web site.

WWII

WHERE WAS CAMP FREELAND?

References:

"Nazi Prisoners of War in America," Arnold Krammer

"Escape from Canada!" John Melady

"Stalag Wisconsin," Betty Cowley

Stuart Frohm, "Midland Daily News," February 24, 2010, "Reporter Visited POW Camp in 1944 For The Daily News"

MICHAEL PETERSON, "Argus-Press," January 1, 2010, "Woman's Hidden History Recalled by Family"

Brian Albrecht, ""Cleveland Plain Dealer," October 15, 2011 "Parma Heights World War II Veteran Recalls Guarding German Pows"

Michael O'Hagan, Blog posts, "POWs in Canada" Entries: "From Port Colborne to Detroit," "Veterans Guard of Canada." "Mapping POWs in Canada," "Mapping Canada's Internment Camps," "Camp 31 Fort Henry: Then and Now," "Sports Behind Barbed Wire,"

"Flint Journal," "For POWs at Owosso, Farm Work Sometimes Provide (Food) Benefits." May 25, 1986

"Owosso Argus-Press," "As Girls Were Arraigned on Conspiracy Charge." July 26, 1944

"Owosso Argus-Press," "Penalty for Foolishness Should Serve as Warning." July 26, 1944

"Owosso Argus-Press," "Four Nazis Flee Guards." August 16, 1944

"Owosso Argus-Press," "Girls Arrested Again in Escape of Prisoners." July 25, 1944

"Owosso Argus-Press," "Girls Cases Before Grand Jury Tomorrow." December 12, 1944

"Owosso Argus-Press," "Girls May Face Treason Charge in Nazi Escape." July 23, 1944

"Owosso Argus-Press," "Girls to Go on Trial Friday." January 2, 1945

"Owosso Argus-Press," "Jury Convicts Owosso Girls of Conspiracy." January 13, 1945

Owosso Argus-Press," "Owosso Girls Get Terms in Federal Prison." February 13, 1945, p. 1.

"POW Camp West of Here Closed." "Argus-Press," December 1, 1945, p. 1.

petawawaheritagevillage.com, "Canadian Internment Camps"

"The Enemy in Our Midst", DVD video production, John Pepin, 2011

Phone conversation with Mike McCollum, Au Train, Michigan, May 5, 2017

Phone conversation with Dan McCollum, Au Train, Michigan, May 19, 2017

Geneva Convention relative to the Treatment of Prisoners of War; Article 13

WWII

THE FOG OF WAR

References:

"The New Namesakes of the Lakes," John O. Greenwood

"New Namesakes II," John O. Greenwood

"Great Lakes Ships We Remember," Vol. I, Rev. Peter J. Van der Lindon

"Graveyard of the Lakes," Mark L. Thompson

"The Ships of the Patterson Fleet," Gene Onchulenko and Skip Gillham

"Lake Superior Shipwrecks," Dr. Julius F. Wolff Jr.

"Record Breakers, World War II U.S. Navy Armed Guard and World War II U.S. Merchant Marine," Thomas R. Bowerman

Jewell R. Dean, "Recovery of the Steamer *Humphrey*," "Inland Seas," Volume 50, Number 4 Winter 1994

Gary S. Dewar, "The US Maritime Commission L6-Type Ore Carriers," "Inland Seas," Volume 49, Number 1, Spring 1993

Paul Wiening, "The Consumers Power, A Great Lakes Anachronism," The Telescope, Volume XXXVI, Number 93, May-June 1987

Charles Asher Jr., "Salvaging the Steamer *George M. Humphrey* Parts I and II," The Detroit Marine Historian, Volume 36, Numbers 3 and 4, November, December 1982

Brookes Scrapbook, 1943, 1944

Dave Swayze Shipwreck Database

maritimehistoryofthegreatlakes.ca

Sources

Author's personal conversation with the late Wally Watkins aboard the J.L. MAUTHE on the subject of loading and unloading sulfur. December 14, 1992

Special thanks to Ric Mixter - Great Lakes historian

WWII

LAKEBOATS OF WAR

References:

"Tin Stackers," Al Miller

"Great Lakes Ships We Remember Vol. III" Rev. Peter Van der Linden

"Ships of the Great Lakes," James P. Barry

"Fresh Water Whales," Richard J. Wright

"Know Your Ships 2016," Roger LeLievre

"Know Your Ships 1978," Thomas Manse

"The Honorable Peter White," Ralph D. Williams

"Namesakes of the 80s," John O. Greenwood

"Iron Fleet," George J. Joachim

"Great Lakes and Seaway News," The Telescope, January-February 1979

"Great Lakes and Seaway News," The Telescope, January-February 1982

"Great Lakes and Seaway News," The Telescope, March-April 1982

"Great Lakes and Seaway News," The Telescope, May-June 1982

"Great Lakes and Seaway News," The Telescope, July-August 1982

"Great Lakes and Seaway News," The Telescope, September-October 1982

"Great Lakes and Seaway News," The Telescope, November-December 1982

Gary S. Dewar, "The Pittsburgh Supers," "Inland Seas," Volume

48, Number 1, Spring 1992

Gary S. Dewar, "U.S. Maritime Commission L6-Type Ore Carriers," "Inland Seas," Volume 49, Number 41, Spring 1993

"Scanner," Volume 13, number 7, April 1981

"Scanner," Volume 18, number 9, Mid-Summer 1986

"Scanner," Volume 20, number 2, November 1987

"Scanner," Volume 20, number 3, December 1987

"Scanner," Volume 20, number 4, January 1988

"Scanner," Volume 20, number 5, February 1988

"Scanner," Volume 20, number 6, March 1988

"Scanner," Volume 20, number 7, April 1988

"Scanner," Volume 20, number 8, May 1988

"Scanner," Volume 20, number 9, Summer 1988

"Scanner," Volume 22, number 2, November 1989

greatlakesvesselhistory.com, The Vessel Histories of Sterling Berry

boatnerd.com

Posting, boatnerd.com, "*Algoma Transfer* Tow Reaches End of the Line", Bill Bird, May 25, 2014

Jim Luke and William J. Luke, The Luke Collection, "Lake File - *Benjamin F. Fairless*"

Correspondence with David "DJ" Story, November 7, 2017

WWII

MIGHTY MAC

References:

"Lake Carriers," Jacques LesStrang

"Steamboats and Sailors of the Great Lakes," Mark L. Thompson.

"Iron Fleet," George J. Joachim

"Freshwater Whales," Richard J. Wright

"The Great Lakes Car Ferries," George W. Hilton

Theodore J. Hull, "The World War II Army Enlistment Records File and Access to Archival Databases," "Prologue Magazine," Volume 38, Number 1, Spring 2006

John H. Wilterding Jr. "The Tacoma-Class Patrol Frigates," "The Nor'easter," Volume 7, Number 4, July-August 1982

uscg.mil

toledosattic.org

sss.gov

shipbuildinghistory.com

core.ac.uk

VICTORY

References:

"Freedom's Arsenal, The story of the Automotive War Counsel," Automobile Manufacturer's Association, 1950

"War in the Pacific," Brigadier General Jerome T. Hagen, USMC

"The Rocket and the Reich: Peenemunde and the Coming of the Ballistic Missile Era," Michael J. Neufeld

"U.S. Air Force Tactical Missiles," George Mindling and Robert Bolton

"The Race for Hitler's X-Planes," John Christopher

"United States Army in World War II, The Technical Services, Ordnance Department: Procurement and Supply," Harry C. Thomson and Linda Mayo

Gary S. Dewar, "The Pittsburgh Supers," "Inland Seas," Volume 48, Number 1, Spring 1992

Gary S. Dewar, "U.S. Maritime Commission L6-Type Ore Carriers," "Inland Seas," Volume 49, Number 41, Spring 1993

disciplesofflight.com/pulse-jet-past-future

Correspondence with Brian Nicklas, National Air and Space Museum.

Author's conversation with Brigadier General Jerome T. Hagen, USMC, Pearl Harbor, Hawaii, January 20, 2014

ABOUT THE AUTHOR

Wes Oleszewski is a research historian, author, cartoonist, professional aviator and life-long spaceflight devotee. As a writer he has composed and has published 18 maritime history books since 1991. He has also authored 6 spaceflight books and is the author of the world's only aviation/aerospace editorial cartoon strip - Klyde Morris. He holds a Bachelor's Degree in Aeronautical Science from the Embry-Riddle Aeronautical University in Daytona Beach, Florida, and is a former airline captain and corporate pilot with thousands of flight hours logged. Currently he lives in the Washington DC area with his wife and two daughters. He often returns to the Great Lakes region to do research, meet his readers, sign books and generally enjoy being far away from Washington DC.

ABOUT THE EDITOR

Christopher W. Rottiers, "Chris" was born in Mid-Michigan and graduated from Birch Run High School in 1975. A true "Jack of all Trades, Master of None" he graduated with an Associate of Arts Degree from Delta College and a Bachelor of Science Degree in Education from The University of  Michigan. His lifelong passions include Great Lakes Maritime History, US Manned Spaceflight, American Military History, Genealogy, and Model kit building and collecting. He is a long time member of The Great Lakes Historical Society, Marine Historical Society of Detroit, Association for Great Lakes Maritime History, and various other Great Lakes Maritime organizations, he is also a member of The United States Naval Institute, the International Plastic Modeler's Society, and a lifetime member of Michigan's Own Military and Space Hero's Museum. Chris credits his knack for doing historical research to Dr. Charles E. Feltner, noted shipwreck hunter and author of Shipwrecks of the Straits of Mackinac who taught him research methodology. Chris was the protégé of the late Ralph K. Roberts of Saginaw, Michigan who was a noted Marine Historian and collector of Great Lakes Vessel photographs. His passion for Great Lakes Maritime history came through his association with Ralph Roberts. Chris is the curator and archivist of the Ralph K. Roberts Great Lakes Marine Collection. Recently retired after a 40-year career with a major Detroit based Auto Manufacturer as a Senior Project Engineer and Subject Matter Expert, Chris and his wife Anne, the parents of 4 adult children, live in Southeast Michigan.